Praise for Charles Lewis
and
The Center for Public Integrity

"There is no more effective public interest watchdog in
Washington, D.C. . . . Where others have put their picks and
shovels aside, the Center keeps digging."
—Bill Moyers

"If Lewis didn't exist, somebody would have to invent him.
His presence underscores an absence:
heavy lifting by most reporters."
—*Chicago Tribune*

"Sometimes I am convinced there is nothing wrong with this
country that couldn't be cured by the magical implantation of
ethical standards on us all—leaders and followers.
Until that becomes doable, The Center for Public Integrity is
about the best thing we have going for us."
—Ben Bradlee, *Washington Post*

"The Center for Public Integrity is the real thing.
Groups of dedicated people who remember that journalism
is about grit and guts and stamina and razor-sharp instincts.
They are, thank heaven, here to stay."
—Diane Sawyer, ABC News

"No other investigative organization shines so many probing
flashlights into so many Washington dirty-laundry baskets."
—Kevin Phillips, author of *Arrogant Capital*

Praise for
THE BUYING OF THE PRESIDENT
and
THE BUYING OF THE CONGRESS

"[*The Buying of the President*] has become an essential reference work for reporters covering the race."

—*The New Yorker*

"[*The Buying of the Congress* is] further evidence that, in today's Washington journalism, nobody else works as hard at investigating the twin roles of money and influence . . . Lewis succeeds where most money-and-politics reportage falls short: showing the link between Capitol Hill and ordinary life."

—*The Washington Monthly*

"Charles Lewis and his colleagues at The Center for Public Integrity think the media should long ago have mastered the collusions of American politics and commerce. Sadly, their book shows that we haven't come close."

—*New York Times Sunday Magazine*

"Lewis and his colleagues at the Center provide many case studies in which money seems to have been decisive in determining public policy. The examples are drawn from both parties, and while it is not absolutely clear that anyone can prove a quid pro quo—cash for a specific vote—the connections between money paid out and legislation show an unsettling linkage."

—Lars-Erik Nelson, *The New York Review of Books*

"Even for those of us who for years have been collecting examples of how legalized bribery works, Lewis & Co. have come up with some fresh and truly outrageous stuff. Some of it is so bad, it's funny."

—Molly Ivins, *Fort Worth Star-Telegram*

Also by Charles Lewis
and The Center for Public Integrity

The Buying of the Congress
The Buying of the President

THE
BUYING
OF THE
PRESIDENT
2000

CHARLES LEWIS
and the
Center for Public Integrity

AVON BOOKS ◆ NEW YORK

AVON BOOKS, INC.
An Imprint of HarperCollins*Publishers*
10 East 53rd Street
New York, New York 10022-5299

Copyright © 2000 by The Center for Public Integrity
Interior design by Kellan Peck
Published by arrangement with The Center for Public Integrity
ISBN: 0-380-79519-1
www.harpercollins.com

Library of Congress Cataloging in Publication Data:

Lewis, Charles, 1953–
  The buying of the president 2000 / Charles Lewis and the Center for Public Integrity.
    p. cm.
  Includes index.
  1. Campaign funds—United States. 2. Presidents—United States—Election—2000
3. Presidential candidates—United States.   I. Center for Public Integrity. II. Title.
JK1991.L5 2000
324.7'8'097309049—dc21   99-055251

First Avon Books Trade Paperback Printing: January 2000

For James R. Soles

Who are to be the electors of the federal representatives? Not the rich more than the poor; not the learned more than the ignorant; not the haughty heirs of distinguished names more than the humble sons [and daughters] of obscure and unpropitious fortune.
—JAMES MADISON

There are only two important things in politics. The first is money, and I can't remember the second.
—MARK HANNA

The Investigative Team

Executive Director
Charles Lewis

Managing Director
Peter Eisner

Director of Investigative Projects
Bill Hogan

Senior Editor
Bill Allison

Senior Fellow
Knut Royce

Senior Researcher
Dan Steinberg

Senior Writers
Annys Shin
Russell Tisinger

Writers
Shannon Feaster
Patrick Kiger
Charles Lewis
Monte Paulsen

Researchers
Megan Chernly
Adrianne Hari
Nathaniel Heller
Marianne Holt
Irene Lin
Lauren Marks
Avril Orloff
Anya Richards
Peter Newbatt Smith
Melanie Strong
Matt Thompson
Derrick Wetherell

The Center for Public Integrity
Hima Jain
Terri Nunn
Regina Russell

Contents

‖‖‖‖‖‖‖‖‖‖

Contents

OTHERS

Introduction

||||||||||

It was a moment that exquisitely captured the state of American politics today.

Last August, nearly half a year before the Iowa caucuses on January 24, 2000, the state's Republican Party staged its quadrennial fund-raising event. This peculiar political carnival—featuring live presidential candidates—fattened the state party's coffers by at least $1 million. Approximately 650 reporters swarmed around defenseless Ames, Iowa, to cover what veteran journalist David Broder of the *Washington Post* branded "the totally unofficial but historically significant straw poll." All of the 23,685 votes cast were paid for, legally. The two candidates who bought the most votes won, and their "victories" were front-page news nationwide.

Nine Republican presidential candidates set up operation outside the Hilton Coliseum at Iowa State University. The campaign of Texas Governor George W. Bush outbid the others and ended up paying $43,500 to rent the prime location—60,000 square feet of grass—for the event. What transpired on August 14 was an orgy of free food, entertainment, walk-around celebrities, and gifts, with each campaign trying to outdo the others. Utah Senator Orrin Hatch's tent had singer Vic Damone and Utah Jazz pro basketball star Karl Malone. Bush had former Dallas Cowboys quarterback

Roger Staubach and singers Tracy Byrd and Linda Davis. Malcolm "Steve" Forbes, Jr., had singers Debby Boone and Ronnie Milsap crooning away in a huge, air-conditioned tent with French doors, which one wag from a rival campaign dubbed "Chateau Malcolm." The multimillionaire publisher also served up 3,100 pounds of pork and set up a miniature amusement park, complete with an inflatable mountain for children to rappel down. Bush and Forbes were the only candidates to have their tents next to the coliseum's entrances.

Candidates were judged in part by the goodies they lavished on caucus-goers. Every campaign had T-shirts. Elizabeth Dole's campaign offered up balloon hats, while Pat Buchanan gave away pot holders. The Bush folks also offered a free lunch and dinner. Hatch provided chicken, Alan Keyes free ice cream. Former Vice President Dan Quayle's low-budget campaign was criticized for passing out bundles of corn.

The Iowa Republicans who were hauled in for the event were pretty much props, too, like the singers and the barbecued pork. The Bush and Forbes campaigns each rented a hundred or so buses to fetch their supporters throughout Iowa. In the evening, inside the Hilton Coliseum, the only people allowed entry were the voters whose $25 entry fees had been paid for by the candidates. Each of the presidential candidates was permitted to speak for ten minutes, and their supporters were then allowed to demonstrate for up to three minutes. Forbes put on the most elaborate show of the night, with thousands of balloons dropped onto the crowd. Because the candidates had bought so many tickets, ordinary, nonpaying citizens who just wanted to listen to the speeches were turned away at the door.

The winner of the Iowa straw poll was Bush, whose campaign had shelled out $825,000 for 7,418 votes—about $111 a vote. "I am proud to be here," Bush told the crowd that night, "for this grassroots exercise in democracy." Broder breathlessly praised his triumph as a "combination of broad public appeal and skillful organization." Forbes finished second, at an even steeper cost: He spent nearly $2 million for 4,921 votes—about $400 a vote.

Welcome to the 2000 presidential campaign. It is disconcerting to behold a political process that so matter-of-factly rewards unabashed, competitive gluttony, a process so utterly devoid of substantive discourse, a process so disdainful of the very people it is supposed to serve. But the lack of self-awareness and independence by the participants themselves is even more stupefying.

Of course, there's much more to electing the most powerful leader on earth than straw votes and sound bites, primaries and party conventions and commercials. Fact is, it takes mammoth sums of money to obtain power. Precisely *how* that all evolves is not always apparent, but one thing is quite clear. As we noted in 1996 in *The Buying of the President,* "Before the first vote is cast in a presidential primary, a private referendum has already been conducted among the nation's financial elites as to which candidate shall earn his party's nomination." Certain candidates are winnowed out, either choosing not to enter the fray at all or attempting it unsuccessfully. And a fundamental determinant in their decision—and in our choices at the polls—is money.

The dirty secret of American presidential politics is that the nation's wealthiest interests largely determine who will be the next President of the United States, in the year *before* the election. As political fund-raising consultant Stan Huckaby has noted, without exception, in every election since 1976, the candidate who has raised the most money by the end of the year preceding the election, and who has been eligible for federal matching funds, has become his party's nominee for President.

The most recent case in point: The two presidential candidates who raised the most money in 1995 and were eligible for matching funds—Clinton and Dole—won their parties' nominations. Both men raised more than $20 million in the year before the election. Of the 16,200 donors who contributed $1,000 to the Clinton-Gore reelection campaign, 15,200, or 94 percent, gave their money early, in 1995. Of the 48,000 donors who contributed the legal maximum of $1,000 to GOP presidential candidates in the 1995-96 election cycle, 39,800, or 83 percent, gave in 1995.

It is the *price* of power that interests us the most in *The Buying of the President 2000.* What accommodations have been made to achieve that power, and with whom? What is the cost to the nation? Who are these presidential candidates, really, and what powerful interests are aligned with them?

For more than a year roughly two dozen researchers, writers, and editors have been analyzing thousands of primary and secondary sources of information, including campaign finance data from the Federal Election Commission and the Center for Responsive Politics, personal financial disclosure forms, and congressional voting records, in some cases going back twenty years. We have interviewed hundreds of individuals. The book has chapters on all major presidential candidates who were active contenders as of September 1999, which explains why we write about Elizabeth Dole and Dan Quayle herein but not Lamar Alexander or John Kasich. Once again, each candidate chapter contains a list of the Top Ten Career Patrons, those most steadfastly generous, important donors who have helped to underwrite the candidate's political career. And, for the first time, we also list the Top 50 Patrons since 1991 (measured in "soft money" contributions) for each of the two major political parties.

"The saddest life is that of a political aspirant under democracy," H. L. Mencken once wrote. "His failure is ignominious and his success is disgraceful." We respect the ideal of public service in the public interest, and we fully recognize that on a personal level, politics can be a brutal exercise. We have tried to be fair to the men and woman who aspire to hold the highest office in the land. For example, every reasonable effort to interview the candidates has been made, over many months. Unfortunately, the candidates *all* declined our repeated requests for interviews. (By way of comparison, for the 1996 book, half of the candidates consented to interviews.)

It should be clear that, simply stated, *The Buying of the President 2000* highlights areas of interest to us, vital information that we believe the American people want—and need—to know. We did not seek to provide *every* detail of the candidates' interactions with their contributors. Nor did we see it as our role to present slick, swooning profiles of the candidates—readers can get that stuff from their authorized campaign biographies or Web sites (which we reference in these pages and on the Center's Web site). Indeed, the book does *not* contain full biographies of the candidates or personal financial disclosure reports, including investments, speaking fees, and all-expenses-paid trips, or specific details about many of the public policy decisions they have made in the past. This kind of information, plus each candidate's "Top 25 Career Patrons" and capsule profiles of those patrons, is at *www.publicintegrity.org.*

We do not live in an inspiring time of candor or contrition when it comes to politics, and to the role of money in politics. Our politicians seem to have become increasingly shameless, arrogant, and loose with the truth. Unfortunately, after the decades of deceit since Vietnam and Watergate, the American people are no longer surprised when government officials ignore or mislead them. It's gotten harder and harder to get straight answers from politicians and those who work for them. Lying is now called "spin" or "damage control," and it's studied, taught, and even admired by many people in Washington today as an effective public relations technique.

We spoke with Archibald Cox, the enormously respected former Watergate independent prosecutor whom President Nixon fired in October 1973, in the opening salvo of the infamous "Saturday Night Massacre." Cox believes there is much less trust in government today than there was during the Watergate years. And he said that campaign finance abuses are "far worse today" than during Watergate, when many unlawful corporate contributions were discovered and prosecuted.

Cox believes that today the threat to the democratic process is even graver. "The abuses are worse partly because there's much more money and . . . there's much more pressure on those who receive the money to yield to the wishes of those who give it," Cox told the Center. "I'm speaking of a lot of elected officials across the board, but particularly in Congress."

Of course, what happens *after* public officials leave government is also troubling, a subject the Center for Public Integrity has investigated frequently over the years. The Washington mercenary culture, absorbing former government decision makers who triple or quadruple their salaries as lobbyists or consultants, grows each year. Thirty years ago there were fewer than 100 registered lobbyists in the nation's capital; today there are approximately 14,000. But we also are seeing more garish profiteering from public service. Some of the nation's most respected political leaders now unabashedly cash in personally as soon as they're off the public payroll.

Some, such as former Governors Ann Richards and Mario Cuomo, have done Doritos commercials. Robert Dole does TV ads about penile erection dysfunction for Viagra (you don't see too many television ads about election dysfunction). Former Senate Majority Leaders George Mitchell and Howard Baker, Jr., recently have made money the old-fashioned Washington way, by lobbying for the tobacco companies.

More broadly, in the three years since the 1996 election we have seen a steady deterioration in tolerable standards of political conduct. What was outrageous yesterday merely seems to be ac-cepted reality today.

In late 1996 and throughout 1997, for example, we learned that President Clinton was personally involved in raising and chan-neling millions of dollars in Democratic Party contributions to his own reelection campaign, with the money spent on television com-mercials that he personally approved and that were aired more than a year before the 1996 election. The Democratic Party ac-cepted millions of dollars in illegal contributions from foreign na-tionals, many of whom met personally with the President. Vice President Albert Gore, Jr., spoke at a fund-raising event at a Bud-dhist monastery in Los Angeles, and everyone from a Colombian drug trafficker to Chinese arms dealers passed through the White House, obtaining access for cash. Separately, from January 1995 to August 1996, the White House hosted 103 coffees—attended by 1,544 people seeking "face time" with the President, the Vice President, and their spouses—who collectively contributed at least $26.4 million to the Democratic Party for the 1996 election. Be-sides being rewarded with overnight stays at the White House and at Camp David, in 1995 and 1996, major Democratic Party donors and fund-raisers rode on Air Force One, Marine One, Air Force Two, and Marine Two (the latter two are the Vice President's aircraft) more than 300 times. In addition, both the President and Vice President solicited campaign contributions by telephone from the White House, Clinton from his residential quarters and Gore from his office. At first Gore said that he dialed for dollars "on a few occasions"; he later acknowledged that he did it fifty-six times. This was the potentially criminal matter that produced the now infamous statement by the Vice President: "My counsel advises me that there is *no controlling legal authority* or case that says that there was any violation of law whatsoever in the manner in which I asked people to contribute to our reelection campaign." [emphasis added]

Sadly, Gore was right. None of this unprecedented activity, which certainly had the stench of misconduct and impropriety, was seriously prosecuted by the Justice Department. Only the small fry were pursued. Attorney General Janet Reno steadfastly refused to name an independent counsel to investigate the various 1996 campaign-finance allegations. And when the Senate Governmental Affairs Committee attempted to investigate the 1996 election abuses, more than forty-five potential witnesses fled the United States or invoked the Fifth Amendment. Months of public hearings were held, but it was painfully obvious that the committee was severely hamstrung by both the White House and the Senate Republican leadership. And there was the hypocrisy of virtually ignoring *congressional* campaign-finance issues, even though, over the years, five of the committee's sixteen members had themselves, through their campaigns, violated federal election laws.

To add insult to injury, the following year, Americans suffered through Monica Mania, ending with the first impeachment of an elected President in U.S. history. Whatever your opinion of Bill Clinton, former White House intern Monica Lewinsky, Independent Counsel Kenneth Starr, or Congress, one thing is clear: In 1998, we reached the lowest point in our nation's political discourse and decorum, including the most blatant, look-you-in-the-eye-with-a-straight-face lying by a sitting President ever. And let us not forget that this whole sordid episode got its start with campaign contributions: Lewinsky became a White House intern in the first place because a friend of her family had given more than $330,000 to the Democratic Party.

In 1999 the presidential election season began with further evidence that the post-Watergate campaign finance system is broken. The son of former President George Bush, George W. Bush, leading all prospective presidential candidates in public opinion polls, set the political world on its ear. Without any detailed policy positions, federal government experience, or stated vision for the future, and while hardly leaving his home in Austin, he raised $37

million in four months. That is more money at that early point in
a presidential campaign than *any* previous White House contender,
more than the ten other Republican contenders *combined*, and
more than either Clinton or Dole raised for their respective campaigns in the *entire* 1995-96 election cycle. Bush's campaign took
in the astonishing sum of $310,748 a day—that's $12,947 an
hour—in contributions. The previous record had been set in 1995,
when Clinton raised $26 million in seven months.

This kind of money isn't raised at backyard barbecues or from
neighborhood bake sales, of course. It comes from thousands of
the wealthiest Americans, many of whom want something from
the government. To be sure, significant cash is, by itself, certainly
not sufficient to ensure future residence at 1600 Pennsylvania Avenue. Just ask John Connally (1980), Ross Perot (1992 and 1996),
or Steve Forbes (1996), to name three well-financed, unsuccessful
aspirants. But without question, money is a *necessary* ingredient
for a candidate, along with a timely, articulate message; credible
professional credentials; confident, attractive presentation; and an
effective campaign organization.

Weeks after his campaign's dramatic disclosure that it had
raised $37 million in the first half of 1999, Bush announced that
he would forgo federal matching funds and the spending limits
that accompany them. In so doing, he can ignore the spending
ceiling of nearly $50 million in the preconvention phase of the
election cycle as well as state-by-state spending caps. Forbes, who
also will forgo matching funds, as he did in 1996, vowed to match
Bush dollar for dollar. Bush put his family's extensive network of
political money-raisers under the charge of his best friend, Donald
Evans, who told a reporter for the *New York Times* that he regards
his work as a form of public service. "Behind every check, there's
a willing heart," Evans said. "To me, it's not a check, it's a person,
someone who cares about this great country."

Bush's calculation that Americans won't mind how much
money he raises, or what rules he plays by, is telling. Simply put,
it marks a new level of political audacity. Heretofore, it would
have been completely unthinkable for a popular candidate with
serious hopes of landing a major party nomination to forsake the

public subsidies established in the wake of the worst political scandal of the twentieth century. But this largely anointed GOP presidential candidate with the famous last name is willing to do it because he thinks he *can* do it. The nation's political establishment even seems to canonize candidates with the Midas touch. The unfortunate wretches who are unable to amass sizable political war chests give off the fetid odor of dead meat, going nowhere fast. The actual merits of the candidates' ideas and backgrounds are largely irrelevant. And meanwhile, there is little public consideration of precisely where the political money has come from or what the donors seek in return.

Certainly, the mutual dependency between politicians and their patrons is nothing new. But one can't help wondering how Abraham Lincoln or Harry Truman would fare in today's political, mega-fund-raising milieu. Would they be willing to dial for dollars for several hours each day and, with frozen smiles, shake thousands upon thousands of strangers' hands at hundreds of fund-raising events throughout the country, a full *year* before the election? It frankly is difficult to fathom.

The stark fact today is that, increasingly, good people are not entering politics for a host of reasons, financial ones chief among them. In 1998 there were more than ninety *uncontested* elections for the U.S. House of Representatives, and the states of Arkansas, Florida, and Louisiana didn't bother to even count votes. In Florida the names of those lucky candidates in uncontested House races didn't even appear on the ballot.

In the past two election cycles we have seen record-shattering sums of private, special-interest money pouring into the political process. We have seen the worst campaign-finance scandals since Watergate. And, at the same time, we have witnessed the worst voter disillusionment in more than half a century.

How did things get so bad?

The short answer is that politicians have become so deeply enmeshed in the money chase and personally tied to powerful economic interests that they have lost the esteem and trust of the American people.

Confidence in government has waned to historic lows. In 1996, 100 million eligible voters declined to participate in this democracy, the lowest turnout (49 percent) in a presidential election year since 1924, and the second lowest since 1824. Only 36 percent of eligible voters went to the polls in 1998, the lowest turnout since 1942.

Meanwhile, the ruling class of politicians and patrons has not felt compelled to open democracy to greater citizen participation. The 1996 presidential election revealed what moneyed interests have done to the political process. "The abuses of the campaign-finance system, as practiced by both parties in 1996 . . . destroyed what was left of this country's campaign-finance laws," journalist Elizabeth Drew observed in her 1999 book, *The Corruption of American Politics.* "There were now effectively no limits on how much money could be raised and spent in a campaign, and the limits on how it could be raised were rendered meaningless. Powerful people had undermined the law. . . ."

The reckless orgy in 1996 between politicians and their deep-pocketed patrons came at the same time the rich were getting richer. More people have become billionaires in the past fifteen years than at any other time in U.S. history, and the 189 American billionaires today (more than twelve times the number in 1982) have well over a trillion dollars in wealth. In Silicon Valley alone, sixty-four new millionaires are made each day. One percent of the population controls 40 percent of the nation's assets, and the United States now has the widest gap between rich and poor of any industrialized country.

Meanwhile, the number of bankruptcy cases has risen almost 70 percent since 1995. One in five American children—a total of 14.5 million children—live in poverty. Every day, 1,827 babies are born in the United States without health-care coverage; 11.3 million children from coast to coast are without health care.

Wall Street bestowed $11 billion in bonuses in 1998, up from $2 billion in 1990. In this new Gilded Age of twenty-something millionaires and ostentatious materialism, from Manhattan to Silicon Valley, we are witnessing almost incomprehensible wealth wash over the political system as well, further transforming it. The same 535 Members of Congress, two political parties, and presidential candidates who raised $2 billion in 1992 and $2.4 billion in 1996 are well on their way to amassing more than $3 billion in this election cycle. And that's just the money we know about.

This game is too rich for ordinary folks. In 1996, for example, only four percent of the American people gave money to candidates for any political office. Only one-fourth of one percent gave $200 or more to candidates for federal office. Our electoral process is now so besotted by big money that millionaires now make up more than a third of the U.S. Senate, even though fewer than one percent of Americans are so fortunate. And while practically no one has noticed, at least ten of the presidential candidates in 1999—Lamar Alexander, Bill Bradley, Pat Buchanan, George W. Bush, Elizabeth Dole, Steve Forbes, Al Gore, Orrin Hatch, John McCain, and Dan Quayle—are millionaires. The richest candidate by far is Forbes, who will tap his personal wealth of more than $400 million to bankroll his own campaign, as he did in 1996. Among other things, he favors eliminating the tax on capital gains.

It is hardly coincidental that over the years, Congress has substantially reduced both the top income-tax rate and the tax on capital gains. Or that Congress and its banking patrons killed legislation that would have eliminated bank ATM fees. Or that Congress has failed to pass legislation that would have required employers to help pay for health-care insurance. Or that Congress has passed special "cheap labor" immigration-exemption laws and Y2K liability exemption laws at the request of Silicon Valley companies. The list of special favors for the privileged few is quite, quite long. As political scientist Louise Overacker wrote in 1932, "Even a dog will not bite the hand that feeds it, and a political party will hardly 'sell out' the person whose money it accepts." And every public policy dispensation for political donors—no matter how crass or narrow the economic interest—is invariably cloaked under some kind of broader, nobler pretext.

At various times in the past century, the American people have expressed their outrage over the deterioration of their political process into a mercenary, pay-to-play culture, and insisted that system be reformed. The most recent eruption of public will was a quarter century ago, in 1974. After two years and hundreds of stories (including many of major campaign contributors getting special government favors), Americans were completely fed up with the widespread corruption and lying of Washington officials. "Watergate" was shorthand for cash contributions in paper bags, illegal corporate donations, secret slush funds, and the like. Just weeks after Richard Nixon's resignation, the new President, Republican Gerald Ford, signed historic campaign finance-reform legislation. "The times," he said, "demand this legislation."

The law created a new regulatory agency, the Federal Election Commission (FEC); contribution and expenditure disclosure requirements for all federal elections; and specific limits on what individuals, political committees, and party organizations could give to federal campaigns. It also set up a system of partial public financing of presidential campaigns—voluntary public matching funds during the primaries and full public financing during the general election. The idea behind the matching funds was to reduce potentially corrosive fund-raising pressures during the late stages of the campaign and encourage small donations in the early going.

No one disputes that the new disclosure requirements dramatically opened up the political process, and the contribution limits prevented the kind of huge donations to candidates that had badly stained the presidential election of 1972. Indeed, for many years, presidential campaigns seemed relatively free of the taint of scandal.

But the authority of this new regulatory system was soon undermined. In 1976, in a landmark case, *Buckley* v. *Valeo,* the Supreme Court framed campaign spending as a First Amendment, free-speech issue. In other words, wealthy individuals can spend as much of their own money as they want on their own campaigns. At the same time, the controversial decision recognized the importance of "the primary purpose" of the 1974 reform law, "to limit the actuality and appearance of corruption, resulting from large individual financial contributions." The Court also held that while advertisements expressly advocating the election or defeat of a candidate for federal office could be regulated, advertisements about issues could not be restricted under the Constitution.

Separately, it soon became obvious that the FEC was incapable of independently regulating the politicians and the political industry. The agency became an easy mark for the aggressive tactics of party lawyers, accountants, and candidates. For example, because of several FEC advisory opinions, approved without hearings or public comment, beginning in the 1980s, the two major political parties were permitted to raise back-door, unlimited contributions known as "soft money." In 1995-96 the two parties raised $262 million in soft money—three times the 1991-92 total. It was mostly raised through large contributions from corporations and labor unions, which are prohibited from making direct contributions to federal candidates and committees.

What is the significance of all this? The post-Watergate reforms have been eroded and trivialized, with debilitating repercussions. Today's unvarnished political realities are:

1. Politicians and their parties can collect and spend as much money as they want.
It's not only soft money that's exploding. In 1995-96, twenty-nine organizations spent $135 million to $150 million on "issue-advocacy" advertising in the presidential and congressional elections; in 1997-98, seventy-seven groups spent roughly $300 million. Those soft-money and issue-ad numbers are expected to go through the roof in 2000. Mel Sembler, the finance chairman of the Republican National Committee, plans to raise a special, new $30 million fund "to support the most aggressive issue-advocacy program in GOP history."

2. Candidates and their campaigns are raising and spending secret money.
Presidential candidates this time around have raised millions of dollars in nonfederal accounts that aren't subject to public disclosure requirements. Their other techniques for hiding money include creating nonprofit organizations. These undisclosed revenue streams render the traditional reporting system a relic.

3. The enforcement of election laws is almost always too little, too late.
After the biggest political scandal since Watergate, not a single White House or Democratic National Committee official was indicted. The FEC is completely captive to the politicians, and would be regarded as a national embarrassment if anyone cared. A case in point: After the 1996 election scandal, even though FEC audi-

tors and FBI agents found that the Clinton and Dole campaigns had misspent tens of millions of dollars, the FEC's six commissioners—three Democrats and three Republicans—ultimately declined to impose fines or other sanctions on either side.

4. Political accountability itself is in danger of becoming a lost virtue. With voter participation and trust at historic lows, the American people have come to expect and accept the worst from their politicians. Public interest and news media interest in politics generally have declined; so has the inclination of citizens to get involved in political causes. Increasingly, the disengagement is making government the exclusive province of vested economic interests and the politicians they support. Politicians do not take responsibility for this reality, nor are they asked to. And as long as no one is marching in the streets, prodigious amounts of money will be sloshing through the system, sometimes secretly, sometimes illegally, sometimes directly influencing life-and-death public policy decisions. We also will continue to have mock sincerity and epidemic equivocation by our elected officials.

All in all, the potential for corruption is enormous, and the immediate prospects for reform are not auspicious. It is against this sobering backdrop that we have produced *The Buying of the President 2000*. We present not only chapters about the major candidates, but also the fascinating milieu in which they exist, the political parties. Ironically, as historian Arthur Schlesinger, Jr., has observed, the Articles of Confederation and the Constitution contained no mention of political parties. And yet throughout the twentieth century no one has been elected President from *outside* the Democratic and Republican parties. The candidates' ideas, organizations, and campaign finances are deeply enmeshed in the culture and daily operations of their respective political parties. We examine some of the practical, grubby realities of the two major parties in Washington, which act as legal conduits between policy makers and the most powerful economic interests affected by their decisions. These special interests open the spigots of cash flowing to the party and its leading members holding public office. And they facilitate access to power by the captains of industry and labor, who have paid handsomely and expect special consideration. Private corporations with public stature and function, these quasi-public institutions are themselves as deeply mired in high-powered influence-peddling in Washington as any lobbying firm. It is long past time that we correct our vision of these American icons.

President Harry Truman once said, "I never give them hell—I just tell the truth and they think it's hell." Over the years at the Center for Public Integrity, we have earned the enmity of a wide array of entrenched interests, and we were once dubbed "the scourge of lobbyists" by *National Journal*.

The Buying of the President in 1996 was the first book to delineate the special-interest sponsors of White House aspirants and to be published before the primaries and caucuses. When our 1996 *Under the Influence* study about campaign advisers revealed that Pat Buchanan's co-chairman, Larry Pratt, was helping hate groups such as Aryan Nation—he was removed from the campaign within hours of our news conference—we received angry calls and letters from extremists around the nation. An issue of the Center's investigative newsletter, *The Public i*, titled "Fat Cat Hotel," detailed the names of seventy-five Democratic Party donors and fund-raisers who'd stayed overnight in the Lincoln Bedroom and other upstairs rooms at the Clinton White House. And these were just three of the six investigative reports issued by the Center in 1996. Two years later, we directed our attention to Capitol Hill, in *The Buying of the Congress*. A spokesperson for Newt Gingrich, then the Speaker of the House, called our book "ridiculous" before it had even been released.

It might not surprise you, then, that we are not part of the Washington power circuit, or invited to dinners at the White House, regardless of occupant. Chances are, neither are you. But by reading *The Buying of the President 2000*, you will at least get a better idea about who is coziest with the next leader of the free world—and why.

THE PARTIES

The Democratic Party

Donald Fowler, the national chairman of the Democratic National Committee, was summoned to the family quarters of the White House on September 10, 1995, for a nine p.m. meeting with President Bill Clinton, Vice President Albert Gore, Jr., White House Chief of Staff Leon Panetta, and Deputy Chief of Staff Harold Ickes, among others.

Fowler had become the chairman of the DNC the previous January, not long after the Democrats' shellacking in the 1994 mid-term elections. While leading his party, Fowler—in the backdoor tradition of half the political party chairmen since 1977—was simultaneously working as a registered lobbyist for various corporate interests. One of his biggest clients: Chem-Nuclear Systems, Inc., a nuclear-waste disposal company that he's represented in his native South Carolina and in Illinois. "I started representing them in December 1979," Fowler told the Center for Public Integrity. "I was just about ready to leave the state [Democratic Party] chair's job here [in South Carolina]. I've been on their dole since then."

Chem-Nuclear's investment in Fowler and other lobbyists (about $350,000 in all, including generous campaign contributions to South Carolina lawmakers) paid off big in 1995, when the state legislature agreed to open the company's nuclear-waste landfill in Barnwell to the entire nation for up to ten years. The deal was "spun" by the company's lobbyists as a boost for education, inasmuch as the nuclear-waste disposal fees paid by Chem-Nuclear to the state were to be earmarked for scholarships and school construction. Fowler acknowledged in the interview that the low-level radioactive waste business is "controversial" and also admitted, referring to his lobbying activities while chairman, that he was "surprised that more of that didn't come up in the various hearings and depositions." He said, "My private business concerns never became an issue while I was there, and really haven't since."

That night at the White House, however, Fowler wasn't being called on the carpet for his mercenary moonlighting. Indeed, his activities as a lobbyist were known and accepted. ("Party chairs," he told the Center, "have historically done that.") No, tonight Fowler was being asked to go along with an unprecedented scheme to route tens of millions of dollars in private "soft money" contributions through the Democratic Party for use in a nationwide TV advertising blitz on behalf of the President. Federal law forbids using party funds in this manner for a presidential election campaign, and before 1996, no incumbent President had ever pushed the envelope so near to—or past—the legal limits.

Such a desperate measure reflected Clinton's precarious political situation. Beset by scandal almost from the moment he'd taken the oath of office, Clinton had seen his chief legislative initiative, health-care reform, die in 1994. And in November of that year, the Democrats had lost eight seats in the Senate and fifty-two seats in the House of Representatives, giving the Republicans control of Congress for the first time in forty years.

Clinton, then, was beginning to look like a one-term President. He secretly turned to political consultant Dick Morris, an old ally and political lifesaver from his Arkansas gubernatorial days. In March 1995, Morris recommended a $40 million paid media campaign that would hit 43 percent of the U.S. population, to begin as soon as possible. Clinton and his advisers toyed with the idea of forgoing federal matching funds and the strict spending limits that come with them, but they ultimately rejected that option as impractical politically. It was also clear, however, that the presidential campaign spending limits precluded an aggressive paid media campaign on behalf of Clinton a full year before the election. Both Morris and Ickes, to this day, remain proud of their solution to the problem: to use soft-money funds routed through the Democratic Party to pay for "issue advertising," thus circumventing federal election laws. That way, the President's image could be refurbished without drawing down his campaign war chest for 1996.

No one at the White House meeting that night questioned the idea of bending the law in this way for political advantage. Hand-wringing over issues of ethics, in fact, has not exactly been a hallmark of the Clinton Administration, to put it charitably. Moreover, the participants had been advised that the ploy was legal. All the President and his White House team needed now was Fowler's expected acquiescence, since the Democratic Party would be the pretext and the conduit for the money scheme. He didn't disappoint them. As Fowler later testified in his Senate deposition, the advertising "was to be funded by the party, but it would focus on the President's program for the party and what he had done. . . . There was a general consensus that this was a good idea."

Weeks later, at a fund-raising dinner at the posh Hay-Adams Hotel in Washington, Clinton proudly described the scheme. "We realized that we could run these ads through the Democratic Party, which meant that we could raise money in twenty and fifty and hundred-thousand-dollar lots, and we didn't have to do it all in thousand-dollar [lots]," he said. "And run down—you know—what I can spend, which is limited by law. So that's what we've done."

Many of the excesses of the 1996 presidential campaign, we now know, were directly related to this conscious decision by the President, the Vice President, their White House and campaign aides, and the Democratic Party to subvert the nation's existing campaign-finance laws. The only way to raise such huge sums of cash, everyone knew, would be for the President and Vice President to get personally involved in fund raising, even by making cold calls from within the White House itself. The garish images of unabashedly selling access to the icons of our democracy persist today, of systematically rewarding large donors with invitations to White House coffees, overnight stays in the Lincoln Bedroom and at Camp David, flights on Air Force One, and so on.

Never have we seen such a dubious array of characters plying our nation's leaders with campaign cash—from an Arkansas restaurateur and an Indonesian billionaire to Buddhist nuns, Chinese arms merchants, and a convicted Colombian drug dealer. All of it distracted us, of course, from the hundreds of millions of dollars invested by powerful economic interests every year in the Washington decision-making process. It's not that other Presidents haven't sold access to their most generous backers in the past; they just haven't done it so systematically, so shamelessly. In retrospect, it was destined to become a national scandal—resulting in congressional investigations, hundreds of hours of hearings, tens of thousands of news stories, and an assortment of little-fish types (nineteen individuals, at most recent count) charged with violating federal campaign-finance laws. And the President's first instinct, when the scandal initially hit the public consciousness, was to disingenuously fob it off on the Democratic Party, a distinction without a difference. "That was the other campaign that had problems with that, not mine."

Presidents have always been the de facto leaders of their respective political parties, and not surprisingly, their White House and political-campaign staffs have exerted substantial influence over the operation and management of the parties. But in 1996 there was such a blurring of responsibility and authority between the Clinton White House, the Clinton-Gore campaign, and the Democratic Party as to make them all practically indistinguishable from each other.

The same company that handled the Clinton-Gore campaign's TV commercials, for example, produced the DNC-sponsored "issue ads." The White House's mammoth database of contacts, built and maintained with millions of dollars in public funds, was meshed with the DNC's donor database. The DNC's Robert "Bobby" Watson was given that sensitive assignment; an internal White House memorandum revealed that Clinton and Ickes personally wanted it done. Watson, who had pleaded guilty in 1992 to distributing an illegally intercepted telephone call of Virginia Governor Doug

Wilder—became the DNC's deputy executive director in 1994; its executive director in 1995, under Fowler; and by 1996 he had left and joined a Washington lobbying firm.

As Morris testified, President Clinton was the "day-to-day operational director" of the DNC-sponsored media campaign. He "worked over every script, watched each ad, ordered changes in every visual presentation, and decided which ads would run when and where." Clinton also was deeply involved in operations and personnel at the DNC, insisting, for example, that a man named John Huang be hired to help raise money. (More than $2 million of the money he helped to raise came from illegal or questionable sources and eventually had to be returned; Huang himself is now a convicted felon.) The President had approved the appointment of Fowler as the DNC's chairman. He had also approved Marvin Rosen, a Miami lawyer, to be the DNC's finance chairman in 1995. Federal regulators had accused Rosen of unethical practices that contributed to the failure of a Florida savings-and-loan institution that he had represented and helped to finance. In 1992 his law firm agreed to pay $8.15 million to the Resolution Trust Corporation, the agency that oversaw the S&L bailout.

Apparently no one found it odd that a registered lobbyist for a nuclear waste-dumping company, a convicted political dirty-trickster, and a key figure in an S&L scandal were running the National Democratic Committee as chairman, executive director, and treasurer, respectively. Perhaps that is some kind of metaphor for Washington today.

Soon after Rosen began collecting campaign cash for Clinton and the DNC, he capitalized on his new status and opened a lobbying office in Washington for his law firm. Among those he hired there were Commerce Secretary Ronald Brown's son Michael and Senator Edward Kennedy's wife Victoria, according to the *New York Times*. Some major party donors began to retain Rosen's firm to do their lobbying in Washington, including controversial oil financier Roger Tamraz, who gave $300,000 to the Democratic Party. He had been ordered by a French court to pay more than $50 million for diverting funds from a French bank that collapsed, and he faced a Lebanese arrest warrant for allegedly embezzling $154 million to $200 million from a bank in that country. Even though he was an international fugitive, Tamraz was invited to six social events at the White House, and he spoke directly with the President about his oil pipeline project in the Caucasus, for which he sought U.S. support. He also attended a dinner with the Vice President at the home of Senator Kennedy. "The only reason to give money is to get access," Tamraz, with brazen candor, later told members of the Senate Governmental Affairs Committee. "I think next time I'll give $600,000."

Tamraz had Rosen and Fowler—two of the Democratic Party's top officials—in his pocket. There is detailed evidence that Fowler contacted officials of the CIA and the National Security Council in his efforts to "clear Tamraz's name," contacts later described by the investigating Senate committee as "*highly* inappropriate." Unfortunately, such intervention on behalf of a donor was no aberration.

The DNC, for example, attempted to influence a decision by the Interior Department's Bureau of Indian Affairs regarding a group of Wisconsin Indian tribes that were seeking to open a casino in Hudson, Wisconsin. Neighboring tribes in Minnesota, worried about the competition, opposed the proposal. The application was eventually denied, even though career BIA officials at the regional and national levels had recommended that it be approved. It was a victory for the wealthier Minnesota tribes, which within months gave more than $330,000 to national and state Democratic Party organizations and hired a former DNC treasurer to be their Washington lobbyist. Representatives of these Minnesota tribes had met with Fowler, who subsequently called Ickes and an official of the Interior Department. "Whatever they contributed or didn't contribute had nothing to do with my actions in that regard," Fowler later told members of the Senate Governmental Affairs Committee. "We are happy to receive contributions that are made honestly and with integrity, and I assumed that those contributions were made in that vein." Interior Secretary Bruce Babbitt gave conflicting testimony to Congress about the affair, and an independent counsel found that there was insufficient evidence to warrant charges against either Ickes or him. The Senate committee's conclusion: "Political donations to the DNC apparently succeeded in purchasing government policy concessions."

It was widely understood in 1996 that both the Clinton–Gore campaign and the Democratic Party were, for all intents and purposes, being run from the White House. Thus, the most significant decisions about soliciting campaign funds, spending that money, and responding to the policy concerns of big donors all ultimately intersected at 1600 Pennsylvania Avenue. Ickes put it this way in his deposition for the Senate committee: "The President . . . is the CEO of the party. If the President says this is the way I want it, it was up to me to see that it was done, and the [DNC] chairman understood that." Indeed, this was so excruciatingly obvious to Fowler that not once did he protest or appeal an Ickes decision to Clinton himself. Not surprisingly, however, Fowler resented how Ickes had usurped his authority as chairman. "I did feel that he was involved in the management of the DNC in a fashion that I didn't appreciate, that I didn't agree with."

Despite that friction, there certainly was unanimous consent that to succeed at the polls, the nation's oldest political party would have to accumulate astounding sums of money. And it happened. Various Democratic Party committees raised $345 million, up 61 percent from $214 million in the 1992 presidential election cycle. The amount of large "soft money" contributions to the party tripled. They couldn't have done it without the President's active involvement: In 1996 alone, Clinton attended more than 230 fund-raising events around the nation, which generated at least $119 million in contributions. "I haven't slept in three days," Morris recalled Clinton complaining. "I cannot think, I cannot do anything. Every minute of my time is spent at these fund-raisers." Vice President Gore, similarly engaged, reportedly came to be called the "Solicitor-in-Chief" within the DNC.

The Democratic Party accepted so many contributions of questionable origin that it ultimately was forced to return at least $2.8 million in illegal or improper donations. This epitomizes the now inexplicable: that in the headlong dash for cash, the Democratic Party's internal vetting process had been quietly eliminated somewhere along the way. After months of hearings and thousands of pages of depositions, it is still unclear how or why that happened.

And so, Americans watched their political process sink to new levels of crassness and absurdity. Who can forget the case of

Johnny Chung, a Taiwanese businessman who, along with his company, made $366,000 in contributions to the Democratic Party from 1994 to 1996? The money was later returned, and Chung was subsequently convicted of bank fraud, tax evasion, and conspiracy. Chung had been inside the Clinton White House at least forty-nine times. "The White House is like a subway," he explained to a reporter for the *Los Angeles Times*. "You have to put in coins to open the gates."

Fowler and his staff at the DNC personally helped Chung slot his token. Fowler met with Chung and a group of business executives from China, and later he personally intervened to make sure that Chung and his foreign guests could attend the President's Saturday radio address at the White House. That day Shi-Zeng Chen, the founder and president of Tangshan Haomen Group, China's second-largest beer producer, was pleased to have his picture taken with President Clinton—a photograph later used to advertise beer in China.

Who knows how many Johnny Chungs were given red-carpet treatment by Fowler and his DNC staff, people and favors that we know nothing about? And, inasmuch as the Freedom of Information Act doesn't apply to White House records, who knows how many lobbyists and CEOs sat down with the President privately, more subtly working the "subway" system, out of public view?

In his prepared Senate testimony, Fowler became the first national political party chairman to unabashedly acknowledge, in broad daylight, what he and other party officials do to "service" donors. "I have long believed that one of the principal functions of a political party is to provide a link between the people and government," he said. "I thus believe it fully appropriate for the head of a national party to secure a meeting for a supporter with an administration official and to advocate a worthy cause. Members of Congress do this, staff members of Congress do this. It is your responsibility, their responsibility, it is appropriate for the head of a national political party to do it."

Stepping past the horse manure, covered as it may be with the shiny gold straw of Washington-speak, the fact is that party officials help pretty much anyone with a big enough political bankroll. Every cause is worthy, so long as the cash rolls in. How else to explain the helping hands for international fugitives or Chinese beer distributors? Fowler was a facilitator between politician and patron, an *enabler* helping politicians to keep drinking in the cash and helping their patrons feel good about giving it. Party chairmen are by definition the best-connected lobbyists in Washington, and their lobbying is done on behalf of the party's most generous donors (though none of that activity must be disclosed to the public, under the current laws). So much for the quaint, civics-class notion that political parties exist almost entirely to elect candidates.

Both parties have, increasingly, bent the nation's campaign-finance laws to their own ends. In the 1995-96 election cycle, for example, they displayed remarkable gumption in using nonprofit, ostensibly nonpartisan organizations to do their political bidding. There was the strange story of Warren Meddoff, who caused President Clinton to do a double take at a fund-raising event in Miami. Meddoff—later described by journalist Elizabeth Drew as "a pudgy man wearing a diamond pinky ring"—gave Clinton his business card, on which he had written, "I have an associate that is interested in donating $5 million to your campaign." Meddoff told the Senate committee that the President of the United States "took two steps, looked at it, came back, and asked if he could have another one of those cards." Days later, from Air Force One, Harold Ickes telephoned Meddoff, who informed him that the donation needed to be made "in a tax-favorable way." Ickes subsequently had his assistant at the White House fax Meddoff a list of four Democrat-friendly tax-exempt groups—complete with the bank-account numbers needed for the wire transfers that Ickes sought.

The Senate Governmental Affairs Committee subpoenaed records of no fewer than thirty-two nonprofit organizations in an effort to determine if they "were genuinely nonpartisan and acted independently of political parties or candidates, as required by federal law" in the 1996 election cycle. Most of the organizations simply ignored the subpoenas, refusing to produce any documents or witnesses. Apparently no organization was more obstinately unresponsive than the AFL-CIO, which the committee's investigators found had coordinated its political activities with both the DNC and the Clinton-Gore campaign.

For decades, labor unions have been a major political presence in Washington, contributing generously to the Democratic Party and its candidates. The AFL-CIO and its member unions have gotten more aggressive under the new leadership of its president, John Sweeney. According to the Center for Responsive Politics, in the 1995-96 election cycle, labor unions spent at least $119 million on federal political activity—nearly $66 million in contributions to political candidates and committees, $35 million on issue ads, and $18.5 million on lobbying at the federal level. But labor has never been truly competitive with business, which outspent it seven to one in 1995-96. Then, in 1996, the AFL-CIO dramatically announced that it would spend $35 million to defeat Republican candidates in seventy-five targeted congressional districts. It planned, as part of that effort, to train and deploy as many as three hundred full-time organizers. In many ways, union members remain, as they have traditionally been, the foot soldiers of the Democratic Party.

In the 1970s the Democrat-controlled Congress exempted labor unions from limits on "in-kind contributions" to political candidates. Consequently, from telephone banks to the daily use of paid union employees, there are virtually no limits and hardly any disclosure. Leo Troy, a professor of economics at Rutgers University, has estimated that the unions provide $300 million to $500 million in such "in-kind" contributions in presidential election cycles, a statistic Republicans quickly point to when they are asked about their substantial financial edge in national elections. In his last months in office, President George Bush issued an executive order that required greater disclosure. But it was promptly voided by President Clinton.

Nonetheless, the actual reported contributions shouldn't be underestimated. Labor unions contributed at least $58.8 million to the two major political parties and to federal candidates and committees in 1995-96—93 percent of it to Democrats—and spent at least an additional $6.8 million on independent expenditures and communications costs, according to the Center for Responsive Politics. The most interesting part of the equation, however, is labor's soft-money giving, which jumped 124 percent from the 1992 to the 1996 election cycles.

Throughout the 1990s, in fact, unions have been among the largest providers of soft money to the Democratic Party. In our "Top Fifty Patrons" list of soft-money contributors to the party from 1991 through June 1999, six of the top ten are labor unions: the American Federation of State, County, and Municipal Employees (AFSCME) was the No. 1 donor, at $3.7 million; the Communications Workers of America (CWA) was No. 2, at $3.6 million; the National Education Association (NEA) was No. 4, at $2.6 million; the American Federation of Teachers (AFT) was No. 5 at $2.1 million; the Service Employees International Union (SEIU) was No. 6, at $2 million; and the United Food and Commercial Workers (UFCW) was No. 9, at $1.8 million.*

Interestingly, the NEA and the AFT—together representing 3.2 million public school teachers and administrators and college and university professors nationwide—have considered merging over the years. If their totals were combined, it means that school teachers nationwide have given the Democratic Party more soft money—more than $7 million in all—than anyone else.

The meshing of Democratic Party, Clinton Administration, and labor union gears has been quite apparent the past seven years. Clinton was never labor's favorite Democrat—the AFL-CIO Executive Council did not endorse him for President until after he'd secured the party nomination. He confirmed labor's worst fears, on the issue of international trade, with his administration's aggressive push for the North American Free Trade Agreement (NAFTA). But union leaders were heartened that he supported one of their favorite issues, national health-care insurance, and they embraced and fought for his proposed plan. By 1995, Clinton, Capitol Hill Democrats, and the unions all especially needed each other after the GOP's stunning takeover of Congress. Facing hostile and newly

---

*In the interest of full disclosure, it should be noted that The Center for Public Integrity accepted contributions from labor unions (and corporations) from 1990 to 1994, totaling $197,500, or seven percent of its total income during that period.

empowered forces in both chambers of Congress, Clinton pledged to veto any attempts to repeal the Davis-Bacon Act, which sets wage rates on federal construction projects, to name one of several very real possibilities feared by the unions.

In the summer of 1996, Congress passed and the President signed into law a bill boosting the minimum wage from $4.25 to $5.15 an hour. The only way Clinton and the unions could get the legislation passed was by bundling it with $21 billion in tax breaks for corporate America, essentially buying off such low-wage employers as pizza chains and convenience-store operators, and by labeling it the Small Business Job Protection Act of 1996. As AFL-CIO President John Sweeney complained to us two years ago, "It wasn't even called a minimum-wage bill."

But that kind of frustrating, back-door progress, from labor's perspective, is necessary these days. Members of labor unions make up only 14 percent of the workforce, and despite all the campaign contributions and an occasional victory on the public-relations front, this actually is one of the low points in the history of the U.S. labor movement. A few unions have practically more retirees drawing pensions than actual dues-paying members. And yet a visit to some of the cavernous Washington buildings that serve as the headquarters of many of the largest unions does make one wonder, as writer Jonathan Tasini has, if union officials do not have an "edifice complex." He calculated the real estate values of union-owned buildings in Washington, D.C., at more than $300 million. And he has written that unions further squandered their resources not on organizing new members but on political contributions at the national level—roughly $250 million from 1979 to 1992.

Some of these buildings seem eerily empty and strangely quiet. As labor lawyer Thomas Geoghegan writes in his poignant book, *Which Side Are You On?*, organized labor is "too old, too arthritic, to be a cause. It was a cause, back in the thirties. Now it is a dumb, stupid mastodon of a thing, crawling off to Bal Harbour to die. . . . I still read in the press about 'Labor' and 'Business' on Capitol Hill, fighting over policy, and I think, '*Labor?* What are they talking about?' . . . Labor cannot even organize the people who want to join."

Meanwhile, the international union presidents are very well-paid, very well-fed, and very well-traveled, with multimillion-dollar annual conventions and meetings in Hawaii and other exotic venues. Robert Georgine, for example, draws one salary as the president of the AFL-CIO Building and Construction Trades Department and another as the chairman and chief executive officer of Union Labor Life Insurance Company, a 1,400-employee health and life insurance company with more than $400 million in annual revenues. Georgine isn't the only union president to fly on a private jet.

The Clinton Administration got NAFTA passed into law, accelerated the privatization of public-sector jobs as part of its "reinventing government" initiatives, and overhauled the nation's welfare system—all of which, ironically, represented labor's worst Republican nightmares and have contributed to the loss of thousands of union jobs. Nonetheless, to the unions, Clinton and the Democratic Party are regarded as infinitely better and friendlier than the alternative. Clinton certainly understands the political reality that unions have nowhere else to go. And, drawing on his remarkable political skills, he has quieted their occasional anger and public criticism with the ego-gratifying accouterments of presidential power and high social status in Washington. Thus, union presidents fly with him on Air Force One and attend various White House functions, from the infamous "coffees" to state dinners and Rose Garden ceremonies. That and access to power throughout the Executive Branch, which for the most part they did not have through twelve cold years of the Reagan and Bush administrations, are tangible benefits to unions of their alliance with Clinton and the Democratic Party.

But that, unfortunately, isn't the worst of it. The White House and the Democratic Party have coddled and collaborated politically with union leaders who are well known to be corrupt. And Clinton and his party have given the impression to the millions of rank-and-file union members nationwide that greed and corruption at the highest levels of the labor movement are no big deal, and are thus acceptable. Indeed, the Center was unable to find a single utterance by President Clinton or Vice President Gore about the vexing problem of union corruption. In an odd way, the White

House, the Democratic Party, and the labor unions have all effectively silenced each other. The President and his party have sought and received hundreds of millions of dollars in political contributions and electioneering from the unions, and are not about to bite the hands that are feeding them. And the unions have sought and received access to power and been able to obtain some policy and even tangible financial gains, and are not about to crow too loudly when the New Democrats enact another pro-business law that's detrimental to rank-and-file union members.

Take the case of Arthur Coia, the president of the 750,000-member Laborers' International Union of North America, which since 1991 has given at least $1.2 million in soft money to the Democratic Party. Coia, who earned more than $420,000 in 1998, was found by his own union to have had "a direct conflict of interest" by jointly owning a Ferrari with a car-leasing company that did business with the union. It fined him $100,000 for engaging in an improper business investment with a union vendor. The Justice Department has had a criminal investigation of Coia and his union for years, and in 1994 it determined that Coia has "associated with and been controlled by" mobsters. In 1995, however, the Justice Department decided to allow the Laborers to attempt to regulate themselves. A group of former federal prosecutors and FBI agents hired by the Laborers has removed roughly 200 union members and officials and taken control of twenty local and district councils. But, as part of this same process, a union hearing officer also decided that Coia was not under the control of organized crime and thus could stay in his position.

Meanwhile, Coia has dramatically increased his political clout in Washington. Besides his union's huge contributions to the Democratic Party, Coia cohosted a 1994 fund-raising event that raked in more than $3.5 million for the DNC, and he was vice-chairman of a May 1996 bash that produced more than $12 million for the party. Not only has Coia been a frequent guest at the White House, but he's also traveled on Air Force One with Clinton several times, including his trip to Denver to greet the Pope. In 1994, First Lady Hillary Rodham Clinton addressed a Laborers' union conference in Florida, ignoring the Justice Department's recommendation that she refrain because of the government's ongoing criminal investigations.

Partisan critics and a few dissident union members have decried all of this, not surprisingly, alleging that Coia and his cronies would have been prosecuted were it not for their close relationship with Clinton and the Democratic Party. The conservative, decidedly anti-union Heritage Foundation actually has documented that in the first two years of the Clinton Administration, the financially desperate Laborers' union received nearly $30 million in grants from several federal departments and agencies, including the Department of Housing and Urban Development and the Environmental Protection Agency. And according to an account in *The Washington Monthly,* Coia personally lobbied Clinton for federal grants at a fall 1994 meeting in the Oval Office; Clinton told Coia that Harold Ickes, his deputy chief of staff, would personally handle it. (Before joining the White House staff, Ickes, a labor lawyer, represented, among others, the Laborers' union.)

Then there is the matter of the 245,000-member Hotel Employees and Restaurant Employees International Union, with decades of well-known corruption and associations with organized crime. Its president, Edward Hanley, ruled the union for twenty-five years, until his forced retirement in July 1998. The union provided Hanley with a luxury condominium in Georgetown, which he used infrequently since he was never in the Washington headquarters more than twenty-five days a year. The union leased office space in Chicago and Palm Springs, California, not far from homes owned by Hanley. The only employee in the latter office was Hanley's mother-in-law, who told investigators that "she would like to be productive." Hanley had a $2.5 million Sabreliner private jet, sometimes used to fly Mrs. Hanley, traveling alone, between Chicago and Palm Springs. The union also maintained a fleet of sixty leased vehicles, in addition to limousines owned in Washington and Chicago. Hanley, a native of Chicago, had more than a hundred well-paid organizers and consultants on his union's payroll, from Jesse Jackson, Jr. (before he was elected to Congress), and former Senator Alan Dixon of Illinois to former House Ways and Means Committee chairman Dan Rostenkowski. Rostenkowski's $150,000 consulting agreement was apparently signed after his indictment by a federal grand jury and was terminated only after he was convicted.

Perhaps Hanley's most stunning indulgence, however, was the $450,000 in union funds that went to building the Edward T. Hanley Basketball Arena outside Dublin, Ireland. In 1993 Hanley led a thirty-four-member delegation of union officials and guests, including his wife, to the dedication of the arena with all expenses paid, of course, by the union.

"This [case] was an eye-opener to me," Kurt Muellenberg, the union's court-appointed monitor, told the Center. (Muellenberg has more than twenty years experience as a Justice Department prosecutor of organized crime and union corruption in Cleveland, Detroit, and Washington.) "Union leadership at all levels was hardly ever challenged. And the level of corruption and in-your-face arrogance are startling." As for Hanley, with whom he had several conversations, "there was never any sense of contrition," Muellenberg said. Indeed, in his formal immunity agreement with the Justice Department, Hanley did not admit any wrongdoing, and the investigative report was sealed until after his forced retirement. He will not be prosecuted.

Like other unions in the AFL-CIO, Hanley's contributed heavily to Democratic Party and Clinton campaigns.

Of course, no union in the United States is considered to have a more notoriously corrupt history than the International Brotherhood of Teamsters. Six of the past eight presidents of the Teamsters union, from Jimmy Hoffa to Ron Carey, were indicted, convicted, or sued by the federal government while in office for such offenses as pension-fund looting and racketeering. In 1989, as part of a consent decree, the union was placed under the control of the Justice Department. But even that did not prevent the fraudulent reelection of Ron Carey in 1996. The onetime "reform" leader was expelled from the Teamsters after three of his top campaign officials pleaded guilty to several felonies for siphoning money from the union's general fund. Nor did federal "oversight" prevent the looting of what was once the nation's largest most powerful union. During Carey's tenure, its treasury plummeted from $154 million to $16 million. From 1991 to 1996, as the union was careening toward bankruptcy, it was spending more than $18 million on a wide range of political activities and borrowing nearly $16 million to help pay for its activism.

Carey's point man at the White House was Ickes, who forwarded a memo to Clinton about the political importance of the Teamsters union and highlighted for his attention language in it that urged Clinton "to develop a better relationship with Carey," which he did. Congressional hearings and reports by two committees have shown at least one way in which Ickes attempted to help Carey. The Teamsters were in the midst of a seemingly interminable strike against Diamond Walnut Growers, Inc., in Stockton, California. Ickes got U.S. Trade Representative Michael "Mickey" Kantor to call William Cuff, the president and chief executive officer of the cooperative, and say that the strike "was interfering with international trade issues." When Ickes stated in his Senate deposition that the Clinton Administration did "nothing that I know of" to help the Teamsters in the Diamond Walnut Growers strike, it became the subject of a preliminary investigation by Attorney General Janet Reno for possible perjury. An independent counsel was not appointed.

By 1996 there had been much mutual back-scratching between the Teamsters, the White House, and the Democratic Party. And so a deal was struck, a complicated scheme that happens to have been illegal. The Teamsters would continue to pour unprecedented sums into the Clinton-Gore campaign and Democratic Party committees, and in exchange the Democrats would help to finance Carey's own reelection campaign. They couldn't do that directly, of course, so the money was laundered through a liberal public-interest organization, Citizen Action, and through other groups, including the National Council of Senior Citizens and Project Vote. Federal law prohibits employers from contributing to any union election. More than $4 million in DNC money moved to Citizen Action and other groups, and at least $885,000 in union funds was illegally diverted into Carey's reelection campaign.

Today, the carnage from this scandal and the continuing federal criminal grand-jury investigation casts a pall over the entire labor movement. Three individuals have pleaded guilty to embezzlement, mail fraud, and conspiracy and have been cooperating with the federal prosecutors. (One of them, Michael Ansara, still does major consulting business with the DNC via his company, the Share Group.) A fourth, William Hamilton, a former political director of the Teamsters union, has been indicted. The AFL-CIO's No. 2 official, Richard Trumka, who as secretary-treasurer signed some of the checks, has asserted his Fifth Amendment right against self-incrimination—to federal prosecutors, to a court-appointed labor investigator, to a congressional committee, and even to AFL-CIO president Sweeney.

It's difficult for many labor insiders to accept that Trumka hatched such a plan. No one seems to know for sure how the high-level labor conversations exactly went with respect to the illegal scheme involving the Democratic Party and the Teamsters, but Gerald McEntee, the president AFSCME and the chairman of the AFL-CIO's political committee (a position he assumed in 1995), certainly was involved. He has had a close personal friendship with Carey. McEntee retained an attorney, paid for by AFSCME, to represent him in the teamsters matter and admitted to federal prosecutors that he sought a campaign donation of $20,000 to the Carey campaign from the owners of a company that does major business with AFSCME. Kelly Press, Inc. is barred by federal law from contributing to a union campaign, and McEntee apparently broke government-imposed rules for union elections by soliciting an AFSCME supplier. Paul Booth, an aide to McEntee who's married to Heather Booth, a former DNC official and a founder of Citizen Action, also has said under oath that he raised thousands of dollars for Carey.

"What we did, according to our attorneys, was nothing illegal," McEntee told the Center. "We cooperated fully and completely with the people who were investigating this case, and that's about the size of it," said Booth.

But there is, as they say, much more to the story.

McEntee has been the president of the nation's largest union of public employees since 1981, following the death of Jerry Wurf. Wurf, who boosted the union's membership from 200,000 to roughly one million—organizing police officers, firefighters, sanitation and hospital workers, and other government employees from coast to coast—was enormously respected for his honesty and his independence. A case in point: He opposed the U.S. involvement in the Vietnam war, to the consternation of George Meany, then the president of the AFL-CIO. Under Wurf, AFSCME became known as a pioneer in aggressively recruiting women and blacks. It is a forgotten footnote of history that the mostly black, striking garbage workers who in April 1968 drew the Reverend Martin Luther King, Jr., to Memphis, where he was assassinated, were AFSCME members. (The day before he was shot, King gave an inspiring speech on the significance of the AFSCME strike in the centuries-long struggle for freedom and civil rights. King's closing words, including the famous "I've been to the mountaintop," seemed to have eerily predicted his tragic death.)

In McEntee's two decades of stewardship, AFSCME's membership has grown only modestly, and no one seems to know the exact number (the union's annual reports to the Labor Department have suspiciously listed the same membership figure for the past five years: 1.3 million). As in many unions today, secrecy continues to reign. It is not well-known that the progressive union respected for its commitment to civil rights and diversity—it once brought Nelson Mandela to speak to its national convention—was sued by ten employees for race discrimination. AFSCME settled all the cases out of court. "McEntee was made aware of the situation and he did not take steps to deal with it," a union insider told the Center. "If you set a permissive environment, if people get a sense that discrimination doesn't matter, then it will reverberate throughout the organization."

Long considered one of the "clean" unions, a cloud of corruption has now begun to surround AFSCME. Besides the Teamsters scandal that's swirling around McEntee and Booth, in recent years no fewer than six AFSCME international vice-presidents have been forced to resign. Consider the following:

In New York City, Stanley Hill, the executive director of AFSCME District Council 37, retired after spending several months on unpaid leave pending investigation. Two of his top aides resigned following their admissions that they had helped to rig the vote on the local's 1996 contract ratification. Also in New York City, Albert Diop was removed last year as the president of an AFSCME clerical workers local. Diop and three others charged more than $1 million in personal expenses on their union credit cards and spent nearly $1.2 million on undocumented "hospitality" payments when traveling. Diop spent more than $600,000 to rent a penthouse apartment and ran up $162,431 in hotel charges in New York City for 446 nights, including 128 on weekends, even though he has a residence in the city. He also spent nearly $135,000 over three years to lease a Lincoln Town Car even though he already had a $665-a-month automobile allowance. In Connecticut, Dominic Badolato was expelled from AFSCME for using illegal strong-arm tactics against his political opponents. In Boston, Joseph Bonavita had to leave his union after an audit revealed he had been paid $82,416 in unauthorized bonuses and undocumented reimbursements. In Iowa, Don McKee was convicted of helping himself to $43,000 in union money. And in Pennsylvania, Earl Stout was convicted of racketeering, embezzlement, and mail fraud.

"Wherever we have found this [corruption], we have rooted it out, and we have either suspended or dismissed the union leaders that were involved," McEntee told the Center. "We are a good union, we are a clean union."

When Wurf died, he was making about $108,000 a year in salary and allowances and had refused a raise. Eighteen years later, McEntee makes $375,000 a year, and he also got his friendly board to adopt a deferred compensation plan so that when he retires he will receive nearly 100 percent of his salary. "I think you ought to get decent pay, a decent pension, decent benefits," McEntee told the Center.

AFSCME also provides McEntee with a car and a chauffeur as well as an $1,800-a-month automobile expense allowance. Sources told the Center that McEntee spends more than $100,000 a year in AFSCME funds to travel around the United States on charter jets and stay in the finest hotel suites, and he is a fixture at such "power lunch" expense-account restaurants in Washington as The Palm, where his caricature is on the wall. None of this information, of course, is in AFSCME's annual reports to the Labor Department.

Referring to McEntee and, in general, the unseemly extravagances of today's union leaders, a veteran AFSCME member who asked that his name not be used told the Center, "They think they're becoming the captains of industry, for chrissakes! . . . I guess they forgot what they're supposed to be doing."

The Center has learned that McEntee personally benefited from the generosity of certain AFSCME vendors, a violation of union rules. Consider the case of Kelly Press, which contributed $20,000 to the Teamster election at McEntee's urging. Over the years, the company has gotten millions of dollars in printing business from AFSCME. McEntee and Paul Kelly, a co-owner of the company, frequently play tennis at Congressional Country Club, in Bethesda, Maryland, where Kelly is a member, and sources told the Center that McEntee has been an occasional guest on the Kellys' fishing boat. The relationship goes back at least a decade. When McEntee was remarried, Kelly arranged for the wedding reception to be at Congressional. "The only way that you can have a wedding there is that a member has to sponsor you," McEntee told the Center. "So the Kellys sponsored us."

No union president is closer to Bill Clinton today than McEntee; the two men have assiduously courted each other for nearly a decade now. AFSCME was the first national union to back Clinton, even before the 1992 New Hampshire primary, when he was still a dark horse. Clinton had spoken to the AFSCME board, and he brought along a letter of support from 840 AFSCME members in Arkansas. He even showed them his own AFSCME membership card. Days later, McEntee assigned three staff members to work for Clinton in New Hampshire. And so it began.

Since 1993, McEntee has reveled in his personal access to the President. From the private St. Patrick's Day party at the White House and various Rose Garden events, to trips on Air Force One and Friday night bull sessions at the White House mess, McEntee, to quote a veteran union insider, "got lost in space over that stuff." ("I've only been on Air Force One maybe six times—that's six times in eight years—so it's not like I take a trip every three weeks," McEntee told the Center.) At McEntee's sixtieth birthday celebration a few years ago at Washington's Capital Hilton hotel, Clinton spoke warmly about how McEntee had always been there for him. McEntee and AFSCME have certainly been there financially for Clinton and his party, more than anyone else in America, to the tune of more than $3.6 million. The union has an elaborate get-out-the-vote operation, a voter registration effort, and an extensive phone bank system, in addition to the contributions to politicians at all levels of government. McEntee led the AFL-CIO's highly publicized $35 million ad campaign in 1996. And McEntee, the Center has learned, called a meeting to personally urge higher-ups at AFSCME to make contributions to the President's legal expense fund.

Unfortunately, such access comes at a steep price. On policy issues of greatest concern to AFSCME's members, in public McEntee has been largely silent. McEntee doesn't criticize Clinton by name, and if he feels obligated politically to criticize the administration, which is rare, he has sometimes called the White House in advance to explain it and quietly warn Clinton and his staff. Take, for example, the subject of national health care insurance. For years AFSCME had advocated the liberal "single payer" plan with the greatest government role—not surprising for a union whose largest contingent is 325,000 health and hospital workers. But under the Clinton-McEntee spell, the union muted its public advocacy for this policy and fell in line behind the White House. As the Center described in its 1994 study, *Well-Healed: Inside Lobbying for Health Care Reform,* just weeks before Clinton's inauguration in January 1993, there was a high-level, unusual confrontation at AFSCME headquarters between Ralph Nader and McEntee.

Nader invoked the example of Franklin Roosevelt, after he had been elected President, telling his supporters, "You elected me, now go out there and make me do it." Nader argued that advocates of a single-payer approach could not squander the opportunity and had a moral obligation to speak out forcefully. McEntee, by contrast, stressed the extraordinary access they all now had after twelve years of being completely shut out. The basic response was, "We're going to handle this our way, behind the scenes."

AFSCME chose not to wage a postcard campaign, or to support a very public bus caravan to Little Rock, Arkansas, to promote the single-payer option. And in early 1993, at a meeting of the AFL-CIO health care committee, McEntee and AFSCME voted in favor of managed competition, abandoning its long-held single-payer position. AFSCME also poured money into television issue ads in support of the Clinton health care plan—ads that were intended to counter the highly effective "Harry and Louise" commercials paid for by the insurance companies. In addition, the Center has learned that when the President and the First Lady embarked on a bus tour "to the heartland" to garner public support for the administration's ill-fated plan, McEntee's union agreed to help pay for it.

The bottom line, however, is that during the 1993-94 struggle over health care reform, organized labor, including AFSCME, was politically ineffective and ultimately unsuccessful. McEntee remains unbowed about his inside approach, however. In the spring of 1996, he met with Clinton, urging that the White House address the public concern over managed health care, and months later the President named McEntee to a commission on health care quality.

The "reinventing government" mantra of the Clinton-Gore Administration has presented McEntee with an interesting problem, as AFSCME faces initiatives nationwide to privatize many traditional state and local government functions—which, on its face, is a direct affront to the union's membership. McEntee's public posture is to support the idea of making government more efficient and responsive by eliminating red tape and redundant management, and to decry privatization when it cheats citizens by failing to provide adequate services by trained employees. AFSCME forged an innovative privatization agreement with the Republican mayor of Indianapolis, Stephen Goldsmith, in which the local union avoided mass layoffs. McEntee has testified before Congress that AFSCME regularly wins back 80 percent of privatized contracts, by bidding successfully or working with management to redesign the system in lieu of privatization.

McEntee was not directly critical of the President when he proposed welfare reform, which union leaders have estimated could cost more than 200,000 jobs, and got it enacted. But he and other union leaders successfully lobbied the administration—over Republican opposition on Capitol Hill—to rule that people who must work for their welfare benefits are protected by federal labor law and entitled to the minimum wage.

McEntee and others were able to gain another back-door concession. In a March 28, 1997 meeting with the President, McEntee, Sweeney, and two other union presidents urged Clinton to reject a request by Texas Governor George W. Bush, a Republican, for federal permission to allow private companies to manage several Texas welfare programs, which could have meant the loss of 5,000 public jobs. Weeks later, Clinton sided with McEntee and labor, which Bush complained would cost the state $10 million a month.

It's one thing to micromanage the national political party from the White House in unprecedented fashion, and unabashedly sell access to the White House, Air Force One, Camp David, and so forth, to the party's biggest patrons. And as we chronicled in *The Buying of the President [1996]*, Bill Clinton has a long history—going back two decades to Arkansas—of accommodating government policies to the agenda of the most powerful and generous corporate angels.

But what if a President's naked malleability, his willingness to bend policies to money, actually violates and jeopardizes our national security? What if a U.S. company headed by the Democratic Party's most generous individual patron in the 1990s violates federal laws involving national security? And after this happens, what if the company continues to get government contracts and even an export waiver signed by the President himself, worth millions of dollars—over the objections of Justice Department prosecutors? All of this did in fact occur, against a backdrop of espionage and intrigue, of dozens of illegal campaign contributions from foreign nationals with no real assets, of nuclear secrets systematically stolen from our most advanced laboratories over many years, and all of it led back to one country—China.

America, however, has barely noticed. While most of the country was distracted by the news media's frothy coverage of the Monica Lewinsky affair in 1998, investigative reporter Jeff Gerth and his colleagues at the *New York Times* uncovered something quite remarkable. Their findings prompted several government investigations and won the newspaper the Pulitzer Prize in 1999. But hundreds of unanswered questions remain, and, unfortunately, no one seems particularly eager to answer them.

After the Tiananmen Square massacre in 1989, the export of American satellites for launching on Chinese rockets was suspended. Since then, such a commercial deal can occur only if the

President of the United States concludes that the export is in the national interest and a waiver is granted.

In 1992, after President Bush had approved a waiver, and an American satellite was subsequently launched on a Chinese rocket, several senators, including Al Gore, wrote to the Bush Administration to complain that China was using the launchings to "gain foreign aerospace technology that would be otherwise unavailable to it." In the final days of the 1992 presidential campaign, Gore, then Clinton's running mate, charged that Bush "has permitted five additional American-built satellites to be launched by the Chinese. . . . President Bush really is an incurable patsy for those dictators he sets out to coddle."

Unfortunately, far more than Chinese leaders were coddled by the Clinton-Gore Administration and the Democratic Party, under vastly more serious circumstances. More chilling, it appears there were no "patsies" involved, only consenting adults. In its first four years, the Clinton Administration awarded ten waivers to China, one more than Bush. But the number of waivers is not really the issue.

Almost as soon as Clinton and Gore took office in January 1993, the Chinese and U.S. corporations doing business in China began lobbying intensely to "educate" the new administration to look beyond the country's poor human-rights record. In the 1992 election, dozens of U.S. companies active in China had given millions of dollars to the Democratic Party. By May 1993 the President reversed his campaign posture and awarded China most-favored-nation trade status. Even though the law requires the President to review the MFN determination each year, it has never been seriously in doubt since Clinton's first months in office.

One of the most aggressive of those companies was Loral Space and Communications Ltd., which manufactures satellites and is headed by Bernard Schwartz. Loral and Schwartz have contributed at least $1.9 million to the Democratic Party since 1991 and are No. 7 on the Center's "Top 50 Patrons" list of soft-money donors.

In 1994, Schwartz was awarded one of the coveted seats on the late Commerce Secretary Ronald Brown's trade mission to China. Brown helped Loral seal a multimillion-dollar mobile telephone satellite network deal in Beijing. Schwartz was understandably pleased, and a few weeks later White House Deputy Chief of Staff Harold Ickes wrote in a memo to the President that Schwartz "is prepared to do anything he can for the Administration." And he did. In the 1995-96 election cycle, Loral and Schwartz gave the Democratic Party more than $600,000, making Schwartz the largest single individual donor to the party that year.

During the 1990s the Chinese government courted companies like Loral to launch its satellites. Both Chinese and American companies wanted the U.S. government to loosen its export licensing rules regarding satellites. Specifically, they wanted satellite export licensing decisions to be made by the Commerce Department, not the more restrictive State Department. Billions of dollars were at stake—an estimated fourteen commercial communications satellite launchings annually, each costing several hundred million dollars. C. Michael Armstrong, then the chief executive officer of Hughes Electronics Corporation, another satellite manufacturer, met with then–Secretary of State Warren Christopher, and requested that satellites be regarded as commercial, as opposed to military, goods. Christopher agreed to conduct a detailed interagency review with officials from the Defense Department, the National Security Agency, the CIA, and other agencies.

Soon, however, a majority of the interagency group, including Christopher, had concerns about the security ramifications, disagreeing with Loral, Hughes, and the aerospace industry generally. They thus recommended that satellites continue to be categorized as military on the State Department's munitions list. Commerce Secretary Brown, a former chairman of the Democratic National Committee and a prolific fund-raiser, appealed the decision to the President. Clinton sided with Loral and the industry, in a decision that was publicly announced in March 1996. The Commerce Department thus was entrusted with the national security issues surrounding satellite technology.

The decision came at an inopportune time. Days earlier, China had heightened tensions in Asia by firing ballistic missiles with dummy warheads just thirty miles offshore of Taiwan. But the United States was now easing technology transfers and loosening the Tiananmen Square killings-era sanctions vis-à-vis China.

Worse, weeks earlier a Chinese rocket carrying a $200 million

Loral satellite had crashed seconds after liftoff in southern China, killing and injuring civilians on the ground. The China Great Wall Industry Corporation—the Chinese government's missile, rocket, and launch provider—asked Loral to help pinpoint the cause of the accident. In the collaboration that ensued, engineers from Loral and other companies identified potential causes that the Chinese engineers had overlooked. As a result, China may be able to improve the accuracy of its intercontinental ballistic missiles (ICBMs), thirteen of which are aimed at U.S. cities. The Pentagon and the CIA found that both Loral and Hughes had "greatly damaged U.S. national security." The State Department warned White House aides that Loral had engaged in "unlawful" and "criminal" activity. The companies have steadfastly denied any wrongdoing. The Justice Department began a formal criminal investigation into the matter.

Amid all this, in the chutzpah department, Loral had another satellite deal pending with the Chinese, and once again wanted a waiver from the President. Samuel "Sandy" Berger, Clinton's national security adviser, and other administration officials recommended that Loral be given the green light, although they acknowledged in a memorandum to Clinton that such a decision might be perceived as letting Loral "off the hook on criminal charges for its unauthorized assistance to China's ballistic missile program." Meanwhile, Justice Department prosecutors warned that approving the waiver request would seriously jeopardize the Loral investigation.

On February 18, 1998, the President approved the deal and signed the waiver. It was treated as an urgent matter inside the White House not because of pressing national security exigencies, but because Loral faced heavy fines if the project was delayed any further.

The wheeling and dealing were not occurring in a vacuum. Months earlier, in July 1997, the President had been briefed that China, through years of spying and outright theft, had obtained some of the most sensitive U.S. military technology, including nuclear weapons design. And the Democratic Party was deeply embroiled in scandal over illegal contributions from China, part of a systematic campaign to influence the 1996 U.S. presidential election. The Senate Governmental Affairs Committee had recently found "strong circumstantial evidence that the Government of the People's Republic of China was involved in funding, directing, or encouraging some of these foreign contributions." Clinton had been criticized for months for repeatedly stonewalling requests from the Senate committee and the news media for information, and more than forty-five witnesses had fled the country or invoked the Fifth Amendment. The President and his administration, the Senate committee found, "took no action whatsoever to persuade such individuals to cooperate." More foreboding, 80 percent of the illegal foreign contributions had been raised by two longtime Clinton friends, John Huang and Charlie Trie; Huang took the Fifth and Trie fled to China. (Huang later decided to cooperate with the Justice Department and pleaded guilty to one felony charge; Trie voluntarily surrendered to U.S. authorities in February 1998 and pleaded guilty to violating federal campaign finance laws the following May.)

At the very least, it strains credulity that any President, including Clinton, would have approved the multimillion-dollar waiver to this company under all these troubling circumstances if no money had passed into the party coffers. In fact, well over $1 million was lavished upon the Democratic Party. No one can plausibly suggest—although the President, his aides, and Loral have vainly tried—that Schwartz and his satellite company did not get special consideration because of the cash.

"I have never spoken to the President of the United States about my interest in this part of our business," Schwartz told the Center. "I think it would be an abuse of the friendship." He stressed that he has been a loyal, active Democrat since the 1950s and has never given money with a notion toward getting something back. "I'm feisty about this," he said. "You know, I don't think it's any of your goddamned business. I am answering these things somewhat reluctantly because it really is none of your business whom I vote for and whom I give money to. I was chairman of a company that had 35,000 employees in the United States, representing one of the most significant industries in America. I could have access to anybody I wanted. . . ."

In 1999, a select House committee chaired by Representative

Christopher Cox, a Republican from California, produced an 872-page report that was unanimously approved by its five Republican and four Democratic members—a rare feat of bipartisanship in Washington these days. The committee found that China's "acquisition efforts [of American military technology] over the past two decades" had been a "serious, sustained" activity. The committee specifically criticized Loral and Hughes for passing "illegally transmitted" information to the Chinese that was "useful for the design and improved reliability" of future Chinese ballistic missiles.

The report said that the Clinton Administration's policy of permitting businesses to police their own technology sales abroad has not worked, because the national security interest "simply may not be related to improving a corporation's 'bottom line.'"

But it sure worked well for the companies, China, and the Democratic Party.

At a fund-raising dinner in the elegant Hay-Adams Hotel, across Lafayette Park from the White House, a major DNC donor brought up a business grievance with President Clinton. The donor wanted to launch a business venture that happened to be opposed by environmental activists, and he was concerned that Interior Secretary Bruce Babbitt might block it.

Clinton asked, "Do you think we can pass a decent bill in this Congress?" When the donor said yes, Clinton responded, "Why don't you give me an outline of what you want and let me work with the government on it?" During that same dinner, the President gave the party patrons his views about money and politics. "I think it's okay if your investment gets you influence," he told them, "but your investment shouldn't get you control."

There may be no more dramatic example of influence and what money can buy in Washington than the case of Atlantic Richfield Company. What follows is a case study of how the enormous ambitions of a multibillion-dollar oil company, and a beleaguered President and his political party bent on maintaining control of both the White House and a governor's seat, converged. The same administration that waxes eloquent about global warming quietly, legally, "worked with the government" at all levels for the fossil-fuels industry, thereby opening up more than 4 million acres of supposedly untouchable federal land.

ARCO was the only oil company to make the Center's "Top Fifty Patrons" list of soft-money contributors to the Democratic Party. (ARCO's total contributions of $1.3 million placed it at No. 17). Oil companies "invested" $35.2 million in national party committees and congressional candidates from 1987 to April 1998, and Republicans received nearly three times more money than Democrats. In fact, the GOP's largest oil company contributor was ARCO, which gave $4.9 million.

In 1988 a former oil man was elected President of the United States. ARCO was the largest soft-money donor to the Republican Party during George Bush's election and tenure as President, contributing $713,470 from 1987 to 1992. At the 1992 Republican National Convention in Houston, who can forget the indelible image of President Bush and Vice President Dan Quayle standing on the caboose of a "Victory Train," waving to a happy, cheering crowd at the lavish ARCO reception? While President, Bush got an ARCO provision to promote reformulated gasoline inserted into the Clean Air Act, and his White House also pushed unsuccessfully for opening up Alaska's Arctic National Wildlife Refuge to oil drilling. About 80 percent of ARCO's oil reserves are in the United States, mostly in Alaska.

In 1993 the company discovered oil in the "Alpine" region of Alaska, on the eastern border of the National Petroleum Reserve. The reserve was created by Congress in 1923, under President Warren G. Harding, for emergency use only. No President and no Congress had ever acceded to the oil interests and opened up this pristine land for commercial drilling—not during the Depression, World War II, or the energy crisis of the 1970s. Ronald Reagan's Interior Secretary, James Watt, held a few lease sales in the early 1980s, but the oil companies weren't very interested at the time. Now, with the exciting Alpine discovery and geological surveys also indicating sizable oil deposits in the adjacent reserve, ARCO wanted to do the impossible: get Washington to reverse more than seventy years of policy and precedent and permit oil production on the reserve.

No plausible case could be made that an energy emergency

existed, however, and by this time ARCO's good friend George Bush had been evicted from the White House. But the company still had some reason for optimism. Its chief lobbyist in Washington, Robert Healy, had helped write the Democratic Party platform in 1992 to include wording "acceptable to energy interests." ARCO loaned the Clinton/Gore 1992 Inaugural Committee $100,000, and had given at least $268,317 to the Democratic National Committee. In addition, ARCO is represented by Washington superlobbyist Charles Manatt, a former chairman of the Democratic National Committee, whose former law partner, Mickey Kantor, had run the Clinton/Gore campaign in 1992 and later served in two Cabinet posts.

Although the Freedom of Information Act has always exempted the White House and Congress from public disclosure requirements, thereby making it more difficult to discern who's actually doing what, we've gotten a few public glimpses of the coziness between ARCO and the Clinton White House. In the 1993-94 election cycle, for example, ARCO gave the DNC $274,500. Then, in June 1994, at a White House luncheon with business executives, the President presented Lodwrick Cook, then the company's chairman, with a birthday cake. Meanwhile, from 1990 through 1994, ARCO was the top political giver in Alaska, contributing about $750,000 to state parties and candidates. In 1994, Democrat Tony Knowles eked out a surprise 536-vote victory to become the governor of Alaska, a traditionally Republican state. He quickly expressed his desire to establish "a new partnership" with oil companies, and soon he had taken up their cause of lobbying Washington to open up the National Petroleum Reserve in his state. (This was regarded as more realistic than opening the more bountiful Arctic National Wildlife Refuge, which the Clinton Administration had declared off-limits to development.) In January 1995, Knowles slept overnight in the White House. In December 1995 the Alaska Democratic Party sponsored a black-tie, $1,000-a-plate fund-raising dinner in Anchorage for the "Governor's Fund"—Knowles's political slush fund. Oil companies poured in $21,000. Three months later, in February 1996, Lieutenant Governor Fran Ulmer attended a White House coffee with the President.

Meanwhile, on the lobbying front, Manatt, ARCO's top hired

gun, attended a White House coffee with Clinton and Kantor in May 1995. In October 1995, Healy, ARCO's top in-house lobbyist, attended a White House coffee with, among others, Vice President Gore and Marvin Rosen, the DNC's finance chairman. The ARCO Foundation gave $10,000 to the Vice President's Residence Foundation, a not-for-profit organization that has raised funds for improvements to the Vice President's official home. And as Clinton and Gore sought reelection in 1996, ARCO nearly doubled its support to the DNC, to $496,072.

The real push from ARCO to open up NPR-A (National Petroleum Reserve-Alaska) began in earnest in late 1996. In November, Air Force One stopped in Anchorage for a few hours to refuel, and Governor Knowles reportedly used the occasion to lobby Clinton to open up the reserve. Days after Clinton was reelected, Brooks Yeager, then the Interior Department's Deputy Assistant Secretary for Policy, informed environmental organizations in Alaska that NPR-A would soon be the subject of an environmental impact statement—the first step toward opening it for leasing.

Internal government documents obtained by the Center for Public Integrity show that five senior ARCO executives—among them J. Ken Thompson, the president of ARCO Alaska, Inc., and Healy—met with Babbitt and other high-ranking officials of the Interior Department in Washington on December 9. The agenda for the meeting consisted of just two items: "Alpine Project Update" and "NPR-A (Federal Lease Sale, State/Native Land Exchange)."

Weeks later, in January 1997, Secretary Babbitt ordered the Bureau of Land Management to begin preparing a draft Environmental Impact Statement (EIS) for the reserve. In February, Knowles met with Babbitt, and on February 12 the Interior Department announced the details of the process by which 4.6 million acres of the 24-million-acre reserve might be opened to oil and natural-gas development. Babbitt personally explored the reserve on foot in July 1997. On August 6, 1998, the review completed, the Interior Department announced that all but 580,000 acres of the 4.6-million-acre tract would be leased. "This is a good plan," Babbitt said in making the announcement, "based on sound science and a very public outreach process."

In November 1998, Governor Knowles was reelected easily. But he wasn't the only winner. The following May, the results of the lease bidding were announced. ARCO tendered the winning bids on ninety-nine of the 133 tracts that were bid on, and if its merger with British Petroleum is approved the new conglomerate would end up with nineteen more. In all, six oil companies spent $104 million on the winning bids.

The Interior Department estimates that the leased land has from 300 million to 2 billion barrels of oil, with a potential value of $2.34 to $36 billion. For a relative pittance and some face time with politicians in Alaska and Washington, ARCO had hit a multibillion-dollar bonanza.

The reversal of U.S. policy on NPR-A went almost unnoticed by the news media, environmental organizations, and the public. There were no dissenting voices at the perfunctory congressional oversight hearings, though since then a number of environmental organizations have sued the Interior Department, alleging, among other things, that its environmental impact statement is inadequate. Internal government documents obtained by the Center show that officials of the Interior Department acknowledged that "the timetable [was] very compressed" and that such a review normally takes roughly three years—twice as long as it actually took. Since when does the federal bureaucracy move so fast? Answer: when the wheels have been greased.

Interior Secretary Bruce Babbitt; former ARCO chairman Lodwrick Cook; Robert Healy, ARCO's in-house lobbyist; and Alaska Governor Tony Knowles all declined the Center's requests for interviews. Charles Manatt, ARCO's outside lobbyist, told the Center that he was not involved in the matter.

Former Colorado Governor Roy Romer succeeded Fowler as the chairman of the Democratic National Committee, which in the 2000 election will almost certainly surpass the prodigious fundraising it did in 1996. (In September 1999, Romer was replaced by Philadelphia Mayor Edward Rendell.) "I have the feeling that the party should be there advocating the general policy interest on behalf of the constituents, the party should be there to help the constituent know how to get access, but I don't think the party should be an advocate of a specific decision, particularly that has financial self-interest of a large sum to the clientele," Romer told the Center weeks before he left the DNC. "I'm trying to make that distinction for the welfare mother. I mean, I think the party has an obligation to help the welfare mother to know where to go now that we've got welfare reform and your checks run out. What do you do?"

Ah, the Democratic Party dilemma, vacillating between "I feel your pain" concern for the poor and persistent pandering to the rich. "I was in the Hamptons this last weekend," Romer told the Center. "You know what I mean? It's a place where the height of the hedges kind of determines the wealth of the occupant in the home. You know what I mean? You see, I'm walking down this hedgerow and I can't see the homes, and I come to a driveway and I lean down to see if I can see the side of the mansion. Well, I'm out there raising money trying to help that welfare mother."

The Democratic Party
Top Fifty Patrons

1. **American Federation of State, County, and Municipal Employees,** Washington
   $3,671,809

2. **Communications Workers of America,** Washington
   $3,593,815

3. **The Seagram Company, Ltd.,** Montreal
   $2,673,983

4. **National Education Association,** Washington
   $2,644,927

5. **American Federation of Teachers,** Washington
   $2,075,913

6. **Service Employees International Union,** Washington
   $1,978,691

7. **Loral Space & Communications, Ltd.,** New York/**Bernard Schwartz**
   $1,949,500

8. **Walt Disney Company,** Burbank, California
   $1,877,605

This list is based on soft-money contributions to the Democratic National Committee and its affiliated committees from January 1991 through June 1999. Sources: Federal Election Commission, Common Cause.

9. **United Food and Commercial Workers**, Washington
$1,789,064

10. **Shorenstein Company**, San Francisco/**Shorenstein family**
$1,660,680

11. **The Connell Company**, Westfield, New Jersey
$1,505,600

12. **AT&T Corporation/TCI**, Basking Ridge, New Jersey
$1,476,138

13. **MCI WorldCom**, Jackson, Mississippi
$1,459,029

14. **The Goldman Sachs Group, Inc.**, New York
$1,456,300

15. **AFL-CIO**, Washington
$1,397,161

16. **Peter, Paul, and Lawrence Buttenweiser**, New York
$1,382,500

17. **Atlantic Richfield Company (ARCO)**, Los Angeles
$1,354,038

18. **Milberg Weiss Bershad Hynes & Lerach**, New York
$1,337,500

19. **Laborers' International Union of North America**, Washington
$1,256,025

20. **Philip Morris Companies, Inc.**, New York
$1,237,582

21. **Thompson Medical Company, Inc.**, New York
$1,233,430

22. **Archer Daniels Midland Company**, Decatur, Illinois
$1,232,000

23. **Bell Atlantic Corporation/NYNEX**, New York
$1,216,872

24. **DreamWorks SKG**, Universal City, California
$1,179,400

25. **Revlon Group, Inc.**, New York
$1,168,599

26. **International Brotherhood of Electrical Workers**, Washington
$1,164,109

27. **FDX Corporation**, Memphis, Tennessee
$1,178,550

28. **Anheuser-Busch Companies, Inc.**, St. Louis
$1,102,764

29. **Association of Trial Lawyers of America**, Washington
$1,149,250

30. **Time Warner, Inc.**, New York
$1,081,333

31. **Leucadia National Corporation**, New York/**Ian Cumming**
$1,066,500

32. **Lazard Freres & Company**, New York
$1,065,356

33. **American Financial Group, Inc.**, Cincinnati/**Carl Lindner**
$1,030,000

34. **International Association of Machinists & Aerospace Employees,** Washington
$1,020,250

35. **Yucaipa Companies,** Los Angeles
$1,006,454

36. **Sprint Corporation,** Westwood, Kansas
$964,033

37. **Williams Bailey Law Firm,** Houston
$954,600

38. **Ernst & Young International,** New York
$897,960

39. **Mashantucket Pequot Tribal Nation,** Mashantucket, Connecticut
$893,625

40. **International Association of Fire Fighters,** Washington
$886,958

41. **E. & J. Gallo Winery,** Modesto, California
$885,700

42. **American Airlines, Inc.,** Dallas
$864,967

43. **Nabisco Group Holdings Corporation/R.J. Reynolds Tobacco Holding, Inc.,** New York
$859,299

44. **Waite, Schneider, Bayless, and Chesley,** Cincinnati
$807,087

45. **Sheet Metal Workers International Association,** Washington
$794,600

46. **United Steel Workers of America,** Pittsburgh
$772,801

47. **Beneficial Management Corporation of America,** Kennewick, Washington
$771,319

48. **Integrated Health Services, Inc.,** Owings Mills, Maryland
$727,000

49. **United Auto Workers,** Detroit
$724,842

50. **David Steiner/Steiner Equities Group,** Roseland, New Jersey
$712,720

The Republican Party

||||||||||||

If it wasn't the "greatest robbery in the history of mankind," it certainly will go down as one of the most morally reprehensible. Switzerland—the Swiss National Bank and its private banks—took in more looted Nazi gold than anyone ever remotely imagined, at least an estimated $4 billion in today's money. It has been suggested on both sides of the Atlantic that World War II may have been prolonged by months as a result. Nearly all of the gold stolen by the Nazis came from central banks in occupied countries or Germany, but one-sixth came from individuals, including Jews who were systematically murdered in Nazi concentration camps. Gold was melted down from wedding rings and gold teeth extracted from corpses at Auschwitz and other Nazi death camps.

In 1995 this story exploded around the world, and soon the United States—with the largest number of Holocaust survivors in the world—became a hotbed of reactivity for the jittery Swiss. The Swiss were concerned about being shut out of U.S. markets. They faced class-action lawsuits and were threatened with sanctions from hundreds of local U.S. officials in New York, California, and Pennsylvania. And they were up against Senate and House Banking Committee investigations.

By late 1996 the Swiss government was reeling from revelations, and the field of action had become the U.S. Congress. Republican Alfonse D'Amato of New York, then the chairman of the Senate Banking Committee, had presented acutely embarrassing information about the Swiss banks in April and October, and hundreds of journalists from all over the world pursued him and his aides in a feeding frenzy. The Swiss were already represented by at least one prominent law firm in Washington, Wilmer, Cutler & Pickering, but clearly they needed more political muscle in the United States.

And to whom did the descendants of "Adolf Hitler's money launderers" turn for help?

The Swiss government retained the lobbying firm of Haley Barbour, the chairman of the National Republican Committee, for $20,000 a month. In a letter of agreement with Ambassador Carlo Jagmetti at the embassy of Switzerland, Lanny Griffith, Barbour's partner, wrote, "We are eager to assist the Swiss government managing the controversy arising out of allegations of Swiss banking practices before, during, and after World War II and relating to the Holocaust."

"Maybe they [the Swiss government] thought if they get the former Republican National Committee chairman, he would have influence over us," Gregg Rickman, then an aide to D'Amato who directed the Senate Banking Committee's investigation, and who wrote *Swiss Banks and Jewish Souls,* told the Center for Public Integrity. "Anyone who thought that was crazy." In an interview with the Center, Barbour said, "Nobody ever asked me to talk to Alfonse, I'd never talk to Alfonse, and if I had talked to him I would have expected him to throw a 'full Alfonse.'" Rickman said that while Barbour himself did not have any contact with him or, to his knowledge, D'Amato, he recalled dealing with Lanny Griffith and Doug MacKinnon of Barbour's firm. ("I did look askance," Rickman said, "at anyone who helped defend these guys.")

One of their assignments was to prepare the top Swiss government spokesman, Thomas Borer, for his congressional testimony. They also gathered intelligence on Capitol Hill, developed and placed questions to be asked of other hearing witnesses, and dispensed "strategic advice" on working with Capitol Hill lawmakers, members of their staffs, and the news media. With the Swiss obviously concerned about secrecy, the Barbour firm pledged complete discretion. "Our firm recognizes that in the course of our representation of the government of Switzerland, we may become aware of information, practices or policies which you may want to keep confidential," the letter of agreement said. "Our firm agrees to maintain that confidentiality."

Hiring Barbour's firm was just one of many damage-control measures employed by the Swiss—for example, they also hired Ruder Finn, a New York City–based public-relations firm that represented the Israeli government and many other prominent Jewish clients—all of which proved remarkably successful. Today, after three years of *Sturm und Drang* for the Swiss government and banks, the heat is mostly off. The banks agreed to pay a lump-sum settlement of $1.25 billion, and the congressional investigations are history.

Barbour's firm began representing the Swiss during his final weeks as the chairman of the Republican National Committee. But the firm, in correspondence to the Justice Department, tried to hide Barbour's financial ties to the controversial foreign client.

But behind the subterfuge was a more serious matter. In December 1996, when Barbour's lobbying firm informed the Justice Department of its new client, papers were also filed there showing that Barbour owned a full, equal partnership in the company. This was not illegal, but it did reveal for the first time that Barbour had lied to the public and his fellow Republicans for four years.

In 1992, when he had campaigned to become the RNC's chairman, Barbour had pledged, if elected, to resign from the lobbying firm he had founded. Within days of his election to the chairmanship in January 1993, Barbour declared on CNN's "Evans & Novak" program: "I'll be selling my interest in my law firm to my partners. I'll sever my relationship with it. I won't have any ties to it, business ties to it at all, or financial ties."

Reminded of these comments in 1997, Lanny Griffith, the managing partner of Barbour, Griffith & Rogers, gave a Clintonesque response: "What he had said when he took over as RNC chairman is he would not become active in lobbying as chairman." At least he didn't say it depends on what the meaning of *is* is.

For his part, Barbour told the Center, he has no objection to a party chairman lobbying. "There's nothing wrong—it's not illegal or anything like that," he said. "But when I ran for chairman, I said I would not actively lobby because I didn't want a Member [of Congress] to wonder whether I was coming down there for the Republican Party or for some business deal that is in Haley's interest. So I kept my equity interest in this firm, but I didn't lobby for anybody the whole time that I was chairman—again, not because I thought that there was something morally wrong with it, [but because] I thought it would confuse the issue."

Throughout his chairmanship of the Republican National Committee, in other words, Barbour also had secretly been deriving income from his lobbying firm. Just two of his firm's clients, Glaxo-Wellcome, Inc., and the Pharmaceutical Research and Manufacturers of America, gave more than $700,000 to the Republican Party from 1993 to 1997 (the span of Barbour's chairmanship), buying access to power via the party and its leaders in the Senate and House; they also were *simultaneously* paying Barbour's firm to promote their interests in Washington. As soon as Barbour returned to his old lobbying firm full-time in January 1997, he added more than a dozen corporate clients, many of them the most generous Republican Party patrons. He and his firm, for example, began representing the five largest U.S. tobacco companies: Philip Morris Companies, Inc.; RJR Nabisco Holdings Corporation, UST, Inc. (the parent of United States Tobacco Company), Brown & Williamson Tobacco Corporation, and Loews Corporation (the parent of Lorillard Tobacco Company). These five companies have contributed at least $13.5 million to the RNC and other national party committees since 1991. By 1998, Barbour, Griffith & Rogers had become one of Washington's hottest lobbying firms, with three dozen clients and $7.4 million in direct lobbying income, having boosted its revenue by more than 42 percent in one year and ranking sixth among Washington firms.

There was no clearer example of Barbour's power broker "sizzle" than in 1998, when he escorted his new client, Microsoft founder Bill Gates—in the midst of the Clinton Justice Department's major antitrust case—into a meeting with Senate Majority Leader Trent Lott. Barbour and Lott are both from Mississippi. In the same year, in response to speculation in the news media that his lobbying firm might be acquired by a much larger New York company, Barbour told the Center: "If the terms and conditions are right, I don't have anything that isn't for sale except my wife and children."

During the time that he was the RNC's chairman, Barbour also served as a director of another lobbying firm, National Environmental Strategies Company, which he had helped form in 1990. At the same time that Republicans in the House were unsuccessfully attempting to rewrite the nation's environmental laws, the Republican Party and a company connected to its chairman separately were getting major cash from corporations seeking to severely reduce or even eliminate federal environmental regulation. In 1998, National Environmental Strategies racked up nearly $1.2 million in lobbying income from twenty-three clients, including such corporate polluter interests as Occidental Petroleum Corporation, Union Carbide Corporation, the Chemical Manufacturers Association, and the National Mining Association. Also while Barbour was the RNC's chairman, the National Policy Forum, a Republican Party "think tank" created by Barbour, held more than a dozen conferences, in 1995 and 1996, in which the industry perspective about the enforcement of environmental laws was ventilated. Marc Himmelstein, a partner of Barbour's in National Environmental Strategies, admitted to a reporter for the *Washington Post* that at these events he did "give some ideas." Barbour, in short, wore two hats—one visible and one invisible.

There has never been any palpable, public sign of disapproval or disappointment over Barbour's conflicts of interest from members of the Republican National Committee. Their silence is golden, literally. The Republican Party requires hundreds upon hundreds of millions of dollars from corporations and individuals, and its leaders have a fundamental responsibility to keep the cash flowing in. Without it there will be no party message going out, no resonance with voters, no victories at the polls. A gifted fundraiser is almost by definition outgoing, gregarious, persuasive, and entrepreneurial. But there are no laws restricting outside income, requiring honest public statements, or mandating full financial disclosure for top leadership positions in either major party today. The news media don't focus closely on these issues—partly because of the paucity of disclosure documents—and most Americans cannot even name their elected officials, let alone the chairman of a political party. In other words, the private financial dealings of a party chairman—no matter how offensive or conflict-ridden—are a nonissue in Washington.

It's almost as though all the hoopla around money, stroking the big donors with special perquisites so that they will give again, may have obscured the actual values and shared beliefs of the party itself. The Republican National Convention in San Diego in 1996, for example, adopted a 98-page party platform that three key GOP leaders—Robert Dole, the party's presidential nominee; then-House Speaker Newt Gingrich; and Barbour—had not even read.

Barbour is widely regarded to have been an exceptionally talented, successful chairman of the Republican National Committee, perhaps one of the best ever. The affable fifty-two-year-old lawyer has a self-deprecating wit, a keen intellect, and a folksy charm, quipping once that "Bill Clinton posing as the poster boy for small government is like my being a poster boy for SlimFast." During his testimony before the Senate committee investigating campaign-finance abuses in the 1996 elections, Barbour drew laughter when he said, "You know, Senators, I was born at night, but it wasn't last night." His leadership helped the party win majority control of the House of Representatives in 1994, for the first time in forty years.

Barbour was a phenomenally successful fund-raiser as chairman, expanding Team 100, the club for those who give or raise at least $175,000 over four years. "The RNC had more than seven million contributions while I was chairman," he once boasted. "They totaled some $330 million, an average contribution of about $45." The RNC also had a rigorous FEC compliance system in place—something glaringly missing over at the DNC—which helps to explain why it had fewer front-page embarrassments in the 1996 elections.

Though he's no longer chairman of the RNC, Barbour continues to raise millions of dollars for the party, frequently hosting dinners for GOP lawmakers at his firm's swank Pennsylvania Avenue offices. Such dedication certainly endears him to the most powerful Republicans in Congress, who are likely to be receptive to a Barbour policy suggestion at the behest of a well-heeled client who can afford him. And no single Member of Congress has benefited more from Barbour's financial wizardry than Trent Lott. In 1998, for example, Barbour was the master of ceremonies and a leading money-raiser at a special tribute honoring Lott for his quarter century in Congress, an event that netted over $1 million. In 1999 he played an instrumental role in helping to raise almost $8 million for a gala at Washington's John F. Kennedy Center for the Performing Arts to benefit the Trent Lott Leadership Institute at the University of Mississippi. Some of Barbour's tobacco clients, including Brown & Williamson and RJR Nabisco, ponied up major contributions for this cause.

Barbour's extraordinary network of contacts as chairman of the RNC, his adroit sense of how to mesh client interests with the party's political strategy, and his ability to raise huge sums of money, all place him squarely in the Washington power-and-profit game. Yet Barbour has somehow managed to escape any real scrutiny of his financial dealings. When he testified before the Senate Governmental Affairs Committee in 1997, he wasn't asked a single question about his firm's work for Switzerland or about his manifold conflicts of interest while chairman of the RNC. That was outside the scope of the Senate investigation, and in the hard-bitten mercenary culture of Washington, it hardly seemed out of the ordinary.

One thing did light up that dim radar screen, however. As Barbour and other leading Republicans denounced Clinton and the Democrats for receiving millions of dollars in illegal foreign contributions, there were suggestions that Barbour could find himself in the same hot seat. In March 1997 he appeared on the NBC News program "Meet the Press" and was asked by moderator Tim Russert: "And yet you will not disclose who gave how much money. Why don't you tell the American people who gave hundreds of thousands of dollars to this National Policy Forum, and did any of that money come from overseas?" Barbour replied, "Well, none of the money came from overseas." Russert: "Period?" Barbour: "Period." Barbour was in a position to know, inasmuch as he created and chaired the National Policy Forum, a now-defunct organization that did not have to disclose its donors and could receive foreign money, legally.

Months later, according to Russert, Barbour called him, apologizing "that he had misled me." Barbour said he had discovered that the Pacific Cultural Foundation, a Taiwanese entity, had contributed $25,000 to the National Policy Forum. What Barbour didn't say—and Senate investigators later discovered—is that the RNC chairman sent a personal thank-you letter for the contributions to Ambassador Jason Hu, the U.S. representative of the Taiwanese government.

But that proved to be peanuts compared to Barbour's relationship with Ambrous Young, a Hong Kong businessman. The National Policy Forum was in chronic financial difficulty. Young had been persuaded to put up $2.1 million in collateral, "posted by a shell corporation that had no assets other than money transferred from Hong Kong," according to the report issued by the Democratic members of the Senate investigating committee. Because of Young's generosity, the National Policy Forum was able to get a $2.1 million loan, but most of the proceeds were promptly transferred to the RNC, which allegedly put the money into congressional campaigns nationwide. Young's lawyer, Richard Richards (a former chairman of the RNC), testified that Barbour had told him the loan was needed to win sixty seats in the 1994 congressional races. Barbour flatly denied that the money was used for this illegal purpose or that he had any knowledge that the funds were foreign, but his assertions were contradicted by other testimony and documentation. Fred Volcansek, a fund-raiser for the National Policy Forum, for example, testified before the Senate committee that he'd told Barbour and other GOP leaders that the $2.1 million loan guarantee was from a Hong Kong corporation.

Informed of Volcansek's testimony, Barbour said: "Fred may be right. But I don't recall him saying that. If he said it, I don't remember him saying it. I knew I didn't understand it. Either I didn't understand what they were talking about or I didn't hear."

This even strained the credulity of fellow Republican Fred Thompson, the chairman of the Senate Governmental Affairs Committee. "When you're sitting on a boat in Hong Kong harbor talking to a gentleman who's a resident of—citizen of—Taiwan,"

Thompson said, "I mean, that does raise certain other potential implications." In fact, besides his conversations with Young in Hong Kong, Barbour also had traveled with Young to China. And he also had squired Young around to meet House Speaker Newt Gingrich and Senate Majority Leader Robert Dole, as "a courtesy call."

According to an internal RNC memo found by Senate investigators, Ambrous Young had actually renounced his U.S. citizenship to avoid taxes. Senator Richard Durbin, a Democrat from Illinois, angrily asked Barbour if at some point he had said to himself: " 'Slow down with Ambrous Young. I'm not sure that we ought to get involved with a man who walked away from his U.S. citizenship to avoid paying taxes and now wants to be a big benefactor of the Republican Party.' I mean, Mr. Barbour, you and I go to a lot of events where we wave flags, and we sing along with Lee Greenwood, and we're all for America. Didn't it just give you some pause or hesitation to say, 'You know, this may be hard to explain to the loyal, patriotic Americans who make up the supporters of the Republican Party—why I'm spending time on a yacht, going to trips to China . . . inviting this man in to have a personal meeting with Newt Gingrich and with Bob Dole?' Didn't it ever dawn on you that this might not be the right approach to fundraising for the Grand Old Party?"

"Senator, I must have misspoken," Barbour replied, referring to an earlier answer. "I intended to tell you that I found out this year, in 1997—when we were getting out all the records to deliver to the committee for this investigation is when I found out—that Mr. Young had given up his citizenship." He never addressed the political and moral issue of attempting to garner cash from someone who had renounced his citizenship to avoid taxes.

Under oath Barbour had boldly proclaimed in his opening statement that "honesty and integrity are my life." Despite occasionally evasive answers and an unctuous, slick demeanor, the former Republican Party chairman nonetheless won plaudits for his performance before the Thompson committee. The *New York Times* characterized him as "one of the most successful party chairmen in modern times" and declared that Barbour had handled himself as "nimbly as a dealer cracks the cellophane from a fresh deck of cards." To the *Washington Post,* "Barbour marshaled careful, chart-aided arguments to rebut every charge, suggested areas where Senators might do more homework, and showed such prodigious command of previous testimony that the nine lawyers and other minions who accompanied him had little to do but watch."

For the next two years, Barbour and the Republican National Committee were under a federal criminal grand jury investigation over that Hong Kong deal. No charges have ever been filed. Despite the Hong Kong episode, however, it is generally recognized that the Democrats were far more aggressive and systematically solicitous in seeking illegal foreign contributions, which helps to explain why, as noted earlier, nineteen individuals have been prosecuted by the Justice Department's Campaign Financing Task Force as of this writing.

But another thing illuminated by the campaign-finance investigations is that the Republican Party pioneered the use of proxy organizations and took it to unprecedented levels in 1996.

For years both parties have had more sideshows than a circus, some mere shakedown operations, others "think tanks" developing policy ideas. For example, the Democrats have the Democratic National Committee, the Democratic Congressional Campaign Committee, the Democratic Senate Campaign Committee, and the fifty state party organizations. Centrist Democrats have had the Democratic Leadership Council, which isn't affiliated with the DNC but consists only of Democrats. There are completely separate, but useful, Democratic-friendly research policy organizations—such as the Progressive Policy Institute and the Economic Policy Institute, among many others in Washington. What's more, the Democratic Party benefits hugely at the national, state, and local levels from the money and grassroots activism of labor unions.

Nonetheless, thirty-one of the nation's fifty governors are Republican, as is a majority of both chambers of Congress. In general, Republicans have consistently raised more money than Democrats for more than thirty years. Republican Party committees have consistently outspent their Democratic counterparts on political commercials disguised as "issue advocacy" advertising. Republicans also have a phalanx of organizations—the Republican National Committee, the National Republican Congressional Committee, the National Republican Senatorial Committee, and the fifty state party organizations. Moderate Republicans have the Ripon Society, and the now-defunct National Policy Forum was created as a GOP alternative to the Democratic Leadership Council. There also is a plethora of Republican-leaning think tanks in Washington, including the conservative Heritage Foundation, the American Enterprise Institute for Public Policy Research, and, on many issues, the Cato Institute, to name just a few. The Christian Coalition in past campaigns has been capable of dropping tens of millions of voter guides days before Election Day, inevitably guiding voters toward Republican candidates. And this isn't even mentioning the political committees used by elected officials in both parties to move millions of dollars to their favored candidates.

Both parties, in short, have developed networks of like-minded organizations that can dispense millions of dollars in campaign contributions or issue-advocacy TV commercials at almost the drop of a hat. The 1997 investigation of the Senate Governmental Affairs Committee found that the RNC gave more than $5 million to tax-exempt organizations, many times more than the DNC. The RNC "undertook a wide variety of specific election-related activities with particular organizations, including joint mailings, joint issue-advocacy efforts, joint media events, joint polling, and more." Why? According to the RNC Coalition Building Manual used in the 1996 election, "Always remember, 'What we say about ourselves is suspect, but what others say about us is credible.'" An added bonus in using third-party proxy groups: donors to such groups can conceal their identities and give unlimited sums of money.

In 1996 many such groups were conduits for Republican money and messages. As noted earlier, the National Policy Forum was founded in 1993, chaired by RNC chairman Barbour and substantially funded by the Republican Party. In mid-1994 Michael Baroody, the organization's president, resigned in frustration, writing that "in recent months, it has become increasingly difficult to maintain the fiction of separation." In 1997 the Internal Revenue Service denied the organization's application for tax-exempt status, holding: "Based on the information you submitted, it appears that you are a partisan, issues-oriented organization. Specifically, your activities are designed to promote the Republican Party and politicians affiliated with the Republican Party." Barbour, however, continues to defend the fiction to this day, and he told the Center that "as far as the National Policy Forum and the RNC, I really wouldn't have done anything any differently in terms of fund-raising and reporting and all that."

Barbour and the RNC also created something called the Coalition for Our Children's Future in mid-1995, and between then and the November 1996 elections it spent more than $5 million on advertising in various congressional districts. Despite its name, it did nothing at all to directly help children, but instead existed solely to produce television commercials promoting Republican Party policies and criticizing Democrats. When Barry Bennett, the executive director of the Coalition for Our Children's Future, discovered that his own organization actually had been funding such ads, he resigned, as did the entire board of directors (all of them Republicans). But how could they not have known the truth? In November 1995, Barbour told the U.S. Chamber of Commerce in a speech, "I do encourage all of you to support things like . . . the Coalition for Our Children's Future, which has been particularly helpful in running hard-hitting advertising that some people feel uncomfortable in doing."

Weeks before the 1996 elections, the RNC transferred $4.6 million to Americans for Tax Reform (ATR), an organization that, among other things, made at least four million telephone calls and mailed nineteen million letters to voters. It also staged pro-Republican media events and paid for television "attack" ads against Democrats. The Democratic members of the Senate Governmental Affairs Committee noted that "ATR undertook all of these activities without registering with the FEC as a political organization, without disclosing its contributors or expenditures, and without admitting any partisan or election-related objectives." Barbour told the committee with a straight face that, "to my knowledge and my understanding, none of it [the $4.6 million] was spent to advocate the election or defeat of a candidate for federal office, that none of it was spent on anything that would be covered that would be part of an election campaign."

Then there is the case of Triad Management, Inc., a for-profit corporation owned by Carolyn Malenick, a Republican fund-raiser. In 1996, Triad was responsible for pro-Republican advertising in twenty-six House races and three Senate races. The company is connected to two not-for-profit organizations, Citizens for Reform and Citizens for the Republic Education Fund, and it is through these front organizations that the TV commercials were broadcast. Neither group has a staff or an office, and both are the exclusive preserve of Triad. The public was kept in the dark about the sources of $3 million in television advertising paid for by Triad-related entities in the closing days of the 1996 campaign. Why? Perhaps because the American people might not appreciate that the nation's largest independent oil company apparently was trying to influence several elections.

More than half the Triad-connected money—$1.79 million—came from the Economic Education Trust, which, the Democratic staff of the Thompson committee suggested, has been funded by Charles and David Koch of Wichita, Kansas. They control the nation's second-largest privately owned company, Koch Industries, Inc., with annual revenues of about $35 billion. Senate investigators found that much of the money spent by Triad and the Coalition for Our Children's Future helped Republican candidates in states where Koch Industries has refineries, pipelines, or offices, including Arkansas, Kansas, Louisiana, Minnesota, and Oklahoma. It certainly is not the first time the Koch brothers have attempted to use stealth and hard, cold cash to influence public policy—for years they've secretly moved millions of dollars into various anti-environmental, antiregulation organizations.

Publicly, at least, Barbour has always supported the noble concept of disclosure, stating just days before the 1996 elections that "disclosure of contributions and expenditures, shining the bright light of public scrutiny, is the fundamental principle underlying our campaign-finance laws." This philosophy is in keeping with the Supreme Court's landmark decision in the post-Watergate case of *Buckley* v. *Valeo,* which held, in part: "Disclosure requirements deter actual corruption and avoid the appearance of corruption by exposing large contributors to the light of publicity. This exposure may discourage those who would use money for improper purposes."

The problem is that privately, Barbour and the Republican Party have found manifold ways to circumvent contribution limits and to shield donors and their motives from public scrutiny. In that sense, they have undermined and at times subverted the fundamental precept of the Federal Election Campaign Act.

Which is not to suggest that disclosure is the only issue on which Barbour and the Republican Party have been shamelessly hypocritical. Take, for example, the overfished red herring, "family values." According to political wordsmith William Safire, the phrase was first used in a contemporary political context in 1976, in the Republican Party platform, as follows: "Divorce rates, threatened neighborhoods and schools, and public scandal all create a hostile atmosphere that erodes family structures and family values." In late 1986 a White House panel chaired by Gary Bauer (then an undersecretary at the Department of Education) produced a report about family policy, which led to an Executive Order by President Ronald Reagan on "The Family." But it was in 1992 that the hooked-together phrase "family values" really became the mantra of Republicans, especially at the Republican National Convention in Houston. There, Patrick Buchanan, Marilyn Quayle, Marion G. "Pat" Robertson, and others began using it as a political attack phrase, implicitly or explicitly denigrating the cultural values of Bill and Hillary Clinton and criticizing everything from "radical feminism" and gay rights to personal "character" issues such as marital infidelity and pot smoking.

For a political party that has so aggressively moralized about the subject of "family values," the Republicans have not been similarly vigilant when it comes to some of the worst home-wreckers of all—drinking, smoking, gambling, and handguns. In the 1997-98 election cycle, the Republican Party and its federal candidates received more than two-thirds of the $18.1 million contributed by the alcohol, tobacco, gambling, and gun industries, according to a 1998 report by Public Citizen, a public-interest group. "In the face of such corrupting influences," its president, Joan Claybrook, said at the time, "we must now question whether decisions by our highest leaders are influenced more by the never-ending pursuit of the almighty campaign dollar than by the real needs of our families."

The money had a direct impact on policy. The Republican Party and its corporate underwriters joined forces to kill reform legislation on drunk-driving standards, tobacco, gambling taxes, and gun-owner liability. For example, beer, wine, and liquor companies gave $2.2 million in soft money to the two major political parties, and another $2.2 million in PAC money to individual candidates—75 percent of which went to Republicans. In the House of Representatives, GOP lawmakers killed legislation that would have set a tougher, national drunk-driving standard (.08 percent blood alcohol content).

But no money is more intoxicating to the Republican Party than the tobacco industry's. It has contributed $14.3 million in soft money to Republican Party committees since 1991, compared with $3 million to Democratic Party committees. Philip Morris is No. 1 on the Republican Party's "Top Fifty Patrons" list, with contributions of $6.2 million in soft money since 1991; R.J. Reynolds is No. 4, at $3.2 million; and UST is No. 8, at $1.9 million. The relationship is so cozy and unabashed that in 1995, Representative John Boehner of Ohio, the chairman of the House Republican Conference, was discovered passing out campaign-contribution checks from Brown & Williamson to GOP lawmakers on the floor of the House of Representatives.

And no one has more tirelessly shilled for the tobacco industry than Haley Barbour. For starters, he represents all five major tobacco companies in Washington. He also presses his Rolodex into service at the state level. In 1997 he went to a conference of the National Governors Association in Las Vegas to sell Republican governors on the merits of the $368.5 billion tobacco settlement, and he personally called Texas Governor George W. Bush about tobacco legislation in Texas, and in fact Bush came through for the companies with a veto. While he was the chairman of the RNC, Barbour lobbied state legislators on behalf of his future clients. He telephoned Arizona House Speaker Mark Killian, for example, to encourage him to vote for a pro-tobacco bill. Killian later said, through a spokesman, that he felt surprised and disappointed that the leader of the party would call him and request his support for such legislation.

U.S. Tobacco flew Barbour on a corporate jet at least once and Philip Morris lent him a helicopter on another occasion, but Barbour isn't the industry's only frequent flier. From January 1997 to May 1998, in fact, Republican party leaders took at least eighty-four trips aboard tobacco-company jets paying cut-rate prices (usually 3–7 percent of what a chartered flight would cost). A report, *Air Tobacco,* by the Democratic staff of the House Committee on Government Reform and Oversight, revealed that "the tobacco industry provides more subsidized campaign travel to congressional leaders and political parties than any other corporate special interest." Approximately 90 percent of all subsidized corporate campaign travel was taken by Republican Party committees and members. John Linder, then the chairman of the National Republican Congressional Committee, flew to San Diego for the Super Bowl on a tobacco-company plane but said he sees "nothing wrong" with this type of travel. It is just "another big perk we get."

Republican leaders on Capitol Hill returned the favor by inserting a $50 billion tax credit for the tobacco industry into a budget bill in 1997. House Speaker Gingrich and Senate Majority Leader Lott slipped a forty-six-word sentence into legislation, with the acquiescence of the Clinton White House. This "orphan provision" became law without debate and without an identified sponsor. Neither Gingrich nor Lott publicly accepted sponsorship of the measure. How did the tobacco industry pull this off? Lott and Gingrich were both approached with the provision by a group of Republican lawmakers from tobacco states, urged on by tobacco lobbyists. In his interview with the Center, Barbour acknowledged for the first time that the entire scheme had grown out of his conversations with Gingrich.

The secret deal, which was discovered shortly after it had passed, caused a public uproar and a backlash on Capitol Hill. Not only was the tax break overwhelmingly repealed in both chambers, but Congress also approved a cigarette-tax increase to benefit child health care and a sevenfold increase (from $5 million to $34 million) in the Food and Drug Administration's budget for ID checks on minors who try to buy cigarettes.

From 1996 to 1997 the major tobacco companies were in negotiations with the state Attorneys General, and Senator John McCain of Arizona introduced his tobacco-control legislation in Congress. During this time, tobacco spent more than $49 million on lobbying, hiring not only Barbour, but every living former Senate Majority Leader save for one, who is ninety-six years old. Washington had never witnessed a lobbying juggernaut like the one tobacco assembled for the settlement and legislation.

At one point Mitch McConnell of Kentucky, the chairman of the National Republican Senatorial Committee, became heavily involved. Behind closed doors before the big vote, he promised his fellow Republicans that the tobacco industry would continue running millions of dollars worth of "issue ads" on television in support of those who voted with him to kill the tobacco legislation. McConnell said that the ads would portray Senators voting to kill the bill as fighting a tax increase on America's working class. McConnell apparently was persuasive, and the bill couldn't get over the sixty-vote hurdle set up by Senate rules.

The Campaign for Tobacco-Free Kids, a not-for-profit organization, learned of McConnell's locker-room pep talk to his GOP colleagues and filed a complaint against the tobacco industry with the Federal Election Commission. It alleged that the issue advertising was offered in exchange for lawmakers' votes—a violation of federal election law. The complaint prompted a criminal investigation by the Justice Department.

The tobacco companies and the Republicans have colluded on a host of other tobacco-related issues, from health care to "tort reform." The Center found an illuminating memo that was written in August 1994 by Craig Fuller, a vice-president of Philip Morris. Fuller had previously been Vice President Bush's chief of staff, and he managed the 1992 Republican National Convention in Houston. "About a dozen Republican types were assembled last night by RNC Chairman Haley Barbour," Fuller reported in the memo. "We discussed various tactics with regard to health care. The group was divided—some wanting to try and block anything from passing. I and several others argued that something should be *allowed* to pass this year if possible. [emphasis added] This is where Haley is at the moment."

Jim Nicholson, the RNC's current chairman, said he sees nothing wrong with his party's alliance with an industry whose products kill 400,000 Americans every year. "We're a huge party," he told the Center in an interview. "There are over fifty million of us. You can find somebody who will have a different view on almost any subject matter. But I've never had anyone suggest to me that we not take money from tobacco companies."

Gambling is another of the issues on which Republicans do not exactly practice what they preach. When he was the RNC's chairman, Barbour declared, "It is not my place to be judgmental about issues when it comes to allowing people to support us." Little wonder: Barbour, according to an account in the *Washington Post,* owned shares in a firm that received $15,000 a month in consulting fees from Video Lottery Technologies, Inc., a Montana-based lottery and gaming machine company that later changed its name to Powerhouse Technologies, Inc.

Barbour's successor apparently prefers not to be "judgmental," either. "It is not talked about very much as I go around the country," Nicholson told the Center. "Again, it is a legal business."

Last year, the National Gambling Impact Study Commission, authorized by Congress in 1996 to study gambling and its effects, reported that more than 125 million Americans gamble. Of that number, the commission found, an estimated 7.5 million adults are either problem gamblers or pathologically addicted to gambling. And children are becoming addicted to gambling at a greater rate than adults: Last year, 1.1 million adolescents from twelve to eighteen years old were pathological gamblers.

The industry, meanwhile, is booming as never before, with Internet gambling, convenience-store gambling, video poker, and the proliferation of more than two hundred fifty casinos on Indian reservations nationwide. Twenty-five years ago, gambling was legal in only a handful of states; today, some form of it is permitted in forty-seven states. The gambling industry employs more than 600,000 people nationwide and generates revenues of more than $50 billion annually. Casinos rake in four times as much as the motion pictures, four times as much as spectator sports, and twice as much as the music industry.

In the early 1990s the gambling industry reacted to the threat of higher taxes and greater federal regulation by becoming a major force in the Republican Party. In 1995 the industry created a Washington presence, the American Gaming Association, and picked Frank Fahrenkopf, a former chairman of the RNC, to run it at a salary of $800,000 a year. "I don't think the vast majority of the American people share that view if you're a candidate for the office and you take [gambling money] that you're doing something inherently wrong," Fahrenkopf told the Center in 1996. "Let's face it, everyone has the right to have their own view of what's moral and what's not moral." One of the American Gaming Association's hired-gun lobbyists is Donald Fierce, a former business partner and colleague of Haley Barbour's at the RNC.

The industry has also dramatically increased its political contributions to both parties and candidates. Since 1995 to 1998 gambling interests have contributed more than $5.2 million in soft money to the Republican Party and more than $4.9 million in soft money to the Democratic Party. The industry's investment has paid off. To cite just one case in point, in 1998 two Senators who enjoy substantial financial support from gambling interests—Majority Leader Trent Lott and Minority Leader Tom Daschle—stopped legislation that would have eliminated federal tax deductions on all gambling losses from reaching the Senate floor.

Gambling interests also have been generously "comping" politicians. Stephen Wynn, the chairman of Mirage Resorts, Inc., is perhaps the most powerful figure in the gambling industry. The Mirage houses a mini-campaign headquarters, with telephone banks used for polling and get-out-the-vote drives. Since 1991, Wynn and his companies have contributed more than $1 million in soft money (including $250,000 in July 1999) to the Republican Party. He's hosted political fund-raising events at the Mirage with such leading Republicans as Barbour, Dole, Gingrich, and McConnell, sometimes flying them to Las Vegas in his corporate jet. Gingrich, on one trip to Las Vegas, dined with Wynn privately and attended a breakfast fund-raiser the next morning. The House had already passed the legislation that created the National Gambling Impact Study Commission and would have given it the power to subpoena gambling-industry executives. In front of Las Vegas contributors, though, Gingrich publicly promised that he would try to take away the commission's subpoena power, and, with a helping hand in the Senate from Trent Lott, he did.

Some Republicans are troubled that their party is so eagerly rolling its dice on the gambling industry. "I start to see all these guys, people whom I had known, many who were out giving—quote—'the pro-family speeches,' that 'we are the Republican Party, we're pro-family,' [and now] we're working for the gambling interests," Representative Frank Wolf, a Republican from Virginia told the Center. "They have attempted to corrupt the process up here. There's a gambling caucus on Capitol Hill. Twenty years ago you wouldn't have had a gambling caucus. Twenty years ago a Member of Congress wouldn't have taken [gambling-industry money], wouldn't have wanted to be in the room with a gambler, and now there's a gambler caucus. Now, they don't call it gambling; they call it gaming. But gaming is kind of the respectable name for it. It's gambling." Wolf is so disheartened by his party's coziness with gambling interests that he's spoken with party officials about it.

"Congressman Wolf has a very strong view, and he has been over here to meet with me and talk to me about it," Nicholson told the Center. "I respect him, and I respect his views. But the rank-and-file people around the country, or even the activists and the members of my RNC, rarely ever bring up the subject."

Gambling, tobacco, and alcohol have all wreaked horrendous havoc on American families, but certainly nothing can snuff out a life—and devastate a family—faster than a bullet. And in no developed country do more children die each year from guns than in the United States. In a 1997 study, the Centers for Disease Control and Prevention analyzed firearm deaths for children under the age of fifteen in twenty-six countries and found that 86 percent of the deaths occurred in the United States. Which makes the close collaboration between the gun interests and the Republican Party of "family values" all the more curious.

In recent years the two political parties have increasingly aligned themselves opposite each other, the Republicans generally with gun owners and manufacturers, and the Democrats with gun-control interests. But now, as children keep shooting children in the nation's schools, the GOP is somewhat less comfortable with its public image as the Gun Owners Party. Last year, in the span of twenty-four hours, after a firestorm of criticism, the Republican-controlled Senate completely reversed itself on a piece of gun legislation. And leading Republican presidential candidates actually *talked* about the subject of gun control.

The first indication that something startling was afoot came when, in the wake of the massacre at Columbine High School in Littleton, Colorado, Elizabeth Dole delivered a speech in New Hampshire in which she said that she favors the existing ban on assault weapons, favors a ban on "cop-killer" bullets, and supports safety locks on guns to protect children. There were some boos from the crowd, and other moments of cold silence, but Dole made her point forcefully: "I don't think you need an AK-47," she said, "to defend your family."

These were mainstream American sentiments before the massacre in Littleton, even if not wildly received by Republican voters in "Live Free or Die" New Hampshire. Indeed, according to the University of Chicago's National Opinion Research Center, 85 percent of Americans support mandatory registration of handguns. An overwhelming majority would require background checks even for private sales and require every gun buyer to have safety training. Even gun owners support some government oversight: 82 percent favor at least some prepurchase criminal background checks, and three-quarters support mandatory registration.

There are not, however, many federal gun laws on the books. In fact, there are more laws today governing safety in the manufacture of teddy bears than of guns. It is hardly a coincidence that federal consumer product safety laws do not apply to guns, an omission for which both political parties bear responsibility. Gun violence in the United States is becoming increasingly bizarre in comparison to other parts of the industrialized world. The *Journal of American History* recently reported that, on average, more people are killed with guns in the United States in a week than in all of Western Europe in a year. A 1998 study in the *International Journal of Epidemiology* found that the firearms death rate in the United States is eight times higher than the average for twenty-five other industrialized countries.

The dearth of laws on gun safety and ownership in the United States is, of course, a direct result of decades of pressure politics by the National Rifle Association and other such organizations, to which lawmakers in both parties have succumbed. We found that the NRA is No. 36 on the Republican Party's "Top Fifty Patrons" list, having contributed at least $982,555 in soft money from 1991 to mid-1999. From 1987 to 1997 the gun lobby pumped more than $12.7 million into congressional campaigns. The NRA gave $1.35 million to Republican congressional candidates in the 1998 elections, nearly five times what it gave to Democratic candidates ($283,000), according to the Center for Responsive Politics. And like many special interests, the gun interests have built up personal relationships with lawmakers over the years.

Members of Congress, for example, have participated in the Great Congressional Shootout, sponsored by the NRA and gun manufacturers and held at the Prince George's County Trap and Skeet Center in Glenn Dale, Maryland. In 1996 and 1997 the "Top Gun" trophy for outshooting his colleagues went to Representative Bill Brewster, a Democrat from Oklahoma. Some 250 lawmakers belong to the Congressional Sportsmen's Caucus, which lobbies on any legislation that might affect hunters. The fund-raising arm of the caucus, the Congressional Sportsmen's Foundation, shares office space in Washington with Olin Corporation, the company that makes Winchester ammunition.

None of the forty Capitol Hill lawmakers who joined President Clinton last year in proposing new gun-control legislation were in Democratic leadership posts. Within a week of the Littleton massacre, Senate Democratic Leader Tom Daschle of South Dakota said on National Public Radio, "I'm not sure that gun legislation is what we need." Daschle eventually supported the legislation that passed the Senate, which would have required registration and background checks for purchasers at gun shows. But the parameters of the debate have been circumscribed by decades of pressure from the NRA and other gun interests. By any objective assessment, the gun-related proposals put forth by the White House and Capitol Hill lawmakers in this decade have been quite modest. It is exactly the underwhelming responsiveness of Congress and the Executive Branch on this public safety issue that has prompted victims of gun violence and local governments to seek redress in the courts, hoping to hold gun manufacturers liable for the carnage created by their products. Gun-rights proponents see all this, of course, as a vast conspiracy by the trial lawyers.

In 1993 a Democrat-controlled Congress passed the Brady bill, which requires background checks and a five-day waiting period for handgun buyers. Congress also enacted a ban on the manufacture, sale, and possession of nineteen powerful "assault weapons." While historic and hard-won, the Brady Act actually was weaker than many state gun-control laws, and only a small percentage of crimes are committed with assault weapons (the law specifically lists 650 sporting rifles that are not affected by the assault-weapon ban).

The NRA, however, went ballistic over the new laws. It targeted lawmakers in TV ads narrated by Charlton Heston (now the organization's president), the actor who played Moses in *The Ten Commandments*, in which he said, gravely, "You went to Washington and voted for the first federal gun ban in American history." The NRA spent nearly $3.7 million in the 1994 elections and claimed credit for winning 211 of the 276 races in which it endorsed candidates—and for giving Republicans their first majority in the House of Representatives in forty years. One of the candidates it helped elect was Republican Bob Barr of Georgia, who received $4,950 from the NRA's political action committee. He got personal campaign assistance from NRA national headquarters, which, Barr later told an NRA conference, "made a tremendous difference in that race, and that personified the tremendous grassroots support and grassroots ability" of the NRA.

Barr soon helped persuade his Georgia Republican colleague, then-Speaker Newt Gingrich, to appoint him chairman of a special seven-member Firearms Legislative Task Force, which met weekly to develop a pro-gun agenda. Barr also secured a seat on the House Judiciary Committee, which has jurisdiction over gun issues. Working closely with NRA officials and consultants, Barr helped plan a series of hearings on guns, focusing on such topics as the Second Amendment and the use of guns for self-defense. In the spring of 1996, Barr helped engineer the 239-173 vote in the House to repeal the ban on assault weapons. The ban still stands, since the Senate did not vote to repeal it. In his 1996 race, Barr received even more support from the NRA: Its PAC spent more than $68,000 to help reelect him.

Despite Barr's success in the House on behalf of the NRA, 1995 was a difficult year for the gun lobby. After the April 1995 bombing of the Alfred P. Murrah Federal Building in Oklahoma City, the NRA's ties to radical militia groups came to light. The Washington-based Violence Policy Center discovered and circulated a fund-raising letter from the NRA that described federal agents as "jack-booted government thugs, wearing black, armed to the teeth," who wear "Nazi bucket helmets and black storm-trooper uniforms." The letter was signed by Wayne LaPierre, the NRA's chief executive officer. In the resulting furor—and a harbinger of cracks in the NRA-GOP relationship—former President George Bush resigned his lifetime membership in the organization. He said the group's inflammatory rhetoric aimed at federal employees "deeply offends my own sense of decency and honor."

Despite such signs of strain between centrist and more conservative Republicans over the gun issue, the 1996 Republican Party platform declared, "We defend the constitutional right to keep and bear arms." Weeks after the Oklahoma City bombing, Senator Phil Gramm of Texas, one of the leading Republican presidential candidates in 1996, told NRA convention-goers, "I own more shotguns than I need, but not as many as I want." At that point he had received $440,000 in actual and in-kind support from the NRA over his career (three times more support than his No. 2 career patron) and been one of the NRA's most loyal supporters in Congress, echoing its positions by introducing, sponsoring, or voting for eighteen key bills concerning gun issues.

Many leading Republicans today are still firmly in the NRA's holster. With most Americans still raw from the massacre in Colorado, in which all four weapons used were bought at gun shows, the first instinct of Senate Majority Leader Trent Lott and Senator Larry Craig of Idaho, a Republican and NRA board member, was to enact legislation to relax existing gun controls. The Senate first killed a proposal to close the loophole in the Brady law that permits criminals and juveniles to buy firearms at gun shows without any background check. It then passed an amendment by Craig riddled with new loopholes. A day later, following the public up-roar, the Senate did an about-face to require mandatory back-ground checks at gun shows and other measures. "You can't defend the indefensible," explained Senator Gordon Smith, a Republican from Oregon.

Lott characterized the embarrassing about-face as merely a "technical correction." And in an interview with a reporter for the *New Orleans Times-Picayune,* he characterized the gun legislation passed by the Senate as "another step in the effort to outlaw guns by the media and Democrats," adding: "We're not going to let that happen. . . . I tell you, there are a lot of people who are going to eat these gun votes."

House Speaker Dennis Hastert's first instinct, after expressing condolences to the Littleton families, was to call for a "National Conference on Youth and Culture." In his floor statement the Illinois Republican talked about media violence, declining morals, and school safety, but the easy access to guns was not mentioned. Meanwhile, Representative Barr's latest salvo on behalf of the gun lobby, shortly before the events of Littleton, was introducing legislation that would block the lawsuits filed by cities against gun manufacturers. According to the *New York Times,* Barr, flanked by gun lobbyists, held up a wooden Louisville Slugger at a March news conference, warning that baseball-bat manufacturers may also be subject to litigation, since bats also "are used in the commission of crimes, with some frequency."

Meanwhile, over in the Senate, Republican Orrin Hatch of Utah, the chairman of the Judiciary Committee, which has jurisdiction over gun laws, is close to the NRA. "It's a welcome change while here inside the Beltway to be surrounded by so many like-minded men and women," he told an NRA conference on the Second Amendment in 1995. "Efforts such as this conference . . . provide us with substantial opportunities to make inroads into the despotism of gun control."

In the early battleground states of Iowa and New Hampshire, there already have been signs of the Republican Party's tight alliance with the gun culture. The chairman of the Iowa Republican Party, Kayne Robinson, is the No. 2 official to Charlton Heston at the National Rifle Association. And in New Hampshire, Steve

Forbes's state campaign manager, Peter Robbio, resigned after his arrest for brandishing a gun in a bar dispute there.

Besides Elizabeth Dole's striking departure from past GOP presidential candidate statements on gun control, in the wake of Littleton the other centrist Republican contenders, Senator John McCain of Arizona and Texas Governor George W. Bush have slightly moderated their positions. McCain—who has echoed NRA positions for years, opposed the 1993 Brady law, and voted with Senators Lott and Craig and others on May 12, 1999 to ease existing gun controls—almost immediately issued a press release reversing himself. Its headline, referring to an amendment he was cosponsoring, read: "McCain Closes Loophole, Requires Instant Background Checks at Gun Shows." The press release went on to quote him as saying: "This is not an overly burdensome requirement in the face of the tragic shootings at Columbine High School. Rather, it is a responsible means of lessening the likelihood of unlawful gun purchases."

Bush has been attempting to straddle the post-Littleton angst over guns and his party's longstanding ties to gun interests. Just days after his father resigned from the NRA, Governor Bush won praise from the gun lobby for signing legislation that allows Texans to carry concealed handguns. Following months of silence on the subject of background checks for people buying weapons at gun shows, Bush said after Littleton that he supported the legislation. Interestingly, according to the *Boston Globe,* in the midst of the Senate debate over gun control in 1999, Senator Craig called Bush, urgently seeking to learn his position on the pending legislation. The Senate Republicans apparently moderated their position after consulting with Bush and his aides.

Most voters find it unseemly for a political party or politician to march in lockstep with a special interest. Americans like to think that their elected representatives are independent protectors of the broad public interest. On the gun issue, many Republicans have had an epiphany that their party and elected leaders have been sitting in the NRA's duck blind a little too long.

But Jim Nicholson, a highly decorated Army Ranger in Vietnam, doesn't see it that way, and his posture echoes NRA talking points for the past three decades in the United States. "There's a lot of discussion in our party about guns," he told the Center. "But usually it bottoms out on the fact that we need to enforce the laws that are on the books about guns, which there are over 20,000. In the last two years we've had 6,000 incidents of people bringing guns onto schoolyards or into school buildings, both of which are against existing federal laws. Only thirteen of them have been prosecuted. So we need to start enforcing the existing laws. Common sense will tell you that if you take away the guns from all the law-abiding citizens in this country, the only people who will be left with guns are the criminals. . . . And, you know, let us not also forget that there is a constitutional issue here."

Begrudgingly, Nicholson added: "If there are certain things that ought to go on, like background checks, limiting the size of rounds you can put in clips, and some of those common-sense things, then, you know, I think we probably ought to have them."

Beyond the gun, gambling, tobacco, alcohol, and other controversial interests that are closely associated with the Republican Party, no company is closer to the GOP than Amway Corporation.

Amway is the largest "direct sales" company in the world. With sales of personal-care products in more than eighty countries, about 70 percent of Amway's sales come from overseas. The company describes its product line as "soap and hope"; the soap is the home-care product, and the hope is the giant rallies run by the company with an atmosphere similar to Christian fundamentalist gatherings. Since hope is generally free, the soap must be selling well; in 1998, Amway hit $5.7 billion in sales.

Amway has had its troubles over the years. In the 1970s the Federal Trade Commission charged that the company was an illegal pyramid scheme. In that case, the company successfully defended itself, but in the 1980s the company paid $58 million to the Canadian government to settle charges of customs fraud.

Amway's support of the Republican Party is virtually unparalleled. The company, its founding DeVos and Van Andel families, and related interests are the Republican Party's No. 2 patron, having made more than $4.5 million in soft-money contributions from 1991 through June 1999. Amway founder Richard DeVos and his wife Helen gave $1 million to the RNC in April 1997 (each wrote a check for $500,000), tying the record for the largest contribution from individuals in the FEC's history.

Amway's ties to the Republican Party extend well beyond mere cash donations. DeVos was the finance chairman of the RNC during the first two years of the Reagan Administration, and his daughter-in-law Betsy chairs the Michigan Republican State Committee. In 1994 Amway gave $2.5 million to the GOP to finance the construction of a television studio at the party's Washington headquarters. Haley Barbour, the RNC's chairman at the time, acknowledged that he had actively solicited the money.

Later, in 1996, Amway became embroiled in a scandal over the Republican National Convention when it tried to give $1.3 million to the San Diego tourist board to televise the entire convention on televangelist Pat Robertson's Family Channel. Once again, the omnipresent Barbour had asked for the money. At the same convention, Amway chartered an eighty-three-foot yacht, *Chere Amie,* to entertain delegates and VIP guests.

Amway has also done its part to help raise funds for the Republican Party. On July 18, 1996, a fund-raising dinner in Detroit to honor Richard DeVos netted the party $3 million. The featured speaker at that event was Robert Dole. A charity fund-raiser in Washington that same month sponsored by Dick DeVos (Richard's son) featured a handful of Capitol Hill lawmakers, including House Majority Whip Tom DeLay, himself a former Amway salesman. Besides DeLay, the 104th Congress featured an actual "Amway Caucus" made up of five former or current Amway salespeople who served in the House. All were Republicans: Jon Christensen of Nebraska, Dick Chrysler of Michigan, John Ensign of Nevada, Sue Myrick of North Carolina, and Richard Pombo of California.

So what has Amway gotten for all its money? For starters, there was a tiny provision in a 1997 budget deal that saved Amway upward of $19 million by allowing it to avoid paying taxes on its Asian subsidiaries. Although the language was designed to benefit only a few select companies, President Clinton declined to use his line-item veto for fear of irritating the Republican Congress before pending appropriations debates. Amway hired former government officials to lobby for the tax break. Robert Packwood, the former chairman of the Senate Finance Committee, who'd been forced to resign in the wake of revelations that he'd sexually harassed employees and campaign workers, was brought in to lobby his former aide, Rolf Lundberg, a staff counsel to Senate Majority Leader Lott. (Welcome to the wacky world of Washington.) And according to the *Wall Street Journal,* Amway lobbyist Roger Mentz, a former Treasury Department official, persuaded the Treasury Department, at Newt Gingrich's urging, to announce that it did not oppose the tax bill containing Amway's clause.

Amway's support of the Republican Party continues into the 2000 election cycle. A new GOP fund-raising machine organized by Tom DeLay and known as the Republican Majority Issues Campaign is set to counter the AFL-CIO's highly publicized 1998 issue ads. Its inaugural event, attended by DeLay, House Speaker Hastert, and J. C. Watts, the chairman of the House Republican Conference, was on an Amway-owned yacht. Karl Gallant, a DeLay operative who will run the campaign, is aiming to raise as much as $25 million. He does not plan to register the organization with the Federal Election Commission and therefore will not be forced to publicly disclose contributions or expenditures.

Meanwhile, the telecommunications industry has stepped up its support of the GOP, to the point where more than 60 percent of its campaign money now goes to the Republican Party. It's not as much a thank-you for the 1996 Telecommunications Act, which was brought to us by a Republican-controlled, deregulation-minded Congress, as it is a greasing-the-skids investment in the race to wire America.

For the first time in the history of telecommunications, the technology now exists to provide the average citizen with super-high-speed, low-cost continual access to the Internet. Known as broadband Internet access, it uses existing technology such as cable television lines and local telephone networks to provide both businesses and residents with on-demand Internet access at up to hundreds of times the currently available speeds. Broadband will eliminate the need for traditional dial-up modems and will offer users the ability to use multiple devices like telephones, facsimile machines, and the Internet all at the same time. The key is high-capacity lines, such as cable television lines or local phone lines, equipped with Digital Subscriber Line technology (DSL). Broadband options like cable and DSL will be the future of the Internet.

They are also the future of telecommunications revenue. One estimate puts the value of on-line commerce at $42 billion by 2002. The Commerce Department estimated that in 1998, information technology accounted for 8.2 percent of the total U.S. gross domestic product. Broadband services, once fully deployed, are expected to develop into a market worth $150 billion. These figures are not lost, obviously, on the telecommunications industry. Companies that can gain an edge in the emerging broadband market stand to secure their position as leaders in the economy of the twenty-first century.

Maybe it should come as little surprise, then, that four of the top ten soft-money donors to either party in the first half of 1999 were giant telecommunication companies: AT&T Corporation, Bell Atlantic Corporation, BellSouth Corporation, and SBC Communications, Inc.

Similarly, many of the Republican Party's top soft-money patrons from 1991 through June 1999 are big players in the telecommunications arena. AT&T (including McCaw Cellular and TCI) is No. 5, at $2.9 million; Bell Atlantic is No. 9, at $1.9 million; MCI WorldCom, Inc., is No. 16, at $1.4 million; SBC Communications, Inc., is No. 21, at $1.3 million; U S West, Inc., is No. 40, at $941,717; and BellSouth is No. 46, at $879,990.

Not surprisingly, one of the industry's top hired guns is Haley Barbour. He represented BellSouth, the U.S. Telephone Association, and U S West in 1998. His now defunct National Policy Forum got $200,000 in 1995 from a coalition of regional Bell operating companies that were lobbying for the 1996 Telecommunications Act. Records also show that from 1993 to 1997, Bell Atlantic gave $100,000 to the Republican Policy Forum and BellSouth another $10,000.

Barbour also reached deep into the pockets of the telecommunications industry to raise money for the Trent Lott Leadership Institute at the University of Mississippi. The official "host" of Barbour's fund-raising gala at Washington's Kennedy Center was Bernard Ebbers, the president and chief executive officer of MCI WorldCom, Inc., which donated $1 million; other donations included $250,000 from BellSouth, $100,000 from SBC Communications, and $25,000 from Bell Atlantic.

Unfortunately, for the American citizen who's in search of someone in Washington who's not beholden to the telecommunications industry, the circuits are busy now. Please hang up and try your call again.

Finally, we come to the No. 3 soft-money patron of the Republican Party in the 1990s. What would it take to get the U.S. government to go to bat for your company before an international trade organization even if there were virtually no American jobs at stake? Only about $4.5 million and some friends in high places. Don't believe us? Ask Carl Lindner, the founder of American Financial Group, Inc., a holding company specializing in insurance that in 1998 posted more than $4 billion in revenue. Lindner's company and family have been among the biggest political donors ever, giving more than $1 million in soft money to the Democratic Party and nearly $3.5 million to the Republican Party from 1991 through June 1999.

Lindner is legendary for using money to influence the political process to his advantage. Said a Republican lawmaker back in 1997: "He's an operator. . . . He uses his money to get access. He's totally practical." Indeed, Lindner is not so close-minded as to completely ignore Democrats. He was a White House sleepover guest and attended a coffee with Vice President Albert Gore, Jr., on February 21, 1995. As the PBS program "Frontline" once showed, at a benefit concert at Ford's Theater in 1996, comedian Paula Poundstone asked President Clinton why someone in the banana business—American Financial owns 37 percent of Chiquita Brands International—was sitting so close to him: "Why does the President know the banana guy?" Clinton laughed but did not answer the question. Lindner also uses his political connections for his own financial benefit. One of his business partners in a Florida home-building company is Terence "Terry" McAuliffe, Clinton's top fund-raiser.

But Lindner's political activities have been aimed chiefly at the Republican Party. Besides the millions showered on the party, Lindner has gone out of his way to provide other gifts and perks for prominent Republicans. Former Senator Robert Dole hitched rides aboard Lindner's corporate jet at least eighteen times during his 1996 presidential campaign. Lindner also gave $100,000 to Dole's Better America Foundation in 1994. In addition, he became embroiled in a 1996 scandal over the RNC's steering of campaign donors to Republican-friendly organizations. At the direction of Barbour and Jo-Anne Coe, a longtime aide to Dole who became the RNC's deputy finance director, two $100,000 checks from Lindner went from the RNC to Americans for Tax Reform and the Right to Life Committee.

But Lindner's biggest coup came in May 1999, when the World Trade Organization ruled in favor of the United States and several Latin American countries that had brought a complaint against the European Union for unfair tariffs on bananas.

In mid-1993, when the European Union imposed a tariff on bananas not coming from former European colonies in the Caribbean, Lindner's Latin American-based Chiquita felt the crunch. He immediately turned to the U.S. government for help, even though 39,000 of Chiquita's 45,000 employees are in Latin America. Lindner met with then–U.S. Trade Representative Michael "Mickey" Kantor on January 13, 1994 to discuss the issue, and would meet with Kantor three more times over the next two years. In August 1994, Dole and eleven other Senators urged Kantor to intervene and on November 17 Dole, Gingrich, and House Democratic Leader Richard Gephardt wrote to the President asking for similar assistance. Kantor was somewhat reluctant, but after Dole wrote him a personal letter asking that he intervene, he did. Kantor was quoted as saying, "This came from the big boys at the top."

By April 1996, Kantor announced that he would bring the U.S.—that is, Lindner's—case before the World Trade Organization. In May 1999, the WTO awarded the United States more than $190 million in punitive tariffs based on European violations of free-trade principles. Lindner's money had bought him access, and the access had bought him action.

For his part, though, Nicholson sees no evil. "We believe that it's an important right protected by the First Amendment for people to express themselves through contributions of money to political parties," he told the Center. "I've been chairman of this party now for over two and a half years and have raised hundreds of millions of dollars in amounts from $25 to a million. I have never yet—I can say this unequivocally—had anybody look me in the eyes and ask me for anything as part of a contribution. Not once."

The Republican Party
Top Fifty Patrons

1. **Philip Morris Companies, Inc.**, New York
   $6,211,508

2. **Amway Corporation**, Ada, Michigan/**DeVos family**
   $4,518,500

3. **American Financial Group, Inc./Lindner family**, Cincinnati
   $3,494,000

4. **Nabisco Group Holdings Corporation/R.J. Reynolds Tobacco Holding, Inc.**, New York
   $3,159,627

5. **AT&T Corporation/TCI**, Basking Ridge, New Jersey
   $2,913,543

6. **Atlantic Richfield Company (ARCO)**, Los Angeles
   $2,295,106

7. **Archer Daniels Midland Company**, Decatur, Illinois
   $2,112,268

8. **UST, Inc./United States Tobacco Corporation**, Greenwich, Connecticut/**Vincent Gierer**
   $1,927,200

This list is based on soft-money contributions to the Republican National Committee and its affiliated committees from January 1991 through June 1999. Sources: Federal Election Commission, Common Cause.

9. **Bell Atlantic Corporation/NYNEX**, New York
$1,910,494

10. **The Seagram Company, Ltd.**, Montreal
$1,629,555

11. **Pfizer, Inc.**, New York
$1,551,704

12. **Brown & Williamson Tobacco Corporation**, Louisville, Kentucky
$1,508,800

13. **FDX Corporation**, Memphis, Tennessee
$1,507,763

14. **Enron Company**, Houston
$1,463,200

15. **Chevron Corporation**, San Francisco
$1,460,906

16. **MCI WorldCom**, Jackson, Mississippi
$1,423,298

17. **The News Corporation, Ltd.**, Sydney, Australia
$1,396,750

18. **Citigroup, Inc.**, New York
$1,391,401

19. **Merrill Lynch & Company, Inc.**, New York
$1,302,900

20. **Cintas Corporation**, Cincinnati/**Richard Farmer**
$1,290,000

21. **SBC Communications, Inc.,** San Antonio, Texas
$1,265,291

22. **The Limited, Inc.,** Columbus, Ohio
$1,237,371

23. **Blue Cross & Blue Shield Association,** Chicago
$1,228,690

24. **CSX Corporation,** Richmond, Virginia
$1,192,045

25. **Forstmann Little & Company,** New York
$1,152,750

26. **The Tobacco Institute,** Washington
$1,147,422

27. **A.G. Spanos Construction,** Stockton, California/**Alex Spanos**
$1,132,100

28. **Bristol-Meyers Squibb Company,** New York
$1,111,224

29. **Waste Management, Inc.,** Houston
$1,099,352

30. **Anheuser-Busch Companies, Inc.,** St. Louis
$1,080,403

31. **Freddie Mac,** McLean, Virginia
$1,080,000

32. **Coca-Cola Company,** Atlanta
$1,068,494

33. **Koch Industries, Inc.,** Wichita, Kansas
$1,062,000

34. **Alfa Mutual Insurance Company**, Montgomery, Alabama
$1,047,881

35. **Glaxo Wellcome, Inc.**, Greenford, Middlesex, United Kingdom
$1,016,726

36. **National Rifle Association**, Fairfax, Virginia
$982,225

37. **Union Pacific Corporation**, Omaha, Nebraska
$953,547

38. **Revlon Group, Inc.**, New York
$950,000

39. **Eli Lilly & Company**, Indianapolis
$948,935

40. **U S West, Inc.**, Denver
$941,717

41. **Golden Rule Insurance**, Lawrenceville, Illinois
$931,375

42. **The Boeing Company**, Seattle
$918,405

43. **United Parcel Service of America, Inc.**, Atlanta
$918,368

44. **Paine Webber Group, Inc.**, New York
$902,150

45. **Tiger Management**, New York
$890,000

46. **BellSouth Corporation**, Atlanta
$879,990

47. **American Airlines, Inc.,** Dallas
    $863,205

48. **HD Vest Financial Services,** Irving, Texas
    $863,045

49. **Burlington Northern Railroad Company,** Fort Worth, Texas
    $858,600

50. **Microsoft Corporation,** Redmond, Washington
    $825,166

The Reform Party

||||||||||||

If you watch the Reform Party's convention on television this summer, you may notice a subtle detail that speaks volumes about the difference between the nascent third party and its established counterparts. In contrast to the splendiferous, multimillion-dollar stages replete with high-tech electronics and giant video special effects from which the Democrats and the Republicans will fete their anointed choices for President and Vice President, the Reform Party's candidates will be unveiled to the nation against a simple, somber black background, with an American flag as the only prop.

To be sure, the no-frills setting is an apt symbol for the Reform Party. Founded four years ago by its first presidential candidate, Ross Perot, it advocates a no-nonsense platform of fiscal austerity, streamlined and simplified government, and curbs on the influence of special interests and big-money campaign contributors. But as Pat Choate, Perot's running mate in 1996, pointed out, basic black has another compelling attraction.

"Our normal [total] expense at a convention will be $50,000," Choate told The Center for Public Integrity, noting that that expenditure is probably what the Democrats or Republicans would spend on one of their VIP receptions ("if," he said, "it's one of the shabby ones, where they're using cheap caviar"). "Basically what we do at our conventions is to negotiate with the hotel to get a rate that everybody could afford—eighty or ninety bucks a room. As a condition of us taking several hundred rooms, they have to provide us the convention space. When we set up the space, it's done in simplicity, the stage with the black backdrop and flag. It looks elegant. It's also cheap."

The need for frugality may seem strange, considering that Perot, the party's founding father, pumped millions of his own money into subsidizing the frenzied, last-second petition drives and infomercials that launched the party in 1995 and 1996. But according to Choate and other sources, Perot has largely withdrawn from an active role in the party and is unlikely to run again for President. All the same, Perot's legacy—official federal status as a political party, based on the eight percent of the popular vote that he claimed in the 1996 presidential race—has propelled the Reform Party into the millennium with newfound promise. Nonetheless, at times in 1999, the party had more the atmosphere of a circus than the aura of a serious political movement.

The Reform Party is what Choate and outgoing chairman Russell Verney like to call "America's first cyberspace party." In contrast to its Democratic and Republican counterparts, the Reform Party not only doesn't have a Washington headquarters, it has no offices at all and no paid staff. It has a telephone number (which patches through to the chairman's home), a post-office box, and a Web site from which visitors can download the party's platform. It holds no primaries; the party uses direct mail to ask its members to suggest potential presidential candidates, and it allows members to vote directly for them by e-mail or letter.

"We do virtually all of our communications with e-mail and conference phone calls," Choate told the Center. "We don't need a $50 million building. Don't need a big staff of lawyers, don't need a big PR staff. You just cut to the essence of politics. It also, by the way, frees us from having to go out and raise massive amounts of money."

That bare-bones approach seems fitting for a party that advocates radically streamlining the structure of government and enforcing fiscal austerity. But it's also a necessity. Perot bankrolled the drive to organize the party and recruit members, but his seemingly bottomless pockets are open no more. And, unlike the Democrats and Republicans, the Reform Party has no real corporate or individual fat cats.

"We're certainly not like the Republicans and Democrats, who are raising $30 million, $40 million, $50 million," Verney told the Center. "But our puny little $80,000 or $100,000 is all ours, and it's all legitimate."

The prospect of a third major political party developing in America may seem remote and bizarre, since Americans have been conditioned to think of politics as a two-party contest, now between the Republicans and Democrats. The perception by Americans that a ballot cast for a third-party candidate is a "wasted vote," a protest rather than a choice, is a powerful disadvantage to the rise of a challenger to the status quo. In 1992, for example, exit polls showed that Perot's 19 percent of the electorate might have swelled to 40 percent had voters believed he had a chance to actually win.

Even so, some suggest that the rise of a major third party could provide an antidote to the disillusionment and apathy that has led to chronically low voter turnout in the United States—and even prod the established parties, which have become more focused on taking in contributors' money than taking action on the nation's problems, to at least clean up their acts. "A three-party system would be driven more by issues, precisely because parties fighting for pluralities can be clearer in their positions," writes political scientist Theodore J. Lowi. "In a three-party system, even the two major parties would have stronger incentives to be more clearly programmatic, since their goal would be more realistic and their constituency base would be simpler. . . . The third party is a liberating rather than a confining force, a force for open debate on policies. Just as the rise of the two-party system fundamentally altered the constitutional structure of our government appropriately for the nineteenth century, so a three-party system would alter the structure appropriately for the twenty-first century."

But is the Reform Party up to that task? Just four years into its existence, the party is at a crucial crossroads. Can it move beyond being a vehicle for the presidential aspirations of its founder, and become a truly pluralistic, bottom-driven institution? Can it successfully navigate a daunting gauntlet of obstacles that the established parties have created across the nation? Can it develop alternative means of funding campaigns—a financial base that doesn't rely on well-heeled donors and corporate political action committees looking to buy influence over government policy? The party's performance in its second presidential-election cycle may well show whether it can fulfill its promise and help revive participatory democracy in the United States, or whether it is destined, like other failed progressive movements, to run out of steam and disintegrate.

The Reform Party actually is the latest in a long history of American third parties. Since 1832, thirteen third-party or independent candidates have garnered at least five percent of the popular vote in presidential elections. The most successful third-party candidate in history was Theodore Roosevelt; after serving two terms in the White House as a Republican and retiring, the trust-busting social reformer grew disillusioned with his ineffectual, conservative-leaning successor, William Howard Taft. After failing to wrest the Republican nomination from him, Roosevelt bolted the GOP to form the Progressive Party. Sucking off votes from his former party, Roosevelt edged Taft for second place behind Democrat Woodrow Wilson in the presidential election of 1912, winning 88 electoral votes. The party withered after Roosevelt declined to run again, but in 1924 the Progressives regrouped and nominated Senator Robert La Follette, the reform-minded Republican from Wisconsin. La Follette's platform called for the conservation of natural resources, the abolition of child labor, and the right of workers to organize and bargain collectively. He managed to win only one state, Wisconsin, but attracted 5 million votes nationwide.

Since then, several independent presidential candidates have attracted enough support to be factors in the outcome of elections. Democratic Governor George Wallace of Alabama—a former segregationist who in 1968 accepted the nomination of the fringe American Independent Party, but essentially ran as an independent— won 13.5 percent of the popular vote and 46 electoral votes in the South. Before an assassin crippled him in 1972, Wallace posed a significant threat to Richard Nixon's plan to transform the white South into a Republican stronghold. Nixon took him seriously enough that he sent IRS examiners on a massive investigation of Wallace and his supporters, and pumped $400,000 in slush funds into the campaign of Wallace's unsuccessful opponent for the Alabama governorship in 1970.

Wallace tried to tap into working-class resentment of the two major parties—he liked to proclaim that there wasn't "a dime's worth of difference" between the positions of Richard Nixon and Hubert Humphrey. But his virulently racist reputation kept him from ever reaching mainstream America.

A quarter century later a very different sort of independent candidate, Ross Perot, captured the largest share of the electorate since Teddy Roosevelt. The Texas billionaire, the founder of the data-processing giant EDS, entered the presidential race in 1992 at the urging of Jack Gargan, a retired investment consultant in Florida, and John Jay Hooker, Jr., a lawyer in Nashville—two political iconoclasts who were convinced that the nation was headed for ruin because of weak leadership. Perot's message was simple: The federal government needed to focus on fiscal austerity rather than appeasing wealthy donors and corporate special interests.

There was a certain irony to Perot's role as the messenger for reform. After all, he was a billionaire who'd amassed his fortune in the 1960s and 1970s by obtaining lucrative data-processing contracts for government benefits programs. Perot himself was accused by critics of using campaign contributions (or the promise of them) to influence government in ways favorable to his business. Perot had a reputation for paranoia—he once claimed, for example, that the North Vietnamese had hired the Black Panthers to assassinate him—and became entangled with bizarre characters and causes. But his combination of fiscal austerity and libertarian social ideas, and the caustic one-liners he delivered with a folksy Texas twang, captured the imaginations of many Americans hungry for change.

Early on Perot garnered astonishing levels of support—in some polls as high as 40 percent. But he squandered his momentum and damaged his image by abruptly dropping out of the race in July, and then just as abruptly reentering in October. Perot's explanations—that he was seeking to protect his family from GOP dirty tricks, and that he feared his popularity would throw the election into the House of Representatives—seemed far-fetched. The real explanation, Verney revealed in an interview with the Center, was less colorful, but says a lot more about the difficulty of mounting a challenge to the two-party status quo.

In their haste to put together a nationwide campaign, Perot's politically inexperienced supporters had run afoul of campaign-finance regulations. "When Perot said in February [1992], 'If you put me on the ballot, I'll run,' people started raising and spending money without any controls," Verney told the Center. "And when he got out in July, one of the many reasons was that these people were all violating the [federal election] law. It had to be organized. So they sent people to every state. Like in Florida, I think they closed down twenty-three bank accounts that had the name 'Perot' attached to them that nobody in Dallas knew anything about. They had to reconstruct, from whatever records they could get in each state, all of the financial activity and make it comply with the FEC regulations, which of course meant rebating to people anything that was contributed in excess of $1,000 or anything that they were doing through their corporation. Say a real estate office that was donating office space but was a corporation had to be reimbursed for it all."

Indeed, FEC records show that Perot's campaign was the subject of ten Federal Election Commission investigations in the spring and summer of 1992, though none of the investigations resulted in the FEC taking action. The FEC also sent six letters to Perot in 1992 from May to July, requesting additional information or requesting the committee to return illegal contributions it had accepted.

Essentially, according to Verney, Perot's organizations in various states had to shut down and start over from scratch and do things according to FEC rules. In fact, Perot first hired Verney, who'd been working for a political software firm, to help straighten out the mess so he could reenter the race.

In the wake of his debate performance, Perot made a surpassingly strong comeback, and won nearly a fifth of the popular vote. After the election, he formed an organization, United We

Stand America, and tried to capitalize on his newfound popularity to become a power broker in national politics. (He underwrote the chapters in each state to the tune of $7,500 a month apiece.) Perot failed in his efforts to derail the North American Free Trade Agreement (NAFTA), which he contended would siphon jobs and wealth out of the United States, but his electoral supporters and their reformist rage were widely credited with a significant role in the GOP's seizure of Congress from the Democrats in 1994. But Perot supporters who hoped, naively, to change Congress' fealty to big corporate interests and wealthy donors were left disappointed. "We had just changed the flies," as Verney put it, "but we hadn't done anything about the manure."

Perot decided to refashion his movement. In 1995 he sent questionnaires to all chapters of United We Stand America, asking them to check their states' laws on the formation of new political parties and to poll members on their desire to join one. That September he announced on CNN's "Larry King Live" that he was forming the Independence Party, and planned to immediately launch party-organizing efforts in California, Maine, and Ohio. (Perot later changed the name to the Reform Party, after running into conflicts with groups that owned the Independence name in California and other states.)

Within minutes of his flashing the number on the screen, his 1-800 line received 800,000 calls from would-be supporters. But building a political party, Perot discovered, was considerably more complex and difficult than running as an independent candidate. Simply getting the party on the ballot was a daunting challenge in many places. In the 1920s and 1930s numerous states passed restrictive election laws—in some places to keep communists and socialists from running for office, in other places to stymie reform candidates. A case in point: "In Maine, you needed 5,000 petition signatures for an independent candidate," Verney told the Center. "But if you wanted to create a party in Maine, you had to first go out and get 25,500 people to sign a voter registration card joining a party that doesn't exist. And getting people to change political parties—it's probably easier to get them to change gender, in many cases. . . . And then you have to get the same 25,500 people to sign a petition asking the state to create the party that they already joined."

Ultimately, the Reform Party got on the ballot in all fifty states and the District of Columbia in 1996, but Perot had to spend $50 million of his own money to do it. In a few states, such as Minnesota and New York, Perot cut deals with legally established local third parties that either joined the Reform Party or agreed to run its nominee as their candidate.

Verney insists that Perot remained unsure whether he wanted actually to be the Reform Party's first presidential candidate. "We were trying to create some method of having a nominating process for '96 if anybody else wanted to come along, because Ross was convinced that with all of the beating he had taken, he wasn't the best messenger to go forward from that." But nobody seemed interested until June, when former Colorado Governor Richard Lamm, a career Democrat, spoke at a California Reform Party meeting and, out of the blue, said he might consider running "under the right circumstances." Perot reportedly met with Lamm and encouraged him to become a candidate. Once Lamm threw his hat in the ring, however, Perot declined to give him access to the party's mailing list and refused to debate him.

Because of its late start, the Reform Party could not even hold primaries; instead, members were asked to vote by e-mail and regular mail. With little publicity and only a faint semblance of a contest, only 50,000 of the party's 1.3 million members participated in the candidate selection, which Perot won by 65 to 35 percent. Lamm, as mercurial in his way as the moody Perot, praised the winner as a "prophet" and a patriot on the level of Paul Revere, but all the same declined to support him for President.

If Lamm had been able to win, of course, the Reform Party would have been in a ticklish spot, with no funds to stage a campaign. Perot, in contrast, had been granted $32 million in federal funds because of his strong showing as an independent candidate in 1992. He intended to use that money as he'd used his own personal fortune four years earlier, to run a campaign over the airwaves, and make a big splash in the presidential debates. "Ross was only at about six or seven percent in the polls," Verney recalled. "So we chose not to spend a lot of money early.

We did some Labor Day advertising, right after Labor Day, to establish he was in the campaign. But we didn't attempt to manage poll numbers before the debates. . . . Because that's where Perot picked up huge momentum in '92."

That plan, however, went disastrously awry. The Commission on Presidential Debates, which had allowed Perot to debate Clinton and Bush in 1992, mysteriously decided to exclude him from the two planned televised debates in 1996. To make matters worse, the broadcast networks were unwilling to sell Perot all of the thirty-minute prime-time slots he wanted to air his trademark infomercials. Perot took the Commission on Presidential Debates to federal court and implored the FCC to force the networks to give him airtime, but on both counts he was rebuffed.

Forced to barnstorm and give stump speeches like a conventional politician, the insular billionaire was out of his element. He sometimes snapped angrily at members of his audiences, and at other times made embarrassing gaffes. The infomercials he was able to schedule garnered disappointing ratings, and his speeches turned into bitter personal attacks on Clinton's moral character—a sad turnabout for Perot, who himself had compared the American political process unfavorably to mud-wrestling. ("Mud-wrestling has rules," he once complained. "Politics has no rules.")

Exit polls on election night showed that much of Perot's 1992 following had drifted away. Of the voters who'd supported him in 1992, 45 percent went to Dole and 23 percent to Clinton, 30 percent sticking with Perot. But Perot's 7,874,283 vote performance, though disappointing for the Reform Party, was still more success than failure. By receiving more than five percent of the vote in 1996, the Reform Party became the first new political party in history to qualify for general-election funding. In 2000 it will receive a $12.6 million federal stipend for its nomination contests, national convention, and general-election campaign.

Thanks to Perot, in fact, the Reform Party is no longer dependent on having the billionaire as its candidate. Lamm's cheeky defiance of Perot encouraged other party activists who were discontented with Perot, and even before the election, breakaway factions began plotting strategies for wresting control of the party away from its founder. In October 1997 dissident activists from twenty-three states actually broke away to form the National Reform Party, a splinter group. But while Perot's personal popularity ebbed, his core philosophy still held a resonant appeal, even to his Reform Party critics. One dissident activist, Nelisse Muga of San Diego, spoke for many when she told the *New York Times*: "Ross Perot had the right message, but he was the wrong messenger."

The following year an unlikely figure emerged to hurry Perot on his way. Minnesota native Jesse "The Body" Ventura was a former Navy SEAL in Vietnam, professional wrestler, movie actor, and talk-radio host. He entered politics in 1991, because he was irritated that the local council in Brooklyn Park, Minnesota, had kowtowed to local real-estate developers and approved storm sewers that threatened to destroy a wetland near his house. Ventura ran for mayor and, to the shock of the local political establishment, won. After serving four years as mayor, he saw campaign signs in Minneapolis for Dean Barkley, who was running for U.S. Senate on the ticket of the Reform Party's predecessor, the Independence Party. Barkley lost, but the Reform Party managed to qualify for state funding for future races. Two years later, in 1998, Ventura ran for governor. He proved to be a master of sound bites, a surprisingly agile debater, and had the self-confidence to run TV commercials that cleverly parodied pro-wrestling histrionics and turned the joke on his opponents. (One depicted "Action Figure" grappling with "Special Interest Man" and telling him, "I don't want your stupid money!")

Ventura shocked the established parties by attracting a 40 percent increase in off-year turnout in many parts of the state. He won the three-way contest with 37 percent to Republican Norm Coleman's 34 and Democrat Skip Humphrey's 28 percent.

"Jesse's win was really important because it validated the party," Choate told the Center. "It said that it's more than an instrument of Ross Perot, as many people accused it of being. It also did something else; it opened up communications for the party. Prior to Jesse's win, the only person the national media would talk to in the party was Ross Perot."

Ideologically, Ventura echoed the Reform Party's founder on issues such as simplification of government, fiscal austerity, and particularly on the need for campaign-finance reform. "When candidates accept special-interest or political action committee money, they are indebted to the group that is funding them," Ventura wrote in his 1999 autobiography. "In effect, they've been bought. It's legalized bribery. Campaigns should be funded only by the people, from small, individual donations, so that only those individuals that the people truly want will participate." All the same, Ventura is no fan of Perot, who declined to give Ventura's gubernatorial campaign a desperately needed loan while it awaited post-election reimbursement by the state. "The Reform Party needs to reinvent itself a bit," Ventura wrote in his autobiography. "If the party doesn't get some fresh blood, it's going to become anemic and die."

In the summer of 1999, at the Reform Party's annual convention in Dearborn, Michigan, Ventura threw his weight around in the vote for a new party chairman to replace Russell Verney, who was stepping down. Ventura sent e-mails to 400 convention delegates in support of his choice, Jack Gargan, over Patricia Benjamin, the pro-Perot faction's favored candidate. Gargan, ironically, had been one of the two men who'd originally cajoled Perot into entering politics in the early 1990s. Since then, however, Gargan—like his patron, Ventura—had come to believe the party needed "a new direction." But the new Reform Party chairman will continue the party's developing tradition of colorfully offbeat leadership. Gargan was the founder of Throw the Hypocritical Rascals Out (THRO), and took out full-page newspaper ads thoughout the nation in 1991 advocating term limits. Previously an unsuccessful candidate for the Florida governorship and Congress, Gargan is a Y2K computer chip-glitch doomsayer who fears a global economic collapse, and reportedly lives in Florida's Cedar Key because it has only one bridge to the mainland and could easily be defended from rampaging interlopers.

When Gargan takes over in January 2000 he'll have to deal with some of the same challenges that the Reform Party faced in 1996. Despite federal recognition as a bona fide political organization, the Reform Party is guaranteed ballot access in just twenty-two of the fifty states. In most places, since the party is not legally recognized, voters still can't even register as Reform Party members. (It's a problem that's plagued other would-be third parties as well; in 1996, Ralph Nader, the presidential candidate of the Green Party, managed to get on the ballot in only twenty-one states and the District of Columbia.)

Outgoing chairman Verney, however, is confident that the Reform Party will get its candidate on ballots nationwide, even if the candidate technically has to qualify as an independent or as a representative of some legally recognized local party. In addition, the party has developed an ingenious incentive for future presidential hopefuls: They can qualify for the nomination in part by mounting petition drives to secure ballot access in states where the party doesn't yet have it.

A bigger problem for the Reform Party is getting its candidate into the televised presidential debates. "There's nothing in the Constitution that gives the two existing political parties the right to control the political process, and every thinking American understands that," Perot complained to a National Press Club audience in January 1998. "You can't be a serious presidential candidate unless you're in the debates. And if the two parties can freeze you out, that certainly makes the status quo permanent."

"In both 1988 and 1992," the Commission on Presidential Debates proudly proclaimed on its Web site, "exit polls showed that more voters based their balloting decisions on the debates than on any other single factor." The commission, however, also decides who deserves the opportunity to benefit from its pervasive influence—and who doesn't. After including Perot in the 1992 debates, the commission decided in 1996 not to invite him, after deciding that he did not have a realistic chance that year of being elected President.

"Basically, [the debate] is not an opportunity to make candidates viable but to give people the chance to see the candidates who are most likely to win the election," Paul Kirk, Jr., a former chairman of the Democratic National Committee and co-chairman of the Commission on Presidential Debates, subsequently explained at a 1997 symposium. The commission's general counsel, Lewis Loss, said that including Perot—who was supported by one in five American voters in the 1992 election—"would have been unfair to the one-hundred-plus other declared candidates who have no realistic chance of being elected but all of whom, presumably, would be eager to receive a debate invitation."

It's doubtful that very many of the Americans who tuned in to the debates knew much about the obscure organization that took such pride in its influence over their decisions. While a single party doesn't control the Commission on Presidential Debates, it is hardly apolitical. It was set up in 1987 by the two major parties as a way of eliminating unseemly squabbles between their candidates about when, where, and how to hold debates. The co-chairmen of the commission, Republican Frank Fahrenkopf and Democrat Paul Kirk, are both former chairmen of their parties' national organizations. They preside over a ten-member board evenly composed of Democrats and Republicans. Independents and members of nonmajor parties are not represented at all. Its lack of ideological diversity was so glaring that even one of its own financial sponsors, the Twentieth Century Fund, candidly noted in a 1996 report that "the Commission has cast itself as a nonpartisan debate sponsor, but it is firmly rooted in the two major parties." The report urged that the commission be expanded to include two members who were not affiliated with the major parties—a suggestion that went unheeded.

Although the two major parties dominate the commission, it is set up as a private, not-for-profit organization and accepts no funds from either party or the government, an ingenious structure that also shields it from legal challenges by third-party candidates. Instead, the debates commission is underwritten by large corporate sponsors, the same sort whose PACs and executives help subsidize the parties themselves, Philip Morris Companies, Inc., Anheuser-Busch Companies, Inc., Sprint Corporation, and Lucent Technologies, Inc., to name just a few. Although the Federal Election Campaign Act of 1971 prohibits corporations from financial involvement in electoral politics, the FEC—whose governance also is divided among members of the two parties—drilled a loophole in its regulations to allow them to underwrite an event that plays a major part in filling the nation's highest office. The FEC's answer is that the debates, at least in theory, aren't automatically limited to candidates from the major parties. Additionally, the FEC said, the participants are selected through "pre-established objective criteria." (Federal law, however, doesn't spell out precisely what those criteria must be. The Twentieth Century Fund defines them as "assessments of a candidate's national organization, other measures of public support, and determinations of a candidate's 'newsworthiness and competitiveness.' ")

In 1992 that theory held true. According to the Twentieth Century Fund study, the commission was uneasy about including Perot, but his astonishingly high poll numbers early in the campaign made it clear that he would be a major factor, at least, in the election's outcome. ("We concluded that his prospect of election was unlikely, but not unrealistic," the commission, somewhat cryptically, explained.)

In 1996, however, the Dole campaign, which wanted to see Perot drop out of the race and throw his support to Dole, was adamantly opposed to his participation. "They [the Dole campaign] were behind, they had to make sure Perot wasn't in it," Clinton strategist George Stephanopoulos later noted at a post-campaign symposium. "As long as we would agree to Perot not being in it, we could get everything else we wanted going in. We got our time frame, we got our length, we got our moderator."

The commission, seemingly eager to keep Dole's handlers happy, unanimously reversed its 1992 judgment. Furthermore, it decided that even though Perot still had the potential to sway the outcome of the election, that no longer was enough. A debater had to have a plausible shot at *winning* the presidency. The two major-party candidates, interestingly, did not have to pass such a test.

The precise equation that led to the conclusion remained mysterious. The commission wrote its rules in advance to make it legally possible for corporations to contribute money, but it also made them purposefully vague, reserving enough wiggle room that the board could justify whatever decision it made. (The commission claimed that it "must retain at least a modicum of judgment in applying its objective criteria so as to ensure the avoidance of a potentially 'bizarre' or unwelcome result . . . based solely on quantitative factors.") The commission's rules allowed it to consider public opinion polls, for example, but didn't specify how they should interpret such polls. In any case, it would have been disingenuous not to invite Perot on the basis of his single-digit numbers in 1996, which were roughly comparable to his ratings on the eve of the 1992 debates, not long after he reentered the race. Similarly, the commission could consider factors such as the amount of column inches and broadcast minutes a candidate had received, and "the professional opinions of the Washington bureau chiefs of major newspapers, news magazines, and broadcast networks." The commission ultimately revealed that it also had consulted with prominent political journalists—though it would not reveal which ones.

With all these troubling vagaries, it's not surprising that when Lawrence Noble, the general counsel to the Federal Election Commission, studied the debate commission's decision, he concluded that its selection process quite possibly had been in violation of federal election law, and recommended an investigation. "Some of the factors appear to be subjective on their face and other factors are so vague as to be imprecise," Noble wrote. He noted that by the standard of whether a candidate appeared to have had a realistic chance of winning, Dole, the Republican nominee, could well have been excluded. He charged that the corporations' underwriting of a debate in which only the Republican and Democratic candidates participated in essence represented in-kind contributions to Clinton's and Dole's campaigns. Nevertheless, the FEC's commissioners—supposed watchdogs who, in reality, have never been inclined to growl at the two major parties—chose to disregard Noble's recommendation, and voted 5-0 that the debates met the legal standard.

By the time the Reform Party's lawyers could mount a legal challenge, the election was over. "Now we have only the right to go back to court to say that the Federal Election Commission acted contrary to law," Verney told the Center. "And we went back to court that time. The Federal Election Commission went to court and said, 'They have no standing because the election is over. There is no relief you can give them.'

"So now we were caught in a Catch-22. You can't go to court before the election because you haven't exhausted your administrative remedies. If you go to court after the election, when you've exhausted your administrative remedies, it gets thrown out because the election is over."

Another obstacle for the Reform Party is the difficulty of financing its candidates and its party-building activities without individual and corporate fat cats. Since 1997, according to a memo by Verney, the party has experimented with several different fundraising approaches, including telemarketing and direct-mail solicitations. The party has accumulated a list of 140,000 donors whom it hopes to periodically tap for small amounts—typically, $40 one or more times a year. Borrowing a technique from the health-club industry and America Online, it hopes to convert as many of them as possible into regular donors who make periodic, automatic payments via credit card. Additionally, unlike their Democratic and Republican counterparts, Reform Party officials will play no direct role in fund-raising. Instead, the party has hired a contractor, Direct Campaign Solutions of Tampa, Florida, which will handle the entire fund-raising process, from pitching donors to dealing with FEC regulations about eligibility and actually depositing the money in the bank at the end.

If the Reform Party is going to fulfill its promise, it has to continue to qualify for federal funds. That necessity, however, creates another problem. The Reform Party can't afford to do poorly in an election. It needs a presidential candidate who's guaranteed to grab the requisite minimum number of voters.

Unlike the two major parties, the Reform Party has had a difficult time even finding someone besides Perot to run. (Just a month before its 1996 convention, the party grew so desperate that it sent a mass mailing to members, asking them to write in names of public figures whom they'd like to see run for the nomination, so the party could try to recruit them.) This time around, with federal funds available, party officials are wary of becoming a vehicle for gadflies. The requirement that would-be presidential candidates recruit new supporters and help the party gain access to the ballot is one way to weed them out. Choate estimates that the cost of staging such a petition drive will run about $2 million a candidate—a serious investment of time, but still a relatively modest amount of money in the hyperinflated fin de siècle of American politics; even rear-of-the-pack major party candidates such as Alan Keyes seem to raise that much easily. "It's the cheapest entry into the general election, where you've got an actual chance to win, of all three parties," he explained.

Even so, there's still the temptation to recruit a candidate who already brings with him powerful name recognition. In October 1999, as this book was going to press, Patrick Buchanan bolted the Republican Party and declared himself a candidate for the Reform Party's presidential nomination. In announcing his decision, Buchanan issued a challenge to the "Beltway elites who think that at long last they have pulled up the drawbridge and locked us out forever." Standing before supporters who were chanting "Go, Pat, go," Buchanan said, "You don't know this peasant army—we have not yet begun to fight."

A *National Journal* poll at summer's end suggested that, as the Reform Party's nominee, Buchanan could score 16 percent of the popular vote—more even than the charismatic Ventura (12 percent), who's said that he does not intend to seek the White House.

One major problem with putting Buchanan on the ticket is that his Religious Right stances on issues such as abortion and gay rights clash jarringly with the secular, pro-choice, pro-tolerance Perot and Ventura. Considering Buchanan's obsession with those issues, would he use the Reform Party nomination as a $13 million soapbox for his social agenda, instead of championing the party rank-and-file's desire for genuine economic, government, and electoral reform?

"Pat Buchanan, I don't believe, is necessarily a good fit because Pat Buchanan puts social issues on the front burner," according to Ventura. "We in the Reform Party do not put social issues as a front-burning item. We're more into the normal political government issues."

Verney discounts those concerns. The candidates from the two major parties, he said, "use the parties as a cash cow, not as a think tank, not as a source of principles or values. It's simply cash that brings them together. And what we have done is said: 'We don't, first off, have the cash. What we are about is principles. And if you want our nomination, first thing you should do is support our party's platform. Don't ask us to support your platform. Support our party's platform.' "

And so if Buchanan can agree to support a balanced budget, abolition of the Internal Revenue Service, campaign-finance reform, and other Reform Party positions, Verney sees no reason why he couldn't fit the bill. "I can see him saying that with a straight face and also having his social issues," he said. "We can have a Jesse Ventura with liberal, libertarian views on social issues and a Pat Buchanan with conservative views on the social issues in the same party because they both agree on the economic and government reform issues that we're for." There are some signs, however, that Perot himself may not be as far removed from the activities of the Reform Party as most people have believed. Verney told the Center, for instance, that he was employed by Perot throughout 1999.

In fact, the Reform Party's long-range plan is to metamorphose from a fan club for a charismatic leader to a true grassroots, bottom-driven national movement. Indeed, if the Reform Party has learned anything from Jesse Ventura, it's that the old truism about all politics being local still applies, even to the cyberspace party of the future. But if it eventually succeeds in breaking the Democratic and Republican lock on the electorate, the Reform Party may well rewrite all those old, accepted rules. In the meantime, when new chairman Gargan comes in, Verney notes with a laugh that "The phone will be forwarded to wherever he wants to answer it."

THE DEMOCRATS

Bill Bradley

On January 24, 1989, members of the Senate Finance Committee, then chaired by Democrat Lloyd Bentsen of Texas, held a hearing to discuss the wave of hostile takeovers and leveraged buyouts that had sent shock waves through the American economy. "In 1981, the total value of leveraged-buyout transactions in this country was $3 billion," Bentsen explained to his fellow committee members. "By 1987 that had increased over ten times, until last year alone, in the acquisition of Kraft and RJR-Nabisco, that acquisition by itself—those acquisitions—were shown to be at $36 billion."

Even more troubling, Bentsen explained, were the rivers of red ink that leveraged buyouts were adding to the bottom lines of so many American companies. "The net result of all these transactions is that you're seeing a corporate debt burden that is being tied to a reduction in corporate equity," he said. "Over the period of 1984 to 1987, the non-financial corporations in this country retired a net of $313 billion in equity, and at the same time borrowed a net of $613 billion in debt."

The surge in corporate debt wasn't the only reason for concern. The leveraged-buyout spree of the 1980s brought an unprecedented wave of bankruptcies, layoffs, plant closings, and financial frauds. A few got fantastically rich. Hundreds of thousands of others—ordinary Americans who'd worked for years for companies that were part of their communities—lost their jobs, their pensions, and their standards of living.

Appearing before the Senate Finance Committee the same day, Treasury Secretary Nicholas Brady discussed the effects that the wave of leveraged buyouts and the growing pile of junk debt had on federal tax revenues. "Since interest payments are deductible but corporate dividends are not, there is a substantial tax advantage that accrues to LBOs and other transactions that effectively substitute corporate debt for equity," Brady testified. In other words, a company that generated profits and issued dividends to shareholders also paid taxes; a company whose profits went to paying off mountains of junk bond debt paid no taxes at all.

It was just the sort of arcane issue that typically fascinated the cerebral second-term Senator from New Jersey, Bill Bradley. As one of the key architects of the Tax Reform Act of 1986, Bradley was familiar with the intricacies of corporate finance. He made it his practice to consult with investors on the state of the nation's economy. (Bradley preferred their views to academics. "I like to talk to people who are betting their own money," he told a reporter for *Dun's Business Month* in 1984. "That doesn't mean I don't talk to economists or money managers, but I like people with their own money at risk.") He was acutely aware of the vast assortment of loopholes, shelters, and other devices that wealthy individuals and corporations used to avoid paying federal income taxes. If anyone was qualified to understand the implications of the shift from equity to debt, it was Bill Bradley.

But rather than address the issue of the unlimited deduction for corporate interest that, as Treasury Secretary Brady described it, allowed the junk bond dealers "to change the rules of the game," Bradley decided to focus on the short-term. Brady suggested that interest deductions be limited to prevent the abuses of the leveraged-buyout artists; Bradley preferred to accentuate the positive. He noted that those who sold companies to corporate raiders earned capital gains, which were subject to income taxes. The bottom line, to Bradley at least, was this: "And well—and so, it's a wash to the federal government in terms of tax revenues."

In this case, however, Bradley, an Ivy Leaguer and Rhodes scholar, was wrong in a big way. In 1994, the most recent year for which complete statistics are available, total corporate deductions for interest came to $611 billion. The sum of long- and short-term capital gains—that is, the amount of money all individual taxpayers earned by selling stocks, real estate, art, and so on—totaled just $150 billion. And the revenue produced by that $150 billion was far less. The maximum tax rate on capital gains in 1994 was 28 percent, meaning that at most the capital gains tax raised $42 billion—less than a tenth of the value of the corporate interest write-off.

For the record, the $611 billion in total interest deductions that year also dwarfed the $173 billion in total federal income taxes paid by corporations. Debt had indeed produced a new set of rules, but Bradley preferred to think of it as "a wash."

Nine months after the hearing, in October 1989, the *Washington Post* reported that takeover artists had flooded Congress with contributions the year before. The top recipient was none other than Bradley, who received $96,000 in contributions—mostly from executives of two firms, Wesray Capital Corporation and Hambrecht & Quist—in a year in which he wasn't even running for reelection. An aide to Bradley told a reporter for the *Washington Post* that the Senator didn't even know whether leveraged buyouts posed a problem.

By 1992, Bradley had made up his mind. In an interview with a writer for the *New Republic,* he said that he opposed any attempt to use the tax code to rein in hostile takeovers. "The challenge is how do you devise something that could stop the bad and allow the good," he said, "and it is difficult to find such a beast."

Perhaps in referring to "good" takeovers, Bradley had in mind the kinds of deals that his patrons in the financial community engineered. Over the course of his political career, Bradley has raised hundreds of thousands of dollars in campaign contributions from officers and executives of firms in the corporate-takeover business. Some highlights: at least $50,000 from Wesray Capital Corporation; at least $65,500 from Hambrecht & Quist; at least $84,250 from Skadden, Arps, Meagher and Flom, a New York law firm that made millions advising corporate raiders; at least

$102,601 from Prudential Securities, Inc. (formerly Prudential-Bache Securities) and Prudential Insurance Company of America; $148,800 from Goldman Sachs; and at least $228,000 from Salomon Smith Barney (now a subsidiary of Citigroup, Bradley's No. 1 career patron). Before it collapsed in 1990, Bradley took in nearly $20,000 from the notorious Drexel Burnham Lambert, Inc. In 1986, Bradley even attended Drexel's Predators' Ball, a lavish party at which Carl Icahn, Victor Posner, Nelson Peltz, and other corporate raiders could rub elbows with junk bond king Michael Milken, savings-and-loan operators, and favored politicians. Few of their endeavors could be described as "good." Consider:

• Michael Milken, who at the height of the buyout binge was paid bonuses of up to $40 million a year, pleaded guilty to six felony counts for violating securities laws in 1990. He was fined $400 million and sentenced to ten years in prison. Milken's junk bonds, which gave corporate raiders like Carl Icahn and Norman Peltz the ready cash they needed to acquire such companies as Trans World Airlines and National Can Company, saddled those same companies with high-interest debt for years afterward.

• In 1986, Salomon Smith Barney, known as Salomon Brothers at the time, turned its attention from manipulating federal Treasury Bond auctions (for which the company was fined $290 million in May 1992) to managing the leveraged buyout of Revco, then the second-largest chain of drugstores in the United States. Salomon made $38 million on the deal. The cost of servicing Salomon's junk bonds was greater than the company's cash flow, however, and it declared bankruptcy in 1988. Two years later Revco's shareholders, bondholders, and creditors sued Salomon Brothers, among others, for fraudulently misrepresenting Revco's financial condition to sell the $1.2 billion worth of junk bonds used to buy the company out. (Salomon Brothers settled the suit for $30 million.)

• Victor Posner, another takeover artist and one of the highest-paid executives of the 1980s, looted some $65 million from the worker pension funds of eight companies he owned as a means of expanding his business empire and paying for his lavish lifestyle. Posner used company funds to pay for a yacht and horses; he was also fond of putting family members on his payrolls. In 1987 Posner pleaded no contest to filing fraudulent federal income tax returns; a U.S. District Court judge ordered him to pay more than $4 million in back taxes, penalties, and interest.

• The 1989 leveraged buyout of RJR Nabisco, Inc.—at the time, the largest such deal in history—led to the layoffs of some 825 salaried employees, 700 hourly wage-earners, and another 115 temporary workers, as the company struggled to pay off the $25 billion in debt it had taken on. When Philip Morris Companies, Inc., bought out Kraft Foods, Inc., that same year for $12 billion, it laid off some 400 Kraft employees; another 2,000 positions disappeared at the company as workers who retired or found other jobs weren't replaced.

Wesray Capital all but invented the leveraged buyout. The firm was started by William E. Simon, who was Treasury Secretary under President Gerald Ford, and Raymond G. Chambers, a tax accountant. It made its first big killing in 1982 when it bought Gibson Greeting Cards, Inc. To buy the company, Wesray put down $1 million of its own money and borrowed another $80 million. A year later Wesray arranged an initial public offering for Gibson, and sold it off for $290 million. Simon's personal profit was estimated at $66 million. As for the $80 million in debt, that stayed with Gibson; the newly public company had to repay the loan.

In 1986, Wesray bought out Simmons Mattress Company, which manufactured the Beauty rest mattress and the Hide-A-Bed convertible sofa, for some $120 million. Wesray sold off the company's overseas operations, slashed its workforce from its peak of 4,000 to 2,500 in 1988, and then sold it for $249 million to new investors.

The new investors were Simmons' own employees, most of whom were not even aware of the terms of the deal. Wesray cancelled the workers' 401(K) plan and put an employee stock ownership plan in its place. The ESOP then borrowed $249 million, mostly from banks, the proceeds of which ended up in the pockets of the Wesray investors. The employees of Simmons, as the new owners of the company, would pay the debt off over ten years. In return for their retirement nest eggs and the debt they were taking on, the workers got shares in the new company valued at roughly $10 each.

By 1990 the shares were worth about 50 cents apiece.

As it turned out, Wesray's dealmakers, to secure the $249 million purchase price, had painted an overly rosy scenario of the company's prospects. When Simmons failed to live up to the fine future Wesray had predicted, it defaulted on the first $15 million of debt repayments in 1990. Irate workers, who only then learned of the bargain that Wesray had struck for them, sued the corporate raiders. In 1993 the suit was settled for $15 million. In the meantime, Merrill Lynch Capital Partners, a division of Merrill Lynch & Company, Inc., rescued the company. It paid $32 million for a 60 percent stake in Simmons—$115 million less than Wesray had charged the ESOP for the same amount of stock.

By 1988, when Wesray arranged the deal with the employees of Simmons Mattress Company, William Simon had largely distanced himself from the leveraged buyout firm. His partner, the media-shy Raymond Chambers, quietly continued to run the company for two more years and then also ended his active participation in the business. Although Wesray still maintains an office in Morristown, New Jersey, the company and its once-famous buyout deals have faded along with so many of the other high-flying firms of the eighties. By 1990, Simon had moved on to other investment endeavors, and Chandler began devoting most of his time to philanthropy. And six years later, Bradley left the Senate, leaving a trail of scorn in his wake.

"The Republicans are infatuated with the 'magic' of the private sector and reflexively criticize government as the enemy of freedom," he said, "and the Democrats distrust the market, preach government as the answer to our problems and prefer the bureaucrat they know to the consumer they can't control." He blamed "the power of money in politics" for the public's mistrust of government. Once out of office, he pledged to "energize movements in states to send Washington a message for radical campaign-finance reform." But Bradley chose an odd way to follow through on his pledge. A month after his retirement from the Senate, he was pulling in hundreds of thousands of dollars in consulting fees from the same Wall Street brokerages whose practices he defended in the Senate. Instead of toiling in the grass roots, he took a job with J.P. Morgan Services, Inc., that paid him $100,000 for consulting work. Morgan Guaranty Trust Company of New York, a J.P. Morgan subsidiary, paid him a $200,000 fee, again for consultations. And Van Beuren Management, Inc., a New Jersey firm closely tied to Raymond Chambers, hired Bradley as well; Bradley has not disclosed what he did for the company or how much he was paid.

What Bradley's financial disclosure statement shows is that after he left the Senate, he wasn't building a movement for reform. Rather, he was doing what he's done best for more than twenty years: chasing down cash.

Bill Bradley is the kind of politician who always seems to be holding his nose when he's around politics. That may be because he grew up in a household that had a hearty disdain for local party hacks. Bradley's father, Warren Bradley, a penny shiner who worked his way up to bank president, so disliked the Democratic Party machine that controlled his small town of Crystal City, Missouri, that he was one of the town's few Republicans.

Warren Bradley relished bucking the establishment, but his position in the community made him part of it as well. He wanted his son to be "a gentleman." Bradley's mother, Susie, enrolled him in lessons for everything from golf and tennis, to dancing and French, in the hope that her son would become "a Christian upright citizen."

An only child, Bradley picked up basketball as a way of getting to know other kids who weren't immediately friendly to the privileged "banker's son." But instead of blending in, his single-minded passion for the game made him stand out.

On a luxury cruise to Europe, Bradley turned the narrow corridors of *Queen Elizabeth* into a nonstop dribbling course. Whether he was on the posh ocean liner or in his driveway, he practiced with cardboard attached to the bottom of his glasses so that he would learn to dribble without having to see the ball. He eventually caught the eyes of recruiters for colleges with top basketball teams such as Duke and the University of Kentucky, but he turned them all down to attend Princeton, a university better known for its ivy than its athletics.

At Princeton, Bradley was the upright Christian of his mother's dreams, much to the amusement of his classmates, who nicknamed him "The Martyr." As his coach at the time, Butch van Breda Kolff, observed: "Basketball is a game. It is not an ordeal. I think Bradley is happiest when he can deny himself pleasure." While his peers were tuning in to the Beatles or the Rolling Stones, Bradley would psych himself up before every game by cranking his stereo to play the song "Climb Every Mountain" from *The Sound of Music*.

After graduation, Bradley confounded the sportswriters and basketball fans alike, who speculated on which professional team would snatch up the Princeton star. Rather than make himself available for the NBA draft, Bradley chose to go to England, and pursue his childhood dream of being a Rhodes Scholar.

When he came back, he was signed by the New York Knicks. On the court, it was clear that all those years of dribbling with cardboard cutouts under his glasses had paid off. Bradley was one of the stars in an era that featured one of the great sports rivalries of all time: the New York Knicks vs. the Boston Celtics. Bradley's team probably wasn't quite as talented as the Celtics, but the Knicks made up for it with cohesive play, great hustle, heart, and smarts. Bradley earned the name "Dollar Bill" for his clutch play when games were on the line. He won two championships with the Knicks, and retired in 1977 at the end of a stellar eleven-year career. Bradley, who was later elected to the NBA Hall of Fame, was already looking to politics, and threw his hat into the ring, running for the Senate in New Jersey.

He won, and arrived in the Senate in 1979, but shunned the daily grind of constituent service and the major controversies of his day for more arcane issues such as water rights, tax reform, and Third World debt. Bradley quickly emerged as a master of domains where few of his colleagues, and few of the journalists covering him, bothered to tread. And while his colleagues got stuck with nicknames like Senator Pothole, Bradley was hailed as an "idealist and cerebral loner" and a "Platonic philosopher/king."

But he also became a creature of Washington, raking in record amounts of campaign cash from special interests and jetting around the globe on more than a hundred junkets. He came crashing back to earth in 1990, when his neglected constituents nearly threw him out of office. Bradley quit the Senate in 1996 with disparaging words for his colleagues. He would jockey for the White House from outside Washington.

In December 1998 he went public with the news that he would seek his party's nomination in 2000. The move puzzled many who had seen Bradley turn down previous chances to run, in 1988 and 1992. But the 2000 election presented the best opportunity to wield his newfound status as an outsider. Only running against a sitting Vice President could diminish the eighteen years he spent inside the Beltway and inside the pockets of special interests.

Bradley, of course, cites different reasons for running in 2000. He has said that he feels like he's at the top of his game. That this is an exhilarating time in the nation's history. That he wants to be a good steward of the nation's economy, and extend opportunities to all Americans. "I want to give people a sense of where we're headed in the midst of all this change that we're experiencing now on multiple levels," he explains on his campaign's Web site. "And I want to do that in a way that allows people once again to regain some faith in their democracy—that their participation actually counts. You don't have to give money. That's important, but your participation also counts. The key to this campaign is going to be to get more and more people who have not been a part of campaigns to get involved because they recognize that something is different."

If the advisory board he's chosen for his campaign is any indication, Bradley hasn't been very successful in reaching out beyond his base of well-heeled contributors. He's surrounded himself with Wall Street insiders, corporate raiders, and high-powered attorneys. His campaign treasurer, Theodore V. Wells, Jr., is a partner in the New Jersey law firm Lowenstein, Sandler, Kohl, Fisher and Boylan, Bradley's No. 12 career patron. Wells made a name for himself defending James Regan, a general partner of Princeton/

Newport Partners, L.P., who was indicted and convicted under the Racketeer Influenced and Corrupt Organizations Act for insider trading. Four other partners of Princeton/Newport, and a trader with Drexel Burnham Lambert, were also found guilty in the case. All six convictions were later overturned on appeal.

Wells has defended a host of other high-profile clients. He represented Exxon Corporation in 1990 when the government launched three separate criminal probes into the company's involvement in an oil spill in the waters that separate Staten Island and New Jersey. Exxon eventually pleaded guilty to reduced charges and paid $15 million in fines. Wells defended Salim "Sandy" Lewis, a Wall Street trader who pleaded guilty to manipulating the share price of Fireman's Fund Corporation in concert with Ivan Boesky, the notorious arbitrageur, who also pleaded guilty to charges of insider trading. More recently, Wells successfully defended Mike Espy, the disgraced former Secretary of Agriculture in the Clinton Administration who accepted more than $35,000 in gratuities from companies his department regulated.

Wells is hardly an anomaly. Bradley's top advisers and fundraisers include Joseph H. Flom, an attorney with Skadden, Arps and a major fund-raiser for Bill Clinton; Louis B. Susman, a partner in Salomon Smith Barney, the Wall Street investment firm; and John W. Jordan II, whose firm, Jordan Industries, Inc., deals in junk bonds and leveraged buyouts. All are among Bradley's most generous career patrons.

Bradley has also added Raymond Chambers, the "Ray" in Wesray, to his board of advisers. Chambers jumped on President Bush's "thousand points of light" bandwagon in 1990 and formed the Points of Light Foundation. Another not-for-profit organization, the Points of Light Initiative, shared the same Morristown, New Jersey, mailing address as Wesray Capital and Van Beuren Management—the same company that hired Bradley as a consultant for an undisclosed sum a month after he left the Senate. Since 1990, Van Beuren has given Republican Party committees more than $190,000 in soft money.

Chambers's newest philanthropic project is the Amelior Foundation, which is dedicated to redeveloping Newark, New Jersey. Amelior is run out of the same Morristown office that houses

Wesray and Van Beuren. The foundation runs Loews Theater Newark Metroplex, a movie house whose opening in 1993 was supposed to spark an urban renaissance. The renaissance never occurred, and the theater, according to the *Newark Star-Ledger*, lost more than $320,000 in 1997, and owes $300,000 in back rent to the city. Chambers and his foundation have turned their attention elsewhere: He's reportedly trying to lure the New Jersey Nets to a new arena in downtown Newark.

Bradley's campaign chairman is Douglas Berman, who as a teenager met Bradley when he was still a star for the New York Knicks. Berman managed Bradley's 1978 and 1984 Senate races; he also managed James Florio's successful 1989 New Jersey gubernatorial campaign. Berman spent one year as the state's treasurer, then went on to work for Wall Street financier Jerome Kohlberg, a former partner of Kohlberg, Kravis and Roberts, which made millions managing the leveraged buyout of RJR Nabisco.

In early 1998 Kohlberg decided to become a political reformer. He launched an attack against soft money by spending $1 million of his own money on political advertising. He hired Berman to head the group he formed, Campaign for America, which ran television commercials in nine states. Kohlberg, a large contributor to the Democratic Party, targeted his ads at incumbent Republican Senators.

One of the ads showed a couple sitting at a table, trying to pay their bills. "Corporate polluters and tobacco companies," an announcer intoned, "get big tax breaks in exchange for huge political contributions."

"We'd go to jail if we did that," the man says.

"They call these contributions soft money and they are legal," the announcer replies.

"That's not fair," the couple responds.

Berman was adamant about the message the commercial conveyed. "These ads give a sense that there is a connection," he told a reporter for the Associated Press, "between very large corporate gifts and policy outcomes."

"The choice of tax reform is that you get lower rates in exchange for giving up certain credit exclusions or deductions,"

Bradley said on the Senate floor on June 11, 1986. "You give up those loopholes which only some people use, so that the tax rates on everyone can be lowered dramatically."

That was the theory behind the Tax Reform Act of 1986. By closing the loopholes that allowed millionaires to pay no taxes, all Americans could enjoy a huge reduction in their tax rates. The particular loophole that Bradley wanted to close that day was the deduction for contributions to Individual Retirement Accounts, a provision in the Internal Revenue Code that overwhelmingly benefited not the wealthy, but the middle class.

Passed in 1981, the IRA deduction was hailed by members of both political parties as a tool to provide additional retirement savings for the middle class. Journalists Donald L. Barlett and James B. Steele reported in their 1994 book, *America: Who Really Pays the Taxes,* that the tax break did just that. Some 90 percent of taxpayers taking the deduction earned less than $75,000 a year—hardly the wealthy. But Bradley didn't see it that way.

He brandished a chart that had a different take on the numbers. "It says that the upper income," Bradley told his colleagues, referring to his visual aid, "those making more than $40,000—15 percent, the top 15 percent of the American taxpayers—take 40 percent of the deductions, contribute 50 percent of all money contributed to IRAs, and realize 60 percent of all tax savings."

In other words, those earning as little as $40,000 a year are in the upper-income bracket. Under Bradley's scheme, they would be treated just like someone earning $400,000, or $4 million. That was, after all, the philosophy behind the Tax Reform Act of 1986. Whereas before the top tax rate of 50 percent applied only to the wealthiest, the plan Bradley crafted lowered it to 28 percent. That new top rate kicked in for married couples earning more than $29,750, and single filers earning more than $17,850. So by Bradley's reckoning, $40,000 was a little too high an income to qualify as middle class.

While Bradley fought to close the IRA "loophole," he chose to leave alone another retirement plan that got special treatment in the tax code. Known as Keogh plans, they can be used only by self-employed professionals such as lawyers, doctors, and investors, and by partnerships such as law firms. Keogh plans allow these better-off individuals to shield up to 30 percent of their incomes from taxes—a far greater amount than the maximum $2,500 that a factory worker or a secretary could save tax-free in his or her IRA. In 1994 those earning more than $100,000 a year shielded $5.7 billion in income by paying it into Keogh plans—and realized, to use Bradley's language, 70 percent of the tax savings.

Of course, even without the tax advantages, one can still open an IRA. But without the tax advantage, it's less desirable. In 1985, before Congress eliminated the deduction, 16.2 million taxpayers took advantage of the tax break to save for their retirements. By 1994 that number had fallen to 3.9 million.

In 1996, when the Center for Public Integrity prepared the first version of this book, Bradley responded in a letter to a series of questions about his role in crafting the Tax Reform Act of 1986 by saying that it was "one of my proudest achievements in the Senate . . . six million working poor people stopped paying income taxes at all as a result of this bill."

Preserving the Keogh tax break for wealthy professionals while killing the IRA deduction for the middle class wasn't the only favor Bradley did for the well-off during his three terms in the Senate. While Bradley may have eschewed constituent services for the many, there were a few New Jerseyans whom he was willing to go to bat for. They just happened to be multinational pharmaceutical companies.

Bradley often pointed to the fact that pharmaceutical companies were one of the largest employers in the state as his motive for protecting their interests. But more than once, his favors for drug makers, who contributed large sums of money to his campaigns, flew in the face of the public interest. On two occasions Bradley even abandoned the public stand he took against tax breaks for special interests to save the pharmaceutical industry's biggest boondoggle, Section 936 of the Internal Revenue Code.

Under Section 936, companies that shift manufacturing jobs to Puerto Rico receive as much as a 100 percent tax break on revenues earned in the territory. The purpose of the tax credit, which first took effect after World War II, was to encourage U.S. companies to invest in Puerto Rico, thus creating jobs and raising wages on the impoverished island. While the standard of living in Puerto Rico remains far below that of the United States, the tax break has proven to be a lucrative way for U.S. companies to boost their profits.

Although any industry that operates in Puerto Rico can benefit from the tax credit, drug makers benefit more than any other. A 1992 report by the General Accounting Office estimated that from 1980 to 1990 the Possessions Tax Credit generated a $10.1 billion windfall—about 56 percent of the tax benefit—for twenty-six pharmaceutical companies. Drug companies not only have factories on the island, but they also shelter income earned in the United States there by transferring patents for highly profitable drugs to their Puerto Rican subsidiaries. Little wonder that one of Bradley's colleagues in the Senate, Democrat David Pryor of Arkansas, branded Section 936 "the mother of all tax breaks."

Bradley first saved the Possessions Tax Credit in 1986, just as Congress was hammering out the details of the Tax Reform Act. By that time, it had become clear that Section 936 was doing little to improve conditions in Puerto Rico, and was costing the Treasury billions. It was just the sort of loophole in the tax code that Bradley said he favored closing so that everyone could enjoy dramatically lower rates.

The drug industry, understandably, moved to save its lucrative subsidy. In a letter to Bradley, the chief executives of nine drug companies made a thinly veiled threat to move their operations to foreign countries if Section 936 was repealed. Bradley later told the Center that he didn't remember the letter, adding that it wouldn't have mattered anyway. He fought to save Section 936 and won. "The pharmaceutical industry is one of the largest employers in New Jersey [50,000 jobs], and I didn't need a letter from the companies to know the importance of the industry to my state and my constituents," Bradley told the Center. The sweeping Tax Reform Act of 1986 left the provision alone.

When "the mother of all tax breaks" came under assault a few years later, Bradley once again came to the drug industry's rescue. On March 11, 1992, Pryor introduced an amendment to do away with Section 936. It was the first step in a larger effort to force drug makers to contain the skyrocketing prices of prescription drugs. (Prescription drug prices have increased 146 percent in ten years—triple the rate of inflation.) Closing the Section 936 loophole would have saved the nation's taxpayers more than $7 billion over five years. But the pharmaceutical industry's allies immediately took to the Senate floor to block the proposal. First up at the podium was Bradley.

Bradley was the second-ranking member of the Senate Finance Committee, the tax-writing panel that had jurisdiction over Pryor's amendment. He was soon followed by Democrat Daniel Patrick Moynihan of New York, the committee's chairman, who made it clear that Pryor's amendment was going nowhere. In a speech filled with historical references, Moynihan lectured his colleagues on the history of the Possessions Tax Credit. Off the floor, he deployed Bradley to finish the job.

When Bradley and Pryor emerged from back-room negotiations, Section 936 emerged with them, largely intact.

Those weren't the only special tax breaks Bradley sought for special interests. From 1986 to 1993, Bradley introduced at least forty-five bills on behalf of chemical companies seeking a reduction or suspension of the taxes they pay on imported chemicals used in a variety of products, from pesticides and drugs to dyes and resins.

Bradley explained away the contradiction between his effort to close tax loopholes embodied in the 1986 Tax Reform Act and doling out corporate welfare to chemical companies by saying: "I think the distinction is, if you believe in open trade, you believe in as low a tariff as possible. You want to get to a world where there are no tariffs."

Bradley was so enamored of free trade that he even tried to eliminate tariffs for the benefit of foreign companies. He cut tariffs for Danish and French firms as well as American corporations, all with dire consequences for the environment and public health. Among the substances Bradley repeatedly sought tariff exemptions for are highly toxic pesticides: ethyl parathion, methyl parathion, and malathion. All three belong to a class of chemicals known as organophosphates, which were originally developed during World War II by the Nazis for use in chemical warfare. The EPA lists all three pesticides as a danger to birds, mammals, and aquatic life. Bradley won the duty suspensions on the pesticides for Cheminova,

Inc., a Danish chemical giant whose U.S. subsidiary is based in Wayne, New Jersey.

When inhaled or absorbed through the skin, ethyl parathion attacks the nervous system, causing nausea, vomiting, headaches, blurred vision, sweating, drooling, muscle spasms, and, in some cases, coma and death. It has been linked to the deaths of at least seventy people and illnesses in thousands of farm workers. In 1991, the Environmental Protection Agency banned the use of ethyl parathion on nine crops in the United States. Cheminova still manufactures compounds containing ethyl parathion in the United States for sale abroad.

Methyl parathion is an agricultural pesticide that has found its way into urban areas with disastrous results. In 1996 an exterminator sprayed methyl parathion in houses and buildings in Pascagoula, Mississippi, causing the evacuation of dozens of families and homes and a $50 million federal cleanup. A similar incident led to the contamination of more than two hundred homes in Ohio in 1994.

The third pesticide that Bradley won tariff exemptions for, malathion, can cause nausea, sweating, and muscular weakness in people even at low levels of exposure. In 1999, health authorites in New York City ordered the spraying of all five boroughs with malathion in an effort to wipe out disease-carrying mosquitoes. In 1998, a similar effort in Florida to eradicate Mediterranean fruit flies led to a class-action lawsuit by residents in the sprayed areas who complained of headaches and respiratory problems. The duty suspension Bradley won for malathion in 1993 alone was worth $1.1 million annually. The tax break on all three pesticides was worth $2.5 million annually.

Bradley has touted his past efforts to keep the waters off New Jersey free of pollution. On the stump, he's even threatened to "slap fines" on polluters "until they go bankrupt." But several of the companies for which Bradley won tariff suspensions have caused serious environmental damage in New Jersey and elsewhere.

In 1993, Bradley won Biocraft Laboratories of Fair Lawn, New Jersey, tariff suspensions for six chemicals. In the mid-1990s Biocraft was responsible for more than half the industrial air pollution in Bergen, New Jersey, releasing nearly 500,000 pounds of dichloromethane, a solvent that can be breathed in or absorbed through the skin, potentially causing cancer and liver and kidney damage. It was the fourth-biggest source of toxic emissions in the state. In 1994 the Food and Drug Administration and the Justice Department also forced Biocraft to recall nine drugs and to stop making five drugs because the company failed to meet testing, quality-control, record-keeping, and manufacturing standards.

Bradley handed out pork to another New Jersey polluter, Merck & Company. In 1992 he won Merck tariff suspensions that are worth $10 million annually. In July 1991 New Jersey Citizen Action listed Merck among ten companies responsible for nearly half of the toxic waste dumped in New Jersey. Also making the top ten polluter list was Givaudan Corporation, of Clifton, New Jersey, a subsidiary of Roche Holding, Ltd., the Swiss multinational. A month later, Bradley won Givaudan a tariff exemption for ethanon-1,2-naphthyl, a chemical used in making scents.

Bradley even won pork for Rhone-Poulenc, Inc., the U.S. subsidiary of the French pharmaceutical giant, which only a year earlier had leaked methyl isocyanate—the same gas responsible for the deaths of thousands in Bhopal, India, in 1984—from its plant in West Virginia. Rhone-Poulenc didn't report the leak for three days.

Rhone-Poulenc is also the world's only producer of aldicarb, which the Natural Resources Defense Council has called "the most acutely toxic pesticide registered for use on food." It is responsible for the largest case of food-borne pesticide poisoning in U.S. history: more than a thousand people fell ill in 1986 for aldicarb-tainted watermelons. Because of the health risks, eleven countries have banned or deregistered the pesticide, but the company still sells it in more than seventy countries.

In all, Bradley won at least $100 million worth of tariff suspensions for drug and chemical makers. Little wonder that the pharmaceutical industry rewarded its most valuable player on Capitol Hill with record amounts of campaign money.

After leaving the Senate, Bradley became an outspoken advocate of campaign-finance reform. But while he was in office, he was one of the Senate's most prolific fund-raisers. In 1984 and 1990 he built huge war chests even though he faced weak opponents. In 1984 his campaign even cooked its own books so that it could raise more money for the general election.

Under federal election law, individuals can give a candidate up to $1,000 for a primary election and another $1,000 for the general election; political action committees can give up to $5,000 per election. After a primary election is over, candidates can raise money for it only if they still have debts incurred for that election. In 1984, Bradley's campaign operatives created the illusion of a leftover debt from his primary campaign by redesignating money spent for the general election as having been spent for the primary. This enabled them to let individuals "max out" with $2,000 contributions—and PACs max out at $10,000—long after the primary election was over.

That wasn't the only irregularity Bradley's campaigns have been accused of. In 1990, contributions from Wall Street made him "the king of bundled contributions," according to the Center for Responsive Politics. "Bundling" refers to donations given to a candidate on the same day by many employees of one company. That year, Bradley collected bundles of at least $20,000 from Salomon Brothers, Smith Barney, and Shearson, Lehman, Hutton (all three firms are now part of Citigroup, Bradley's No. 1 career patron); Merrill Lynch (his No. 2 career patron); Goldman Sachs (his No. 3 career patron); Morgan Stanley (No. 4); Time Warner (No. 5); and Prudential Securities (now part of Prudential Insurance Company of America, his No. 6 career patron).

Some time later, the bundled donations from Prudential caught the eye of FEC lawyers. In 1994, they determined that the securities firm had violated federal campaign-finance laws when its president, George Ball, instructed employees and vendors to donate to Bradley and other candidates. Prudential-Bache, which raised $140,000 for Bradley from employees, vendors, and other securities firms, eventually paid a $550,000 fine, the largest ever levied by the FEC. Bradley immediately announced that he would return Prudential's money. But he kept the bundles he received from other Wall Street patrons.

As a presidential candidate, Bradley has resumed taking money from Prudential. Employees of the company gave him more than $27,000 in the first half of 1999, bringing their total contributions to Bradley over his career to more than $100,000.

According to Bradley, the cash from Wall Street that's flowed into his political bank accounts is a consequence of geographic coincidence. "I received more money from these sectors in 1990 than other candidates because the bulk of my contributions came from New Jersey and New York, the financial center of the country," he said in a 1995 letter to the Center for Public Integrity. But Wall Street's investment in Bradley has yielded dividends.

Before he left the Senate, for example, Bradley sided with Wall Street in supporting legislation—now law—to insulate securities firms from class-action lawsuits. In 1994, Orange County, California, had gone broke, making the record books as the biggest local-government bankruptcy in U.S. history. The county lost $1.6 billion and at least 1,200 county employees lost their jobs. Within weeks, the county sued its investment manager. Merrill Lynch eventually agreed to pay the county $437 million to settle the suit and $30 million to end a criminal probe by the county's district attorney. The securities industry wasted no time in pressing Congress to limit such lawsuits, and Congress passed the Securities Litigation Reform Act. Bradley voted for the bill and voted to override President Clinton's veto of the legislation.

Bradley's prowess in raising money from Wall Street was evident even from his first reelection bid. By Election Day in 1984, he'd collected a total of $5,142,316, while his opponent, Mary Mochary, raised only $956,398. Bradley got 64 percent of the vote to Mochary's 35 percent.

But Bradley was just getting started. When he returned to Congress, he immediately began raising money for his 1990 reelection campaign. By the end of 1989, Bradley had a cool $9 million in the bank, while his opponent, a little-known county official named Christine Todd Whitman, was on her way to raising a grand total of $801,660. He eventually collected nearly $13 million.

As Bradley would later admit, money had become an end in itself, the ultimate benchmark of political strength. Looking back in one memoir, he wrote, "How could you have too much money?"

The $13 million war chest, however, quickly turned out to be the benchmark of his arrogance, which Bradley reinforced with his own actions and his own words.

In early 1990, Whitman proposed that she and Bradley each limit their campaign spending to $3 million, but he refused. When she stopped taking PAC money and called on him to do the same, he refused again.

After all the talk of wanting to stay in touch with his constituents, he spent much of the final weeks leading up to the election in Washington. Bradley's heart and mind were clearly not in New Jersey, but on the national stage. He later revealed that the true goal behind all the fund-raising frenzy was to have enough leftover to jump-start a White House bid. During the 1990 race, he already began to invest heavily in national polling and sophisticated software and computers that could track contributions in thirty states.

Perhaps that's why he never saw the statewide tax revolt coming. Grappling with a $3 billion budget deficit, New Jersey Governor James Florio, a Democrat for whom Bradley had campaigned, laid the biggest tax increase in his state's history on middle-class taxpayers. Income taxes and property taxes shot up, and new taxes were added to the books, including one on toilet paper. Whitman tapped into voter anger over the tax hike with bumper stickers that read: "Get Florio, Dump Bradley." Bradley refused to take a position on Florio's tax increase, saying that he'd traditionally stayed out of state tax matters. But Whitman continued to pester him for a response in ads and during debates. As she put it: "He is a tax expert. . . . This is the biggest tax increase in New Jersey history. I'd like to know what he thinks, how he differs from the governor, if at all." But Bradley refused to answer.

His famous reticence almost cost him the election. All the dodging and sidestepping only solidified the impression that Bradley was firmly entrenched in the ways of Washington. On Election Day, Bradley squeaked by with 50 percent of the vote to Whitman's 47 percent, even though he'd outspent her sixteen-to-one. The close result tarnished his political reputation and launched the career of Christine Todd Whitman, who in a few years would get Florio by dumping him from the governor's mansion. Bradley's victory was at best a poor showing for a candidate with all the advantages of incumbency, name recognition, and money, and was certainly a factor in his decision not to seek the Democratic presidential nomination in 1992.

Since then Bradley has worked hard to distance himself from the establishment he spent so much time grooming himself for. When he returned to the Senate, he tried tempering his reserve with a little fire. A day after the Los Angeles riots of 1992, he took to the well of the Senate and banged his fist fifty-six times on the podium, once for every blow that L.A. police officers had delivered to Rodney King's body.

As if to pay penance for his recent excesses, he made a public show of pushing fervently for campaign-finance reform. He argued for a constitutional amendment to overturn the Supreme Court's decision in Buckley v. *Valeo*, and for public financing of general elections. While his proposals were tabled or disregarded, he decided to make the ultimate statement.

In the fall of 1995, he announced his retirement from the Senate with a fiery denunciation of American politics. "We live in a time when, on a basic level, politics is broken," he said. "People have lost faith in the political process." He blamed the power of money in politics for public mistrust. In an interview with Jack Germond, a columnist for the *Baltimore Sun,* in August 1995, he spoke of his "disgust" with both parties.

But all this fury merely signified the beginning of a long-anticipated presidential bid. "What people don't understand or what they misunderstood when I said I wasn't going to run again, was I wasn't leaving in disgust or anger or sadness," he told a reporter for the *Bergen Record* in December 1996. "I was leaving to do other things in the public interest that I couldn't do if I was putting in thirteen, fourteen hours a day for the people of New Jersey in the United States Senate." Of course, Bradley's idea of what was in the "public interest" was little different from what it had been when he was a Senator: collecting cash from special interests.

During his brief retirement before he ran for President, Bradley raked in millions in speaking and consulting fees. In addition to the $300,000 in consulting fees he got from J.P. Morgan and its subsidiary, Morgan Guaranty, he was paid $131,250 by the Gartner Group, Inc., a consulting company in Stamford, Connecticut, during the same period. Neither J.P. Morgan, the Gartner Group, nor Bradley's campaign would tell the Center what he did to earn those fees.

Whatever he did for the more than $400,000 they paid him, neither was a full-time job. He still had time to be a visiting scholar at no fewer than four universities, from East Coast (the University of Maryland) to West (Stanford University). His traveling around the country as an itinerant scholar also proved lucrative: Private companies were willing to pay $30,000 a pop for a chance to hear the ex-Knick and ex-Senator. One company, KeyCorp, a Cleveland-based bank and financial services firm that ranks among the Fortune 500, paid him an estimated $300,000 to $400,000 to speak at thirteen of its branches.

In response to the Center's request for more information about Bradley's speaking engagements with the company, Laura Scharf, a public-affairs officer for KeyCorp, told the Center in an e-mail message: "Presidential candidate Bill Bradley is one of many speakers Key has hired over the past seven years as part of its Corporate Speaker Series to address clients across the country on issues of general interest. Bill Bradley participated in the 1998 Speakers Series at a time when he did not hold public office."

Travel was nothing new to Bradley; during his three terms in the Senate, he went on one junket after another—more than 160 in all. In 1996 alone, he took more all-expenses-paid trips than any U.S. Senator. He went on twenty-nine trips, worth at least $42,031, including a $10,462 excursion to Davos, Switzerland, for the Annual World Economic Forum Meeting, underwritten by the World Economic Forum of Geneva, Switzerland. In September 1996 the Carl Jung Institute of San Francisco spent at least $2,335 to send Bradley to a two-day conference on "The Presidency: Myth, Psyche & Politics." In December 1996, the Walt Disney Company (Bradley's No. 8 career patron) and Smith-Hemion, a Los Angeles film production company, spent at least $3,045 to fly Bradley to the City of Angels to present an award at Disney's Seventh Annual American Teacher Awards. Bradley has longstanding ties to Disney;

Michael Eisner, the company's chief executive officer, personally raised nearly $1 million for Bradley's 1990 Senate race.

In 1997, Bradley was also following the presidential candidate's playbook. He took the remains of his 1990 war chest and turned it into a PAC, Time Future, Inc. He raised money for another PAC, Participation 2000, which trains young people to work on Democratic campaigns around the country. He stayed in the public eye by appearing as an essayist for CBS News. He promoted his two memoirs, *Time Present, Time Past* and *Values of the Game.*

Since hitting the campaign trail, Bradley has tried to paint his candidacy with broad brush strokes, countering the poll-driven obsessions of the Clinton administration. "We are at a time when the idea of winning an election . . . by simply using a focus group phrase or a small program that rhetorically is strong but won't make a real difference on the ground is past," Bradley said in March 1999, during one of his first swings through Iowa. "I think we need to do some bold thinking." He has contrasted his own ideas with those of Vice President Albert Gore, Jr., who he accuses of being part and parcel of a "nickel and dime" policy operation that's ducked the big challenges of the day to take credit for piece-meal achievements.

Thanks to his own Wall Street backers, there's nothing "nickel and dime" about Dollar Bill Bradley.

BILL BRADLEY
Top Ten Career Patrons

Ranking	Company/Individual/Family Name	Total
1	Citigroup, Inc., and affiliated companies, New York	$454,065
2	Merrill Lynch & Co., Inc., New York	$169,500
3	The Goldman Sachs Group, Inc., New York	$148,800
4	Morgan Stanley Dean Witter & Company, New York	$129,675
5	Time Warner, Inc., and affiliated companies, New York	$112,770
6	The Prudential Insurance Company of America, Newark, New Jersey	$102,601
7	Printon, Kane & Company, Short Hills, New Jersey	$97,915
8	The Walt Disney Company and affiliated companies, Burbank, California	$95,415
9	The Equitable Companies and affiliated companies, New York	$94,100
10	Lehman Brothers Holdings, Inc., New York	$91,250

This list is based on individual and PAC contributions to Bradley's Senate campaigns from 1977–1996; individual contributions to Time Future, Inc., from 1997–1998; and individual contributions to Bradley's presidential campaign through June 30, 1999. Bradley no longer accepts PAC contributions.
Sources: Federal Election Commission; Center for Responsive Politics.

1. Includes contributions from employees of Citigroup and the companies that have contributed to the creation of Citigroup, including Citibank; Citicorp; Travelers Corporation; The Copeland Companies; Salomon Smith Barney (and its predecessors, Salomon Brothers and Smith Barney); and Shearson Lehman Hutton (and its predecessors, including Shearson, Hayden & Stone and EF Hutton). From 1981 to 1993, Shearson was owned by American Express. Contributions from individuals who identified themselves as

Shearson employees during this period are also included in the Citigroup figure. Contributions from individuals who identified themselves as American Express employees are not.

4. Includes contributions from employees of Morgan Stanley Dean Witter; its predecessors, Morgan Stanley and Dean Witter Reynolds; and its subsidiary, Van Kampen Investments.

5. Includes contributions from employees of Time Warner and its subsidiaries, including Warner Communications; Warner Brothers; Warner Brothers Records; Warner Brothers Studios; WB Television Network; Warner Chappell Music; Time, Inc.; HBO; TBS, Inc.; Six Flags; Castle Rock Entertainment; and New Line Cinema.

6. Includes contributions from employees of Prudential and its subsidiaries, including Prudential Securities (FKA Prudential-Bache Securities) and Jennison Associates. Does not include contributions from Prudential-Bache Securities employees from 1986-1990, which Bradley voluntarily returned following an FEC investigation into Prudential's fund-raising activities. There was no suggestion from the FEC that Bradley had acted improperly. Including these contributions would move Prudential to No. 2 on this list.

8. Includes contributions from employees of The Walt Disney Company and its subsidiaries, including Walt Disney Pictures; Walt Disney Imagineering; Walt Disney Television; Walt Disney Studios; The Disney Channel; Disneyland; ABC, Inc.; ESPN; Buena Vista Music Group; and Infoseek Corporation.

9. Includes contributions from employees of Equitable and its subsidiaries, including Equitable Life; EQ Financial Consultants; Equitable Capital Management; Donaldson, Lufkin & Jenrette (73 percent owned by Equitable); and Alliance Capital Management (57 percent owned by Equitable).

10. Includes contributions from employees of Lehman Brothers and its predecessor, Lehman Brothers Kuhn Loeb. From 1984 to 1990, Lehman Brothers was part of Shearson Lehman, which was at that time owned by American Express. Contributions from individuals who identified themselves as Shearson Lehman employees during that time are counted in the Citigroup figure above, and are not counted here. Contributions from individuals who identified themselves as Lehman Brothers employees from 1990 to 1994, when Lehman Brothers had stand-alone status within American Express, are included in this Lehman Brothers figure. Contributions from individuals who identified themselves as American Express employees during this time are not.

Albert Gore, Jr.

||||||||||||

"We raised him for it."
—Senator Albert Gore, Sr.,
*when asked in 1992 if his son
was presidential material*

On September 7, 1995, Vice President Albert Gore, Jr., stood on the White House lawn and talked in sweeping terms about ending the era of big government. He touted a list of recommendations formulated by the National Performance Review, an initiative Gore directed that, he claimed, streamlined the federal bureaucracy, cut unnecessary waste, and helped make the government "work better and cost less." Gore said that his report, delivered to President Clinton that day, would continue the drive to "reinvent government."

Gore did not mention that his recommendations to the President included a plan to give oil companies access to thousands of acres of oil-rich, publicly owned land that the U.S. Navy has held as emergency reserves since 1912. Ever since the federal government earmarked the reserves for military emergencies, the oil industry had tried and failed to pry them away from the Navy.

In 1922 a couple of oil men—Edward L. Doheny and Harry Sinclair—bribed Albert Fall, the Secretary of the Interior in the Harding Administration, for secret leases to drill on two of the fields, the Teapot Dome field just outside of Casper, Wyoming, and the Elk Hills field in Bakersfield, California. Doheny and his Pan-American Petroleum and Transport Company (later Atlantic

Richfield Company, or ARCO), paid $300,000 to Fall in exchange for the rights. When the bribes were uncovered, the ensuing Teapot Dome scandal forced the resignations of Fall (who later went to prison) and Edward Denby, the Secretary of the Navy.

In 1973, during the Arab oil embargo, the Nixon Administration tried to lease Elk Hills to boost domestic oil production. In 1984, 1986, and 1987, the Reagan Administration proposed selling Elk Hills for a lump sum payment of $1.5 billion that would go toward reducing the federal budget deficit. Each time, Congress wisely blocked the sale of Elk Hills.

But where Fall, Nixon, and Reagan had failed, Gore succeeded. Despite the history of the naval petroleum reserves, despite the royalty revenues that the field continued to generate, Gore recommended that the government put Elk Hills on the auction block. President Clinton took Gore's advice and approved a deal to let oil companies buy some of the reserves. The White House then pushed to have language authorizing the sales inserted in the 1996 defense authorization bill, which Congress ultimately approved. Oil companies bid on the field and, finally, on October 6, 1997, the Energy Department announced that the government would sell its interest in the 47,000-acre Elk Hills reserve to Occidental Petroleum Corporation for $3.65 billion. It was the largest privatization of federal property in U.S. history, one that tripled Occidental's U.S. oil reserves overnight. During the months after the sale, Occidental tripled the amount of natural gas extracted from the field.

Although the Energy Department was required to assess the likely environmental consequences of the proposed sale, it didn't. Instead it hired a private company, ICF Kaiser International, Inc., to complete the assessment. The general chairman of Gore's presidential campaign, Tony Coelho, sat on the board of directors.

Just hours after the announcement of the Elk Hills sale, Gore stood across town on the campus of Georgetown University and delivered a speech to the White House Conference on Climate Change on the "terrifying prospect" of global warming, a problem he blamed on the unchecked use of fossil fuels such as oil. Even as Occidental was moving forward with plans to boost oil production at Elk Hills, Gore told his audience: "If we ignore the scientific warnings and continue stubbornly on our current course, we'd better begin to prepare what we would like to say to our children and grandchildren, because if they encounter the terrible conse- quences the scientific community is saying now come as a result of global climate disruption, and then look back at the evidence which was clearly laid out for us in our generation, they might fairly ask, 'If you knew all that, why didn't you do something about it?' "

If there is one oil company that Gore might ask "our children and grandchildren" to forgive, it is Occidental Petroleum. The company has been a steady supplier of campaign funds to Gore and to the Democratic Party, though its relationship with Gore goes far deeper. Armand Hammer, who built Occidental Petroleum into the behemoth it is today and who's been described as "the Godfather of American corporate corruption," liked to say that he had Gore's father, Senator Albert Gore, Sr., "in my back pocket." When the elder Gore left the Senate in 1970, Hammer gave him a $500,000-a-year job as the chairman of Island Coal Creek Com- pany, an Occidental subsidiary, and a seat on Occidental's board of directors. By 1992, Gore owned Occidental stock valued at $680,000.

Al Gore, Jr., is known as an earnest politician who takes an intellectual interest in arcane areas of legislative policy, including the "reinvention of government," telecommunications systems, suburban planning, and the Internet. Over the course of his career, Gore has bolstered his Boy Scout image by publicly identifying himself with various hot-button issues. In a 1985 Senate hearing he attacked record-company executives, music retailers, and "heavy metal" bands after his wife, Tipper, and a group she headed called for warning labels on record albums for violent and pornographic lyrics. In an emotional speech to the 1996 Democratic National Convention in Chicago, he related how his sister Nancy, who started smoking when she was thirteen, died of lung cancer in 1984, and how her death—and the prospect that others like her would die from smoking-related diseases—led him to put his "heart and soul into the cause of protecting our children from the dangers of smoking." And for most of his career, Gore has warned of the dangers that modern civilization poses to the environment. His 1992 book argued that an environmental holocaust is inevitable unless society changes its ways.

But Gore is hardly a Boy Scout, and long before he became Clinton's running mate, he proved that he was willing to put aside conscience, or at least political conviction, to raise money for his campaigns. In October 1987, for example, Michael "Mickey" Kantor, the Los Angeles lobbyist, fund-raiser, and later chairman of the 1992 Clinton-Gore campaign, arranged a private meeting for Gore and his wife in the executive dining room of MCA, Inc., with a group of entertainment industry bigwigs. At the meeting, which was described as a "clear the air" session, Tipper Gore averred that the Senate hearings attacking the music industry were "a mistake" that "sent the wrong message." In February 1988, four years after his sister's death from lung cancer, Gore, then a presidential candidate, hollered to an audience in Greenville, North Carolina: "Throughout most of my life, I raised tobacco. I want you to know that with my own hands, all of my life, I put it in the plant beds and transferred it. I've hoed it, I've dug in it, I've sprayed it, I've chopped it, I've shredded it, spiked it, put it in the barn, and stripped it and sold it." Gore proclaimed his support that day for federal tobacco subsidies, but he didn't holler that he also was happy to take money from the tobacco industry. His sister's death notwithstanding, since 1985 Gore has collected at least $65,490 in contributions from tobacco interests. As for the environment, Gore was happy to recommend selling the Elk Hills field, which Occidental quickly snapped up.

Nonetheless, Gore somehow managed to maintain, as a reporter put it at a press conference in 1997, an "impregnable reputation for being above the fray and for being ethically someone who really hasn't been questioned" about his fund-raising practices. But all that ended with the disclosure in March 1997 that, from his office in the West Wing of the White House, Gore had telephoned fifty-six well-heeled donors in 1995 and 1996, hitting them up for soft-money contributions of up to $100,000 apiece—in seeming violation of both the Pendleton Act and the Hatch Act, which prohibit soliciting contributions from government buildings. To raise money for his reelection in 1996, he opened up the residence at the Naval Observatory, the taxpayer-supported home of the Vice President, to wealthy contributors. He and Tipper hosted White House coffees. He attended a fund-raising event at a Buddhist temple that turned out to be implicated in violations of federal election laws. And on March 3, 1997, Gore held a press conference to announce that he did not regret a thing. "I'm very proud that I was able to be effective in helping to reelect President Clinton," he said. "And I was very proud that I was able to also, as part of that effort, help raise campaign funds."

As for whether he had broken any laws, Gore insisted with practiced assurance some seven times in the course of the press conference that "no controlling legal authority" applied to his activities. "As a matter of law," Gore explained at one point, "there is no—according to my counsel—there is no controlling legal authority, no case ever brought, ever decided, that says that this is a violation of the law." In other words, in the 114 years since Congress passed the first law that barred federal officials from soliciting contributions on government property, no person had ever been caught and tried for doing it.

Attorney General Janet Reno sympathetically split legal hairs in the Vice President's favor. She ruled that since Gore wasn't raising hard money (contributions that are regulated under the Federal Election Campaign Act) but rather soft money (contributions that aren't regulated), he was in the clear. It was fine for the Vice President to call from a government building and ask a fat cat for $100,000, but he would have been in trouble had he asked merely for $1,000. Gore's own staff had come up with various other subterfuges to justify his calls. He typically dialed for long distance dollars with a telephone calling card supplied by Clinton/Gore '96 (although in August 1997 the DNC quietly sent the Treasury Department a check for $24.20 to reimburse it for the costs of some of Gore's fund-raising calls), and as Vice President he was exempt from the provisions of the Hatch Act (although in 1995, then-White House Counsel Abner Mikva had sent a memo to all Clinton Administration officials in which he argued exactly the opposite).

Gore's eager participation in the 1996 no-holds-barred dash for cash—he was even dubbed "solicitor-in-chief" by staffers at the

DNC—was part of a pattern stretching over his twenty-two-year career in Washington. In 1987 he was the presidential candidate of choice of Walter Mondale's moneymen, and he agreed to run for the White House only after they wooed him with the promise of millions in funds. Within twenty-four hours of being named Clinton's running mate in 1992, Gore proved his worth to the ticket by raising $1 million in soft money for the campaign. And in advance of the 2000 presidential election, Gore has constructed one of the most formidable fund-raising machines in the history of presidential politics.

As his father said, he was raised for it.

Gore spent most of his childhood on the top floor of the Fairfax Hotel in Washington, D.C., which was owned by relatives and in later years would bear the name Ritz-Carlton. When Gore was born, Albert Gore, Sr., had already served ten years as a U.S. Representative from Tennessee. In 1952, when young Gore was four years old, his father won a seat in the U.S. Senate. The young Gore spent his childhood in Washington admiringly watching his father go about the business of being a Member of Congress. From early on, Gore wanted to follow in his father's footsteps and make a career out of politics. "He was my hero," Gore said of his father in a 1986 interview.

In high school at the exclusive St. Albans School for Boys, Gore's classmates tagged him with the nickname "Ozymandias," a reference to the poem by Percy Bysshe Shelley about a ruler who touts his own power, declaring, "Look on my works, ye Mighty, and despair!" It was apparent even then to Gore's schoolmates that he was headed for a career in politics.

After four years at Harvard (during which time he continued to date his prep-school girlfriend and future wife, Mary Elizabeth "Tipper" Aitcheson), Gore found himself in danger of being drafted into military service. He opposed the Vietnam war, but his father was facing a difficult reelection campaign in Tennessee, where support for U.S. involvement in Indochina ran strong. In what Gore later called "one of the most difficult decisions that I've ever had to make," he opted to enlist. Newly married to Tipper, he received his papers in September 1970, just in time to make campaign appearances with his father in his Army uniform. He arrived in Saigon on December 26, and served seven months as a reporter for Army publications. Although Gore never saw combat there, he wrote a friend that he would pursue divinity school in part to "atone" for what he had witnessed in Vietnam.

In May 1971, Gore returned to Nashville, Tennessee, where he found a job as a reporter for *The Tennessean*. While working at the newspaper, he enrolled in Divinity School at Vanderbilt University. Three years later, in 1974, he took an active step toward a career in politics by transferring to law school at Vanderbilt, much to the delight of his father. Gore Sr. disapproved of his son's decision to work at *The Tennessean,* having always encouraged him to attend law school as preparation for a political career. During Gore's second year of law school, he found himself with an opportunity to run for Congress, and he jumped at it.

In February 1976, Democrat Joe Evins announced his intention to retire from the House of Representatives. Over the course of two days, Gore withdrew from law school, resigned from *The Tennessean,* trimmed his hair, put on a suit, and announced his candidacy. "On, like, Friday afternoon Al was—his hair was a little long, and he was working away as a reporter," a friend of Gore's who was working at the newspaper later told a reporter. "But on Monday morning he had a navy-blue suit and a haircut, and was announcing for Congress."

Once Gore came back to Washington as a U.S. Representative in 1977, he proved far more politically cautious and calculating than his father. Pauline Gore, in a 1988 interview, summed up her son's approach to politics in this way: "Al by nature is more of a pragmatist than his father. As am I. I tried to persuade Albert [Sr.] not to butt at a stone wall just for the sheer joy of butting."

Pragmatist or not, the son often pays homage to his father, a fiery-tempered populist on the campaign trail in his home state who occasionally played the fiddle at political rallies. The elder Gore was not afraid to speak his mind; at a time when most Tennesseeans supported U.S. military involvement in Vietnam, he opposed it. At a memorial service for Gore Sr., who died on December 5, 1998, his son said simply, "My father was the greatest man I ever knew in my life." In his own campaign appearances,

Al Gore frequently invokes the career of his father. In an August 3, 1999, speech to the Progressive National Baptist Convention, a meeting of black religious activists, Gore stressed his father's crusade against bigotry and his three-decade-long commitment to civil rights. "He supported the Voting Rights Act in 1965 and lost his next reelection," Gore said. "But conscience won and he taught me that [that] was worth more than any election."

In truth, however, Gore's father had something of a mixed record on civil rights. In 1964, a reelection year for the Senator from Tennessee, he voted against the Civil Rights Act, a far-reaching piece of legislation that outlawed racial discrimination in schools, in workplaces, and in neighborhoods. Recalling the vote in his 1970 memoir, *The Eye of the Storm: A People's Politics for the Seventies,* the elder Gore explained his opposition to the legislation. "Because of this arbitrary grant of power and because I doubted the justice of, for example, denying federal funds to a hospital filled with sick people because the waiting rooms did not comply with undefined guidelines, I opposed the bill," he wrote. "Now I acknowledge that many people disagreed and will disagree with this point of view. I concede them their point of view but I feel very deeply that I was right." While Gore's father opposed opening the doors of hospital waiting rooms to African-Americans, he was passionately committed to providing access to the corridors of power to wealthy white industrialists like Armand Hammer.

For part of his career, Albert Gore, Sr., received two paychecks: one from the taxpayers, and another from Armand Hammer. Hammer, who raised prize bulls, met the elder Gore at a Tennessee cattle auction in the 1940s. He put Gore, who was then a member of the House, on the payroll of his New Jersey cattle business. Thus began a cozy relationship between the two men that would last until Hammer's death.

Hammer personified the worst excesses of both capitalism and Communism. In his biography of Hammer (*Dossier: The Secret History of Armand Hammer*), Edward Jay Epstein notes that Hammer built a pencil factory outside Moscow in 1926 and returned to the United States soon after that to launder funds for the Communist Party. In the 1930s, Hammer marketed something he called the "Romanoff Treasure," a collection of fake Russian art that he passed off as genuine. Much of the proceeds of the sales went to Joseph Stalin's government. Hammer helped recruit Soviet spies and position them in the U.S. government. At one time he even had a contract to train dogs for the Soviet police.

FBI Director J. Edgar Hoover wanted to prosecute Hammer for his activities on behalf of the Soviet government. But Hammer had friends in Congress whom Hoover believed would attempt to protect him from prosecution; among them was Gore, who took to the floor of the Senate once to defend Hammer against allegations of bribery (later proved to be true) in obtaining government contracts.

Gore's job as a Senator was even more useful to Hammer the capitalist. In January 1961 the most sought-after ticket in Washington was to John F. Kennedy's inaugural ball; Gore made sure that Hammer got one. A few months later Gore successfully lobbied the Commerce Department to back Hammer's visit to the Soviet Union. The Kennedy Administration had banned the importation of Soviet crabmeat on the ground that it was produced with slave labor; Hammer reported that he had found no evidence to support the ban, which was soon lifted. Gore even suggested to President Kennedy that Hammer, whom the FBI had long known was an agent for the Soviet Union, act as an envoy to Nikita Khrushchev should any crisis erupt between the two superpowers.

In April 1968, Senator Gore stood by Hammer's side when the industrialist officially opened his Libyan oil fields. Occidental was not a player in world crude-oil markets until Hammer bribed King Idris and some of his officials to gain a concession to the huge reserves there. Two years after Gore left the Senate, Hammer placed him on Occidental's board of directors, where he earned a much higher salary than he had as a U.S. Senator.

By the time the younger Gore was elected to the U.S. House of Representatives, the Gore relationship with Hammer had already begun to transfer from father to son. In the 1960s, Gore informed Hammer that zinc ore had been discovered near the Gore farm in Smith County, Tennessee. Hammer, who owned Occidental Minerals (a subsidiary of Occidental Petroleum), bought the land for $160,000, twice the only other offer. But after buying the land,

Hammer made a strange decision—at least from a business stand-point. Rather than mine the zinc-rich land, he offered instead to let Gore buy it from him. Then, once ownership transferred to Gore, Occidental starting paying Gore $20,000 per year for the mineral rights to mine it. After the first payment, Gore Sr. sold the land to his son for $140,000. Gore has received a $20,000 check in the mail almost every year since.

Perhaps even more astounding than Hammer's decision to sell the land and pay royalties is that Occidental never actually mined the land. In 1985, Gore began leasing the land to Union Zinc, Inc., a competitor of Occidental's. Gore still receives $20,000 a year in royalties. In all, the Hammer-engineered sweetheart deal has put hundreds of thousands of dollars in profits in Gore's pocket.

The relationship between Hammer and Al Gore, Jr., continued. Gore and his wife once caught a ride across the Atlantic Ocean on Hammer's private jet; they hosted Hammer at Reagan's 1984 inauguration and President Bush's in 1988; and they attended Hammer's ninetieth birthday extravaganza in Washington on May 21, 1988. When Hammer came to Washington for business, he and Gore frequently lunched together in the company of Occidental's lobbyists.

In return, Hammer and members of his family bent over backwards to get money into Gore's campaigns.

Gore recognized that his relationship with Hammer, who died in 1990, and his company did not look good. In 1992, before President Clinton settled on him as his running mate, Gore's father wrote a memo for Clinton on his ties to Occidental to prepare him for possible questions about it. After the election, however, Gore resumed his old relationship with the company and its new chairman, Ray Irani.

Occidental, for example, loaned $100,000 to the Presidential Inaugural Committee to help pay for the ceremony and the cele-brations surrounding it. And Gore used his connections to bring in money from Occidental for the Clinton–Gore reelection campaign. According to a memo from White House Deputy Chief of Staff Harold Ickes, Occidental gave $50,000 in response to one of Gore's "no-controlling-legal authority" telephone calls from his office in the White House. Indeed, since Gore became part of the Democratic ticket in the summer of 1992, Occidental has given more than $470,000 in soft money to various Democratic committees and causes.

Irani may lack Hammer's high profile—the old chairman traded quips with Johnny Carson on *The Tonight Show*—but he has been as cozy as his predecessor was with occupants of the White House. Two days after he slept in the Lincoln Bedroom of the White House, Irani's company dropped $100,000 on the DNC. He was also one of 130 guests at Clinton's second official state dinner, on September 27, 1994, where Russian President Boris Yeltsin and his wife were the guests of honor. Occidental had some interest in Russian oil; in the spring of 1994, Irani had traveled with Commerce Secretary Ronald Brown on a trade mission to Russia.

In 1993, Vice President Gore boarded Air Force Two and flew to Moscow for meetings with Russian Prime Minister Victor Chernomyrdin about the vitally important task of protecting nuclear weapons and nuclear material in the newly decentralized former Soviet Union. It was a natural mission for Gore; during his tenure in the Senate, he had become something of an expert in arms control agreements and, thanks to the patronage from Hammer, had already met with Anatoly Dobrynin, Moscow's longtime ambassador to Washington.

Many defense experts consider Russia's nuclear arsenal to pose the greatest immediate threat to U.S. security, of even greater concern than China's acquisition of U.S. nuclear secrets. The Chinese will no doubt develop sophisticated warheads and the missiles to launch them over the next decade or two; the Russians already have them. The fear of loose nukes grew as economic conditions in the old Soviet republics deteriorated in the early 1990s. Gore's mission was to reach an agreement with Russia on a way to manage all those weapons in a post–Cold War world.

Gore and Chernomyrdin discussed a twenty-year, $12 billion deal—signed just months earlier—under which Russia would ship its weapons-grade uranium to the United States. The U.S. Enrichment Corporation (then a government-owned corporation) would buy the highly enriched uranium, process it into lower grade, reactor-friendly uranium, and sell it to nuclear power plants in the United States. The cash-starved Russian government would get much-needed dollars to pay its nuclear scientists, those scientists would not be tempted to offer their services around the world, and nuclear material would be under the protection of the United States.

It looked good on paper, but it didn't work out that way. In 1996, Congress passed a bill to privatize the U.S. Enrichment Corporation (USEC), a move that threatened the Gore-Chernomyrdin agreement, though one that in fact would ultimately benefit Gore.

Some leading foreign-policy experts warned that privatization threatened the deal. Thomas Neff, a senior researcher for the Center for International Studies at the Massachusetts Institute of Technology, who conceived of the uranium agreement, told The Center for Public Integrity that he raised such questions as he briefed members of the Vice President's staff throughout 1997. A privatized, profit-seeking USEC would pay Russia far less cash for its uranium than the amount Gore and Chernomyrdin had originally agreed on. Although Gore was in a perfect position to lobby against the privatization scheme, he didn't. Instead, the Clinton-Gore administration wholeheartedly supported privatization of USEC as part of its efforts to "reinvent government."

USEC's board of directors, led by William Rainer, a large donor to the Presidential Inaugural Committee in 1993, had decided to consider two options: Sell the company to a behemoth like Lockheed Martin Corporation, or go it alone with an initial public offering. Rainer and the board chose the latter course. In 1998 the U.S. government got $1.9 billion from the sale of USEC to private investors. Clinton rewarded Rainer for presiding over USEC's privatization by nominating him to serve as the chairman of the Commodities Futures Trading Commission. At his Senate confirmation hearings, Rainer said, "I thought it was the right decision, and one year later, I look at the decision and I still think it was the right decision."

The decision was certainly right for some of Gore's biggest benefactors, which quickly cashed in on what turned out to be a

$75 million bonanza. Wall Street firms such as Morgan Stanley, Dean Witter & Company; Merrill Lynch & Company, Inc.; and Goldman Sachs & Company, Gore's No. 3 career patron, collectively raked in at least $42 million in underwriting fees. Well-connected law firms, among them Skadden, Arps, Slate, Meagher & Flom and Patton, Boggs earned nearly $11 million for their part in privatizing the company. USEC retained J.P. Morgan & Company, Inc., as its adviser in the deal; J.P. Morgan, in turn, hired Greg Simon, Gore's domestic policy adviser, for a fee of $10,000 a month to help it select the new, privatized company's directors.

As Neff and other experts had predicted, however, the deal soon began to unravel. Later in 1998 USEC announced that it had received shipments of uranium from the U.S. Department of Energy. The sudden glut caused the worldwide price of uranium to plummet, and the Russians suddenly stood to receive less money than they had been promised. Yeltsin's government cried foul and threatened to sell its nuclear material to other countries, including Iran. The White House scrambled to come up with the money the Russians demanded, and managed to quietly slip an extra $325 million for the Russians—a taxpayer-financed bailout—into an omnibus appropriations bill before Congress.

Neff, the architect of the plan to ship Russia's weapons-grade uranium to USEC for reprocessing, estimates that it will cost taxpayers $140 million a year for fifteen years to continue purchasing the Russian nuclear material, for a total cost of $2.1 billion—or $200 million more than the sale of USEC brought in.

Gore's "reinvention" of USEC made a lot of money for some of his most reliable political patrons. It also endangered nuclear arms control and left in private hands the management of facilities that are contaminated with deadly substances.

On June 16, 1999, when he officially announced in Carthage, Tennessee, that he was a candidate for President, Gore promised to "bring revolutionary improvement" to the nation's public schools. No doubt he had in mind one of his hot-button issues, which he never tires of hyping: connecting every school in the United States to the Internet. The campaign's Web site spells out

Gore's vision for pushing schools into the world of high technology, including promises that "every classroom and library [will be] wired to the Information Superhighway" and of "new educational software for all schools." In the few years since Gore took office the Internet has grown into a significant sector of the U.S. economy. Gore no doubt understood what that could mean for his presidential campaign: a mother lode of money.

Since early 1997, Gore has been holding monthly meetings with a group of executives from Silicon Valley. They reportedly talk about the "high-tech" issues of the day; Gore feeds his interest in the Internet, which he once notoriously claimed he took the lead in creating, and the executives get to advise the Vice President on matters that interest them.

Both Gore and the executives have said that the meetings are not about fund-raising. But Silicon Valley is home to the youngest fat cats in America. The "Gore-tech" group, as it has been called by Gore's staff, consists of about fifteen core visitors (at least nine of whom have made political contributions to Gore), and others from time to time. The "regulars" include Marc Andreessen, a founder of Netscape Communications, Inc., and later the chief technology officer at America Online, Inc., which acquired Netscape in March 1999; Scott Cook, the chairman of Intuit, Inc.; Charles Geschke, the president of Adobe Systems, Inc.; Sanford Robertson, the founder of Robertson Stephens & Company, a Silicon Valley–based investment bank, and a founding investor of E*Offering, which helps on-line investors participate in initial public offerings via the Internet; and L. John Doerr, a partner in Kleiner, Perkins Caufield & Byers, a Silicon Valley venture capital firm.

All of them made $5,000 contributions—the maximum under federal law—to Leadership '98, the political committee that Gore used to warm up for his presidential campaign. Doerr and Robertson managed to persuade members of their families to do the same. Until Clinton and Gore took the White House in 1992, Robertson had never made political contributions to Democrats. Since then, however, he has given at least $503,100 to the Democratic Party and to individual Democrats running for federal office.

Overall, the Silicon Valley "Gore-tech" group has given Democrats at least $1,397,373 since 1993—most of it to the DNC.

Gore's high-tech friends have gotten something for their money, chief among them a new market for their products—courtesy of every telephone customer in the United States.

On January 1, 1998, the federal government imposed a flat tax of 3 percent on every telephone call as a means of raising money to make every school in the nation Internet-accessible. Gore and Reed Hundt, then the chairman of the Federal Communications Commission, had dreamed up the idea the year before. (Gore and Hundt are old friends, having been classmates at St. Albans.) The tax raises upward of $2.3 billion a year, which is to be released to the nation's schools through a program called "E-rate." Gore and Hundt didn't have to fight with Congress to get the extra money; the FCC imposed the tax by an act of bureaucratic fiat.

Both long distance telephone carriers and the regional Bell operating companies complained about the tax from the get-go. Then the "baby Bells," as the local phone companies are commonly called, persuaded the FCC to allow them to pass most of their share of the tax to the long distance carriers. Under the plan, the baby Bells (chief among them BellSouth Corporation and Bell Atlantic—Gore's No. 2 and No. 13 career patrons, respectively) would pay relatively little. Long distance companies were left to shoulder most of the cost of the "Gore-tax" —at least 80 percent, by their estimate.

When AT&T, MCI Communications Corporation, and other long distance carriers started itemizing the cost of the tax on telephone bills, drawing furious responses from customers who were paying the tab, the FCC responded swiftly. It didn't repeal the tax. Instead, the FCC stipulated that the long distance carriers couldn't itemize the charge. As long as the people paying it didn't know about it, there was no harm done.

The tax costs the average American about $30 a year. The money goes to schools, eventually. Before it gets there, it sits at something called the Schools and Libraries Corporation, one of three not-for-profit operations set up by the FCC to administer the "E-rate" program. From its inception in November 1997 until September 1998, Ira Fishman, a fund-raiser for Gore and a former

White House lobbyist, was the president of the Schools and Libraries Corporation. His salary was $200,000 a year—the same as President Clinton's. His contract also included a $50,000 "performance bonus." But Fishman had trouble getting the operation off the ground, and when he resigned after just nine months on the job, the Schools and Libraries Corporation had yet to release any funds to schools.

Fishman did, however, find ways to spend money. In the first quarter of its existence, Schools and Libraries Corporation projected its expenses to be $2.7 million; when the receipts were added up, the cost of administering the E-rate program—which hadn't done anything yet—came to $4.4 million. FCC Commissioner Harold Furchtgott-Roth called the costs "exorbitant and unjustified."

Now that the "E-rate" program is up and running, some of Gore's top patrons have climbed aboard the gravy train. BellSouth and Bell Atlantic each made millions of dollars from providing telephone lines to schools. So did software companies like The Learning Company, a division of Mattel, Inc., which makes educational software and Cyber Patrol, a program that blocks students from accessing pornographic sites from school. The Learning Company, Gore's No. 7 career patron, offers a discount on its Cyber Patrol program to schools participating in the E-rate program. And, of course, connecting all those classrooms—some two million of them—to the Internet won't accomplish much without the computers, monitors, hardware, and software needed to surf the Web. Hundreds of high-tech companies—from chip makers like Intel Corporation to software companies like Netscape and Microsoft Corporation—stand to profit handsomely from E-rate.

Whether those profits, and the Internet connections that lead to them, will ultimately help America's chronically undereducated children, many of whom can't even read, seems to be of secondary importance. Steven Jobs, the founder of Apple Computer, Inc., has donated computers to schools for years, but in a 1996 interview he voiced doubts about hooking up schools to the Internet. "What's wrong with education cannot be fixed with technology," Jobs told a writer for *Wired* magazine. "No amount of technology will make a dent. It's a political problem."

While Silicon Valley has ardently supported a regressive tax even on the poorest American with a telephone, it's quite opposed to any sort of tax on the wealthier consumers who shop on-line. On February 27, 1998, President Clinton spoke to an audience of high-tech executives and announced his support for the Internet Tax Freedom Act, which would ban new state or local taxes on goods and services sold on-line.

It was just what the industry wanted. "We've been pushing for this for nine months," said Eric Schmidt, the chairman and chief executive officer of Novell, Inc., which manufactures computer software and hardware. "This is a big deal. We're talking about billions of dollars in taxes not happening for high tech. Everyone in the industry is happy."

"The most you can ever expect from any political contribution," Jeffrey Hirschberg, the national government relations director for the international accounting firm Ernst & Young told a reporter for the *Washington Post* in 1996, "is an audience with someone to state your case."

Ernst & Young, like the Gore-tech group, has spent handsomely to win audiences with Clinton, Gore, and those who work for them. The firm's partners and their spouses gave nearly $140,000 to Clinton/Gore '96. At the time, the firm was actively lobbying Congress for legislation to limit damages in cases where accounting firms are found to have misled investors about the financial condition of a company. (Under heavy lobbying pressure from the nation's trial lawyers, Clinton vetoed the Private Securities Litigation Reform Act of 1995, but Congress overrode his veto.)

Hirschberg, who was a national finance director of Clinton/Gore '96, is now one of Gore's top twenty-five fund-raisers, each of whom has promised to raise $100,000. Hirschberg has already exceeded his goal; Ernst & Young is Gore's No. 1 career patron. Gore is already expressing his appreciation.

Ernst & Young counts among its clients multinational corporations whose interests range from international taxation to tort reform. The firm also represents some clients with narrower interests. The National Association of Independent Colleges and Universities, for which Ernst & Young has lobbied, advocates tax-free accounts that would enable parents to save for their children's college tuition. So does Gore. "We help people save for retirement tax-free, and help them pay their mortgages tax-free," he said in a May 16, 1999, commencement speech at Graceland College in Lamoni, Iowa. "Now we must help them save tax-free for one of the biggest expenses most families will ever face in life: sending a child to college."

It's not clear, however, that parents of college-bound children would actually benefit from the subsidy. A 1997 report on tuition tax credits by the Joint Committee on Taxation, the congressional committee that studies tax legislation, makes exactly that point. "Some believe that such incentives, by increasing the demand for post-secondary education, would drive up the prices that educational institutions and their employees charge for their services," it said. "To that extent, higher prices could transfer the benefit from the taxpayer to the educational institution." Little wonder, then, that the nation's universities and colleges, which regularly increase tuition far faster than the rate of inflation, support the proposal.

Colleges and universities are not the only clients of Ernst & Young's with an interest in tax legislation. In June 1999 the Advisory Commission on Electronic Commerce—a panel created by Congress to study the issue of Internet taxation—began meeting in Williamsburg, Virginia, to consider whether to impose levies on sales over the Internet. Among the materials that the commissioners—some appointed by Congress, others by President Clinton—received was a study prepared by Ernst & Young for a group of companies that included Time Warner Inc., Gore's No. 12 career patron, America Online, Intuit, and Microsoft, titled, "The Sky Is Not Falling: Why State and Local Revenues Were Not Significantly Impacted by the Internet in 1998."

Ernst & Young has even won free advertising space for its point of view on Gore's campaign Web site, which lists as one of his priorities pursuing "an international agreement to make 'cyberspace' a permanent 'duty-free zone,' so that U.S. companies can sell goods, around the world, via the Internet, without duties."

*　　*　　*

In late October 1995, Sally Aman, Tipper Gore's chief press aide, telephoned John Cooke, then the executive vice-president of the Disney Channel, to ask for a favor. The Gores had no costumes for their annual Halloween costume party, she explained. Could Disney help them out?

Disney did just that. A team of costume makers in Los Angeles made a pair of outfits, based on the main characters in Disney's motion picture version of "Beauty and the Beast," to the Gores' precise measurements. The day before the party, the costumes arrived in Washington, along with a makeup artist to apply the mask that the Vice President would wear.

The total tab for Disney's end of the Gores' Halloween party topped $8,600. But the Gores didn't ask for a bill, and Disney didn't bother to send one. At the time, Disney was awaiting approval for its $19 billion acquisition of American Broadcasting Company, Inc., from the Justice Department and the FCC, chaired by Gore's longtime friend Reed Hundt.

When the *Washington Post* reported on the gift of the costumes, the Gores claimed they had no idea what the costumes were worth and blamed an unnamed staff member for not finding out whether the gifts were improper. Under the Ethics in Government Act, neither the President nor the Vice President may solicit gifts. After they got caught, the Gores announced that the costumes would be paid for—by the Democratic National Committee.

The FCC approved Disney's acquisition of ABC in February 1996.

The Halloween-costume episode offers just a hint of the Gore-Disney relationship. The Walt Disney Company is Gore's No. 9 career patron. The company's support of Gore goes back to 1988, when he made his first run for the White House. John Cooke sat on Gore's executive campaign committee, and took on the role of top fund-raiser in California. When Gore became Vice President, Cooke's wife started raising money for him, too. Diane Cooke is a trustee of the Vice President's Residence Foundation, a not-for-profit operation that's raised hundreds of thousands of dollars for a host of improvements to the Naval Observatory mansion that the Gores have called home since 1973. The Cookes donated $10,000 to the foundation in 1997. A day after Cooke attended a

White House coffee with Gore in 1996, Disney gave $50,000 to the DNC.

Cooke isn't the only Mouseketeer with a direct line to Gore. Michael Eisner, the company's chairman and chief executive officer, has also been a big contributor to Gore and other Democratic candidates (including Gore's rival, Bill Bradley). On June 16, 1994, Gore accompanied Eisner to the Washington premiere of *The Lion King*. At the time, Disney was seeking approval from the Interior Department, which oversees national parks, for its plans to build an amusement park called "Disney's America" next to the site of the historic Battles of Bull Run, two of the bloodiest conflicts in the Civil War, in Manassas, Virginia. Eisner was in the nation's capital to round up support for the project. Eventually, public outrage led Disney to cancel its plans in late September 1994, but not before top officials of the Interior Department went on record as saying that the theme park could spark "a livable, vibrant community located between Disney's America on the west and Manassas National Battlefield on the east."

The nature of Gore's relationship with Disney came into sharp focus in late 1998, when Members of Congress were coalescing behind the Child Online Protection Act, which would have imposed criminal penalties against commercial Web sites that display pornography without trying to weed out Web surfers under the age of seventeen. Disney opposed the legislation, largely because it feared some of the bill's provisions might interfere with its own lucrative Web site.

David Beier, Gore's domestic policy adviser, led a White House team in fighting the legislation, which had been rolled into the huge omnibus budget bill—the sort of awkward legislation that no Member of Congress reads and every Member wants to pass just to get it out of the way. During last minute, behind-the-scenes negotiations between the White House and Republican leaders in Congress, the Beier-led forces lobbied to kill the bill. Representative Michael Oxley, the bill's original sponsor, told a reporter, "[They] tried like hell to take [the language] out."

When Disney's and the White House's efforts became public, both claimed that they had been trying to "modify" the bill, not defeat it. Disney released a public statement on October 7:

"Whether those [requested] improvements were made or not . . . we supported the bills."

Ultimately, Disney lost the battle. Not only did the language stay in the bill, but Disney appeared to be against protecting kids from harmful Internet content. Gore did his best to help preserve and protect Disney's squeaky-clean image. He invited executives from the company to a White House "summit" on protecting children from Internet pornography. Jake Winebaum, the president of Disney's Buena Vista Internet Group, participated in two days of presentations and panel discussions on keeping children away from adult material on the Internet.

If there were any doubts about Disney's financial interest in deregulating the Internet, they fell away last year. In July 1999, Disney announced that it had completed a deal to buy Infoseek Corporation, which operated a popular Internet search engine, and organized its Internet interests around the new acquisition. The resulting product was the "GO Network," a kind of all-service Web site that offers a search engine, directory services, personalized web pages, and links to Disney's own Web sites, including Disney.com and Family.com.

Consider the lineup: Tony Coelho . . . resigned in disgrace from the House of Representatives amid charges that he was involved in a sweetheart deal with Michael Milken, the notorious junk-bond dealer. Nathan Landow . . . investigated for trying to influence the testimony of Kathleen Willey, the White House volunteer who alleged that President Clinton groped her in a corridor outside the Oval Office. Franklin Haney . . . indicted on forty-two counts of making illegal contributions to Tennessee politicians and investigated by Congress for financial irregularities in the lease of a Washington office building that is now home to the FCC. Maria Hsia . . . indicted for making improper campaign contributions. Howard Glicken . . . convicted of persuading a foreign national to contribute to a campaign. Mark Jimenez . . . indicted for making illegal campaign contributions, and currently a fugitive from justice living in the Philippines.

What do they all have in common?

Albert Gore, Jr.

Some are currently employed by, or otherwise involved in, Gore's presidential campaign. Others are past associates that Gore would like the public and the press to forget as he pursues the highest office in the land. Consider the case of Tony Coelho. When the California Congressman's $100,000 junk-bond deal with Milken, then Drexel Burnham Lambert's leveraged buyout operator, was disclosed in 1989, Coelho resigned from the House rather than face an ethics investigation. He violated federal campaign-finance laws by using a private yacht, *High Spirits,* owned by Donald Dixon, who looted the Texas-based Vernon Savings & Loan Association. Two political committees that Coelho ran paid a total of $48,451 to reimburse the thrift for use of the yacht; taxpayers spent an additional $1.3 billion bailing it out after it collapsed amid the savings-and-loan crisis. When the House check-bouncing scandal broke in 1992, Coelho was among the top offenders: He'd written $293,000 in rubber checks—more than three times his congressional salary—in a single year.

So when Gore needed to kick-start his campaign in May 1999, to whom did he turn to head his organization? Coelho. The reason is simple: Coelho has few equals in shaking the political money tree. In 1980, when Democrats were reeling after losing both the White House and the Senate in the Reagan landslide, Coelho took over the Democratic Congressional Campaign Committee (DCCC), where he pioneered the use of soft money in congressional elections. In return for huge contributions, Coelho was only too willing to cut special deals.

The Tax Reform Act of 1986 was a case in point. The theory behind the law was simple: By closing a vast number of loopholes that favored a few, everyone could enjoy lower tax rates. Coelho did his best to preserve the breaks for the few. He was the driving force in the House of Representatives for what Robert Dole once called "the Gallo amendment"—an estate-tax break made-to-order for the owners of the California winery that would save their heirs up to $34 million in inheritance taxes. He fought to preserve tax breaks for independent oil companies, and for sellers of real-estate tax shelters. All the while, Coelho said that he opposed the bill because it was a giveaway to the rich.

Under Coelho's stewardship, the DCCC grew from an organization that held one fund-raising event a year to a money machine for House Democrats. In the process, Coelho trained Terry McAuliffe, his finance director at the DCCC, in the ways of extracting large sums of cash from fat cats. McAuliffe learned his lessons well. He was the force behind the White House coffees at which Bill and Hillary Clinton and Al and Tipper Gore hosted wealthy donors with pressing matters before the federal government. An autographed photograph of the Vice President hangs on the wall of McAuliffe's office, with an inscription thanking him for "being the best finance chair in this or any other universe." In the spring of 1999, McAuliffe signed on to do for Gore 2000 what he had done for Clinton/Gore 1996.

As for Nathan Landow, were it not for him there might not even be a Gore 2000. Back on March 25, 1987, when presidential hopefuls were testing the waters, Gore had decided not to run for President, and made public statements to that effect. But two days later something happened that changed his mind. Landow met with Gore and offered to provide him at least $4 million if he would run. It wasn't an idle promise. Landow had been Walter Mondale's top fund-raiser in the 1984 election, and he'd organized his network of wealthy friends into a political action committee called IMPAC. All he needed was a candidate. Gore fit the bill.

Landow, a real-estate developer and self-styled Democratic kingmaker, had decided that Gore was just the kind of moderate Democrat who could win. On the day of his meeting with Landow, Gore publicly backpedaled on his decision not to run. Instead he said he would "seriously consider making the race." Two weeks later Gore was off and running, with Landow and his moneymen behind him.

Over the years, Landow's money apparently has been the glue that's tied him and Gore together. The Vice President called him from the White House as part of his fund-raising phone-call campaign to ask for $25,000. "You'll have it in hand," Landow replied, "in one hour." He apparently kept his promise, because Gore later wrote him a thank-you note that said, "Thanks! One hour is a record!"

Landow's involvement in national politics goes back to the 1970s. He helped bankroll Jimmy Carter's presidential campaign, and Carter repaid him with a nomination for an ambassadorship, though Carter withdrew his name after the *Washington Post* revealed that Landow had tried to hire Joe Nesline, an illegal-gambling kingpin and Washington organized-crime figure, as a consultant on an Atlantic City casino project. Landow raised money for Carter again in 1980, for Mondale in 1984, and for Gore in 1988. In 1992, Gore brought him on board the Clinton campaign; Landow backed his first winner in a dozen years. He expected to be rewarded for his success.

For years the Cheyenne-Arapaho Indians struggled to regain a parcel of land in Oklahoma seized by the federal government, in violation of a treaty, in 1869. Frustrated time and again in their fruitless attempts to reclaim the mineral-rich land, the tribe's elders decided to play the Washington game. In June and August 1996 they depleted their welfare fund, which paid for medical costs and food for the impoverished tribe, by making $107,000 in contributions to the Democratic National Committee. Representatives of the tribe were invited to attend a luncheon at the White House for their largesse, but nothing else happened.

Then the tribe's lawyer, Richard Grellner, was told to contact Landow, who suggested that they pay a $100,000 retainer and $10,000 monthly fee to Peter Knight, Gore's former Senate chief of staff and the chairman of Clinton's 1996 reelection campaign. Landow wanted his own cut as well: ten percent of anything that the Cheyenne-Arapaho earned, including any revenues from oil and natural gas. Short on cash, the poor tribe declined and took the matter to the Senate Governmental Affairs Committee, which concluded its investigation by determining that "a collection of Democratic fund-raisers and operatives" had "fleeced" and then "abandoned" the Indians. In March 1998 the DNC offered to return the tribe's contribution.

Asked about his role in the Cheyenne-Arapaho deal by a correspondent for "Frontline," the PBS program, Landow blamed the Indian tribe. He told interviewers from the show, "They want the land given back to them on a platter. . . . They brought in innocent people like me. They're a bunch of goddamned uneducated Indians."

Landow isn't just a man looking out for his own interests. He's happy to help out a powerful public servant whenever a problem arises. He tried to arrange a real-estate deal involving a Washington office building for Webster Hubbell after the former associate attorney general had pleaded guilty to bilking his partners in the Rose Law Firm out of more than $400,000 and was under investigation by Independent Counsel Kenneth Starr for understating his income to the Internal Revenue Service by $750,000. Landow also flew Kathleen Willey in a private jet to his Maryland home when he learned that Paula Jones's attorneys wanted her story. When asked about the trip by Starr, Landow cited the Fifth Amendment and declined to testify.

Not everyone is so reticent to talk when asked questions by prosecutors. On June 28, 1999, in a federal courthouse in Washington, Donald Condra of Chattanooga explained how Franklin Haney, a wealthy Tennessee real-estate developer and longtime friend of Al Gore, had given him $1,000 to contribute to the 1996 Clinton–Gore campaign. Haney's administrative assistant, Gloria Thurman, told Condra not to mention the source of the donation. "She said, 'Treat it as a gift from Mr. Haney, and since you'd received the gift, you'd decided to contribute to the campaign,'" Condra testified.

In 1998, Haney was indicted on forty-two counts of making nearly $100,000 worth of illegal contributions to political campaigns. He'd funneled the money through straw donors to various Democratic party candidates, including Clinton and Gore. Government prosecutors produced ledgers from Haney showing payments made to employees and friends, and indicating that they were reimbursements for political contributions.

In 1999 a jury acquitted Haney on all counts, accepting the argument that while Haney may have broken the law, he was not aware he was doing so. "Nobody committed a crime because nobody thought they were doing anything wrong," Ted Wells, Haney's defense attorney, told the jury in his closing statement. Ignorance of the law, in the case of Haney, a longtime political fund-raiser who ran for Congress in the 1960s and governor of Tennessee in the 1970s, turned out to be an excuse. Chris Lehane, a spokesman for Gore, announced that the Vice President was "pleased for Franklin and his family."

While Haney may not be an expert in campaign-finance law, he knows enough about the ways of Washington to have arranged for buildings he owns to be leased by the Tennessee Valley Authority and the Social Security Administration. And in 1995, Haney hired Peter Knight to help him close a real-estate deal in the nation's capital with the FCC. Knight delivered. The FCC signed a lease to occupy the Portals, an office complex in southwest Washington, D.C., that guaranteed it would pay rent even if it wasn't occupying the building. Haney's company was paid $19 million in rent before the FCC's first moving truck pulled up to the front gate.

Haney rewarded Knight for his work: On the day that officials of the FCC signed the contract to move, Haney sent Knight a check for $1 million. Haney maintains that the payment to Knight was for a variety of services over a number of years. But the House Commerce Committee concluded in December 1998 that "Mr. Haney paid his representatives millions of dollars in fees upon the successful closing of the Portals transaction, in which the federal government agreed to specific lease changes sought by Mr. Haney." The House passed its evidence on to the Justice Department, which, after launching a preliminary investigation, dropped the case the following month—in January 1999.

Like Haney, Maria Hsia was indicted on multiple (six) counts of making illegal contributions. (Her trial is scheduled for January 2000.) Hsia arranged the infamous Buddhist temple fund-raiser of 1995, at which Gore was photographed walking out of the temple, wearing a lei and shaking hands with monks. Hsia stood next to Gore in the photo.

Gore originally met Hsia at a fund-raising event for his 1988 presidential campaign. She had moved to the United States as a student in 1973, earned a hefty sum of money by bringing new clients to immigration lawyers, and by 1982 had begun raising money for Democrats. Shortly after meeting Gore in 1988, she wrote to a handful of Senators, including Gore, asking them to participate in a "cultural and educational" trip to China. She did not make the exact purpose of the trip clear. But she did make it understood that if Gore would participate, she and her "colleagues" in California would help contribute to his presidential campaign.

"If you decide to join this trip," she said in a letter to Gore, "I will persuade all my colleagues in the future to play a leader role in your presidential race." All of the Senators she asked declined the invitation—except Gore.

During the same year that Hsia met Al Gore, she began a business relationship with two men who would be implicated in the Clinton-Gore fund-raising fiasco of 1996: Indonesian businessman James Riady and his right-hand man, John Huang. It was Hsia who helped Riady and Huang learn the ropes of political fund-raising in the United States. Together they organized a political action committee, the Pacific Leadership Council, to raise money for politicians in Washington.

After the trip, Gore and Hsia worked out a mutually beneficial business relationship: Gore would serve as her principal contact on Capitol Hill; Hsia would help line up contributors to Gore's Senate campaigns. In 1996, when Gore was scrambling to raise money for the Clinton-Gore ticket, Hsia came to his aid. She organized an event for Gore at His Lai Buddhist Temple in Hacienda Heights, California. There was, however, a big problem with the fund-raising event: The temple is a nonprofit religious organization and so by law cannot make political contributions. In February 1998 a federal grand jury indicted Hsia for soliciting $65,000 in illegal contributions from the temple for the DNC. The indictment also included her solicitations from the temple for other Democratic campaigns from 1993 to 1996.

What did Gore know about the event and when did he know it? At first he said that it was only a "community outreach event" and that "no money was offered or collected at the event."

Later he called it "a political event" and acknowledged knowing "that there were finance people who were going to be present." Finally he admitted that his participation in the event was "inappropriate."

Along with Haney and Hsia, Howard Glicken and Mark Jimenez have two things in common. Both of them have helped raise money for Gore, and both have been indicted for violating federal campaign-finance laws. Jimenez was indicted for laundering money to the Clinton-Gore campaign in 1996. Glicken was indicted for laundering money to the Democratic Senatorial Campaign Committee in 1993.

Glicken and Gore are friends. Glicken, the president of the Miami-based Americas Group, which helps small Latin American companies go public in the United States, has two expensive Jaguars in his garage with license plates that read "GORE 1" and "GORE 2." Glicken has been one of Gore's political benefactors since his first run for the presidency in 1988. Months after Gore moved into the Vice President's residence in 1993, Glicken donated a $6,000 pool table for the house.

During Gore's first term, when Glicken was a finance vice-chairman for the DNC, he became the insider's insider. In 1996 he raised $2 million for Clinton, Gore, and other Democrats; he visited the White House seventy times, spent at least one night in the Lincoln Bedroom, and even flew on Air Force One. On more than one occasion he has hosted Gore in Miami.

In 1998, in Washington, D.C., Glicken pleaded guilty to two misdemeanor counts of soliciting political contributions from a foreign national. Not only had he asked Thomas Kramer, a German citizen working and living in Florida as a real-estate developer, for $20,000 in contributions, but Glicken had also told him how to evade the law by funneling the contributions to a Democratic Party committee through Kramer's secretary, a U.S. citizen. A judge sentenced Glicken to eighteen months probation, fined him $80,000, and ordered him to perform 500 hours of community service. After Glicken was sentenced, a Gore aide who refused to be identified told the Associated Press that Glicken would have no role in the Vice President's future campaigns.

In 1996, Mark Jimenez was an eager Democratic donor. As the majority owner of Future Tech International, a Miami-based company that exports computers to South America, he was in a position to give much of his money away and still lead a very comfortable life. On March 23, 1995, Jimenez gave $20,000 to the Vice President's Residence Foundation.

But in 1998 he became a fugitive. A grand jury in Washington, D.C., indicted Jimenez on seventeen counts of illegal political contributions. He'd allegedly laundered $39,500 through his employees at Future Tech. After the indictment, Jimenez turned up in the Philippines, where he reportedly was an unpaid special adviser to Philippine President Joseph Estrada. Jimenez has since been indicted on additional charges of tax evasion and fraud. In late 1999, the Justice Department was negotiating his extradition.

On May 8, 1996, at a DNC fund-raising dinner in Washington, President Clinton praised the man he had chosen to head his reelection effort. "Any man who can pick your pocket and still win your applause," he said, "deserves to be the campaign manager of the Clinton-Gore campaign." Clinton was describing Peter Knight, to whom Gore has turned in 1999 to raise money for his own presidential bid.

When Gore started his political career in Washington in 1977, he hired Knight, a graduate of Georgetown Law School who had already been working for two years as an aide on Capitol Hill, to be his administrative assistant. The two have been joined at the hip ever since. Knight followed Gore to the Senate in 1985 and then managed Gore's 1988 presidential campaign. After that he became a lobbyist, and in January 1993, with the inauguration of Clinton and Gore, he became the best-connected lobbyist in Washington.

In 1991 Knight had joined Wunder, Diefenderfer, Ryan, Cannon and Thelen, a Washington law firm that had a roster of corporate clients with both the means and the incentive to throw money at politicians. Among them: tobacco companies (RJR Nabisco and Philip Morris Companies, Inc.), oil companies (Ashland, Inc.), and timber companies (Kimberly-Clark Corporation and MAXXAM, Inc.). As a lobbyist, Knight found himself ideally situated to ask his clients for contributions to his former boss, and eventually Knight cemented a new role for himself as Gore's unofficial "chief of fund-raising."

In 1992, Gore picked Knight to run his Vice Presidential campaign, and in 1996, Gore persuaded Clinton to make Knight the chairman of the 1996 Clinton-Gore campaign. In that capacity, Knight raked in about $19 million in soft money for the DNC.

Knight also was Gore's choice to raise money for the Vice President's Residence Foundation, originally organized by Dan Quayle in 1990 and charged with "preserving and furnishing" the

Vice President's official residence. The fund also served as a convenient way for donors to gain direct access to Gore. In the two years that he raised money for the foundation, Knight collected more than $300,000.

Three of Knight's clients—Bell Atlantic, Fluor Corporation, and West Publishing Corporation (by way of its chairman, Vance Opperman)—made $10,000 contributions to the foundation. In response to the Center for Public Integrity's faxed questions about his contribution to the foundation, Opperman's secretary said: "Mr. Opperman did see the fax, and he chose to disregard it. He threw it away, so you won't be hearing from him."

The list of $10,000 donors to the Vice President's Residence Foundation also includes ARCO, the Coca-Cola Company, the Walt Disney Corporation, MCI (now MCI/Worldcom), Time Warner, and Franklin Haney. Bill Gates, the chairman of Microsoft Corporation, donated a sculpture valued at $30,000.

Knight's handiwork paid off when it was time to raise money for Clinton's reelection. He organized a June 6, 1995, dinner for Gore's top financial supporters at the Naval Observatory. The event was well-choreographed, as a memo to Gore that included these instructions on how he was to behave makes plain: "During the cocktail party, please mingle with guests . . . please engage in conversation with guests . . . please be sure to thank everyone for generous support. . . . This is a very core group of supporters who are very enthusiastic about supporting you."

Among those attending the dinner were Disney's John Cooke; Jim Free, a Washington lobbyist for the American Petroleum Institute and R.J. Reynolds Tobacco Company, among other interests; Howard Glicken; Franklin Haney; and James Edwards, then the chairman of ICF Kaiser International, Inc., whose directors included Tony Coelho.

Also attending the affair were William Haney III and Victor Gatto, two executives of Molten Metal Technology, Inc., of Waltham, Massachusetts. William Haney, who is not related to Franklin Haney, was among the first to pledge $50,000 to the Clinton–Gore 1996 campaign. On May 1, 1995, Knight wrote Haney and Gatto an appreciative thank-you note that read, in part,

"Your participation in this program will give you a special place of significance with the Vice President and put you first in line."

That "special place of significance" was worth millions to Molten Metal. The company is one in a long line of firms that have attempted to reprocess liquid nuclear waste into nonradioactive solid materials. Since the advent of nuclear energy, government officials and private companies have promised that reprocessing would eliminate the threat that nuclear wastes, some of which remain lethal for thousands of years, pose to people and the environment.

Unfortunately, reprocessing has never worked, either as a commercial or a government-sponsored enterprise. In the 1960s, 1970s, and 1980s, various companies, sometimes with the aid of the Department of Energy, have tried—and failed. General Electric Company built a plant in Morris, Illinois, that employed a process that worked in the laboratory but not in the factory. The facility never opened. Getty Oil Company got into the business in 1969, and quickly realized it couldn't make a go of it. In the 1980s, Allied-General Nuclear Services operated a facility in Barnwell, South Carolina, which wouldn't have opened without massive government aid. By 1983 the plant had notified its 300 employees that it was going out of business.

Nonetheless, on April 18, 1995, Vice President Gore stood alongside Haney in Falls River, Massachusetts, at one of Molten Metal's factories and announced: "Molten Metal is a success story, a shining example of American ingenuity, hard work, and business know-how."

Molten Metal was a success of sorts, but not at reprocessing. It received by itself more research grants from the Energy Department during the Clinton Administration than the seventeen other companies that applied for such grants combined. Molten Metal even won some $27 million worth of contracts after November 1995, the month experts at the Department of Energy concluded that the company's technology did not work. Despite the recommendation from inside his agency that all further contracts with Molten Metal be suspended, Energy Undersecretary Thomas Grumbly, a former aide to Gore and a close friend of Peter

Knight's, continued to approve government grants for the company.

Knight himself was on the payroll of Molten Metal. Haney, the company's chairman, paid him $7,000 a month plus lucrative stock options. Haney even gave a gift of 640 shares of the company's stock, worth some $10,000 at the time, to Knight's thirteen-year-old son.

The shares, however, soon depreciated in value. In October 1996, Molten Metal announced that it had overestimated the amount of money it would realize from Energy Department contracts by some $12 million; the price of the company's stock plunged with the news. Irate investors initiated a shareholders suit, claiming that some insiders sold out just before the announcement was made. By December 1997 the company was forced to file for bankruptcy, and a share of its stock, once valued at nearly $40 on the strength of the company's revenue from government contracts, could be had for less than a nickel.

The House Commerce Committee investigated the dealings of Knight, Grumbly, Gore, and Molten Metal in November 1997. Knight was indignant that the members of the committee questioned, among other things, the gift of stock the company had made to his son. "Any suggestion that stock was given to my thirteen-year-old son for improper purposes is patently false and outrageous," he said in a statement to the committee. He offered no explanation for the gift other than his friendship with Haney. Neither did Haney, although an April 8, 1996 letter he wrote to Knight sheds some light on his motive. "Our objective is to keep you and other of the more talented people with us right up until you are Secretary of State."

In 1998 the Justice Department, after conducting its own investigation of Knight, closed the case, which gratified Gore. "Peter Knight is one of the most honorable, honest men I have ever known in my life," he told a reporter for the *New York Times*. He didn't mention what position Knight would hold in his administration should he win the presidency.

ALBERT GORE, JR.
Top Ten Career Patrons

Ranking	Company/Individual/Family Name	Total	Soft Money to Democratic Committees, 1991–June, 1999
1	Ernst & Young International, New York	$125,200	$897,960
2	BellSouth Corporation, Atlanta	$104,000	$614,379
3	The Goldman Sachs Group, Inc., New York	$99,250	$1,456,300
4	D.E. Shaw & Company, New York/Shaw and Kobliner families	$98,000	$557,000
5	Citigroup, Inc., and affiliated companies, New York	$91,950	$648,547
6	Viacom, Inc., and affiliated companies, New York	$89,750	$356,900
7	Mattel, Inc., El Segundo, California/The Learning Company	$76,000	$137,425
8	Eskind family, Nashville, Tennessee	$74,500	$173,050
9	The Walt Disney Company and affiliated companies, Burbank, California	$68,000	$1,877,605
10	Olan Mills family, Chattanooga, Tennessee	$67,950	$200,000

This list is based on individual and PAC contributions to Gore's House campaigns from 1977–1984; individual and PAC contributions to Gore's Senate campaigns from 1983–1992; contributions to the Vice President's Residence Foundation from 1993–1998; individual and PAC contributions to Gore's 1988 presidential campaign; individual and PAC contributions to Leadership '98 from 1997–98; and individual contributions to Gore's 2000 presidential campaign through June 30, 1999. Gore's presidential campaign is not accepting PAC contributions. The second column is based on soft money contributions to Democratic committees from 1991 through June 30, 1999.

Sources: Federal Election Commission; Center for Responsive Politics; Vice President's Residence Foundation.

1. Includes contributions from employees of Ernst & Young; its predecessor Ernst & Whinney; and its subsidiary, E&Y Kenneth Leventhal.
3. Includes contributions from employees of BellSouth and its predecessors, South Central Bell and Southern Bell.
4. Includes contributions from employees of D.E. Shaw & Co.; from employees of Juno Online Services, which was founded by D.E. Shaw; from David E. and Beth Kobliner Shaw; and from their family members.
5. Includes contributions from employees of Citigroup and the companies that have contributed to the creation of Citigroup, including Citibank; Citicorp; Travelers Corp.; Salomon Smith Barney (and its predecessors, Salomon Brothers and Smith Barney); Shearson Lehman; and EF Hutton.
6. Includes contributions from employees of Viacom and its subsidiaries, including Paramount Pictures (formerly Paramount Communications); Showtime Networks; MTV Networks; Nickelodeon; Spelling Entertainment; and Simon & Schuster.
7. Includes contributions from employees of Mattel and its Broderbund subsidiary. Primarily, however, this money is from employees of The Learning Company, which was acquired by Mattel in 1999.
9. Includes contributions from employees of The Walt Disney Company and its subsidiaries, including The Disney Channel; Miramax Films; ABC, Inc.; and Buena Vista Publishing.

THE REPUBLICANS

Gary Bauer

▐▐▐▐▐▐▐▐▐▐▐

When President Ronald Reagan picked Gary Bauer to be his chief domestic policy adviser in 1987, Bauer wasted no time in steering the conservative Reagan White House even further to the right. "I'm just going to do things until someone tells me to stop," Bauer said at the time. "When these two years are over, whatever criticism I may get, I don't think anyone will apply the adjective 'passive' to my time here."

In the ensuing decade, Bauer has tackled all things conservative. He shows no sign of slowing down, much less stopping. He took a moribund think tank and built it into one of the nation's most influential "family values" advocacy groups. He created the nation's second-largest political action committee. And now the bantamweight Republican is running for President in the shadow of his lifelong hero. "I'm a Reagan conservative," Bauer often boasts. "All of my views are in line with where his were."

Bauer's views are without doubt the most distinct—some would say the most extreme—of any of the top-tier Republican candidates. He supports school prayer, school choice, tougher obscenity laws, the death penalty, and a family-oriented tax plan that would set a flat tax rate of 16 percent, eliminate inheritance taxes, and cut payroll taxes as part of an overhaul of Social Security. He opposes gay rights, gun control, and most of what Hollywood produces.

He also opposes assisted suicide and has the strongest opposition to abortion of any of the leading candidates. He would make his "pro-life" view a litmus test for all Supreme Court appointees, and would push a "human life bill" that would define unborn children as persons under the Constitution. He would outlaw the medical procedure that critics call "partial-birth abortion" and would prohibit any U.S. foreign aid from being used to pay for abortions.

But perhaps none of Bauer's views set him apart as much as his hard-line stance against the People's Republic of China. He routinely describes "Communist China" in the same hyperbolic way that Reagan famously referred to the former Soviet Union as an "Evil Empire." And he would block free trade with the nation he calls "the world's gravest threat to American values and national security."

Bauer has proven that he can raise enough money to stay in the race through the early primaries—he had collected $3.4 million through the first half of 1999—and he has run his campaign in the same ideological fashion that he ran his advocacy groups: He embraces highly controversial social issues, and speaks loudly about them every chance he gets. He politely makes bitter enemies of those whose ideas he opposes, including many within his own party.

Bauer compares himself to Reagan in nearly every speech he gives. He even steals Reagan's best lines: Three times during his speech at the August 1999 Iowa straw poll he described his vision of America as "a shining city on the hill." But while Reagan was a former movie star with a smooth voice and a magnetic stage presence, Bauer is a squeaky-voiced policy wonk with high, almost comical, eyebrows. The resulting owl-like look often lends Bauer's broad face a bemused expression, as if he is silently wondering whether someone is going to tell him to stop. So far, no one has.

Gary Bauer is a good kid from a bad town. Born on May 4, 1946, he is the only child of a blue-collar Kentucky couple. His father, a former Marine known as "Spike," worked at the local steel mill when he wasn't drinking heavily. His mother and grand-mother attended First Baptist Church, and brought Gary with them. Nearly everyone the young Bauer knew was a Democrat. And many of them were crooks.

Newport, Kentucky, slouches along the south shore of the Ohio River, just across the wide muddy river from Cincinnati. The locals used to call it "Sin City," and for good reason: Newport was home to everything the squeaky clean corporate home of the Procter and Gamble Company didn't want: strip bars, whorehouses, drug dealers, gambling, and organized crime. In the evenings, Ohioans would fly south across the glimmering metal "airplane bridge," so dubbed for the sound a car made as its tires squealed over the open metal grate. And late at night, after they'd had their fill of Kentucky hospitality—or run out of money—they drove back north, leaving behind a town dominated by bookies, pushers, pimps, and the gangsters that more or less ran the place.

The cops were corrupt, and everyone knew it. Shootings were common. But few folks in working-class Newport were willing to stand up to the cabal that ran the town. Many worked for mob-run operations, as waitresses or bouncers, and were afraid to lose their jobs. Others were running their own illegal businesses on the side, squirreling away as much cash as they could before leaving town. Even today, folks in Newport still joke about "digging up the money to buy a new house."

While Bauer was still in high school, however, a flock of re-form-minded conservatives banded together. They called them-selves the Committee of 500. And they pledged to clean up Newport. They elected a new sheriff, and joined him in raiding juke joints and whorehouses. Gary Bauer was one of only three or four Newport High School students to join the committee. They were the first Republicans he'd ever known.

"That set him on a course," recalls classmate Tete Turner, now the principal of Newport High. Turner thought Bauer was a bit radical back then, and he thinks Bauer's positions on issues such as abortion are a bit radical now. But Turner has never doubted Bauer's sincerity or his commitment to the causes he believes in. So he supports Bauer anyway. He counsels his old friends in Sin

City that they "don't have to support Gary's positions, but they should support Gary."

Bauer graduated near the top of his high school class in 1964. And that fateful summer, his new Christian conservative friends took him to the Republican National Convention. There he heard a speech by actor Ronald Reagan. Back then, Senator Barry Goldwater of Arizona was the party's idol, and its presidential nominee. But Bauer decided right there that one day he would work for Reagan.

After graduating from Georgetown College—a Baptist school in Georgetown, Kentucky—Bauer moved to Washington, D.C., where he earned a law degree from Georgetown University in 1973. While in law school, he worked as an opposition researcher for the Republican National Committee. Also during this time he married Carol Hoke, with whom he has three children.

After law school, Bauer landed a job as a lobbyist for the Direct Mail Marketing Association, a Washington-based trade group. There, he developed connections across the burgeoning direct-mail fund-raising industry. Pioneered by Goldwater direct-mail maestro Richard Viguerie, the widespread use of computerized mailings was a stealth weapon that helped build Reagan's national profile between his 1976 and 1980 campaigns.

Bauer returned to Sin City in the spring of 1999 and kicked off his presidential campaign from Newport High School. A hometown crowd of roughly 1,000 turned out. They were met by the same Gary Bauer who helped clean up Newport. He decried births out of wedlock, pornography, drugs, abortion, and racist hate crimes and pledged to reverse the erosion of American values. "This," he told them, "is the good fight I am ready to wage with heart and soul."

True to his 1964 pledge, Bauer left the direct-mail group to work as a policy analyst for Reagan's successful 1980 campaign. He served on Reagan's transition team, and in 1982 was made a deputy undersecretary at the Department of Education. His focus was on restoring discipline and patriotism to America's classrooms, as well as on pushing Reagan's notions about vouchers and tuition tax credits.

Bauer was an ideologue from the start. He attacked the National Education Association almost from his first day on the job. In 1983 he blasted an NEA-sponsored curriculum unit on nuclear war as "an incredibly obvious drive to bring political indoctrination into the classroom," and as "leftist indoctrination aimed at turning today's elementary students into tomorrow's campus radicals." The following year, Bauer wrote a report on school violence that became the basis for Reagan's focus on discipline and curbing crime in the classroom. Remarkably, Bauer retained good personal relations with leaders of the NEA and allied institutions even as he lambasted them in public. His ability to gain the respect of even his fiercest adversaries has become a hallmark of his lobbying style.

After he was promoted to undersecretary in 1985, Bauer continued to advocate the teaching of morality and religion-based values in schools. He also chaired a twenty-two-member White House panel that authored a report on the state of the American family. The controversial report blamed broken families for poverty and crime and encouraged women to stay at home with their children. It concluded that the "easy availability of welfare in all of its forms has become a powerful force for destruction of family life through perpetuation of the welfare culture."

Bauer was promoted again in 1987. As director of the Office of Policy Development for the Reagan White House, he was in charge of shaping Reagan's domestic policies. It was here that he promised to "do things until someone tells me to stop." And that's just what he did.

Banning abortion was one of the causes closest to Reagan's heart, and Bauer poured much of his effort into chipping away at the 1973 Supreme Court decision that legalized the procedure. He helped the Reagan Administration impose numerous restrictions on abortion, worked to keep birth control out of public schools, fought any mention of condoms in high school sexual education classes and pushed the teaching of abstinence. And in 1988, Bauer sent a memo to Otis Bowen, M.D., the Secretary of Health and Human Services, proposing an executive order that would ban federally funded research from using fetal tissues obtained from abortion.

Even more controversial was Bauer's stance on AIDS-related

issues. He supported routine testing for HIV, the virus linked to AIDS, during all hospital admissions and physical exams. This brought him into fierce conflict with AIDS activists and public-health professionals, who feared that mandatory testing would discourage many sexually active people from seeking health care of any kind. That conflict heightened when Bauer effectively blocked White House support for a federal law banning discrimination against AIDS victims. In 1987, in the course of opposing the direct mailing of a publication on AIDS, Bauer asked: "Is there a breathing American who doesn't know that you get AIDS from sex or a dirty needle? If there is, he probably is not the kind of person who reads his mail."

Bauer was lured away from the Reagan White House in 1988 by James Dobson, one of the nation's most influential Christian conservative leaders. Dobson's not-for-profit organization, Focus on the Family, has an annual budget of more than $100 million.

Dobson asked Bauer to take over the Family Research Council, a dormant subsidiary of the organization. When Bauer arrived, the council had four employees and a budget of a couple hundred thousand dollars. Within a decade it would have 110 employees, a budget of $14 million, and a mailing list of more than 400,000 supporters. Bauer separated the council from its parent organization. And with financial help from the DeVos and Prince families of Michigan, the Family Research Council recently bought a six-story building in Washington for its national headquarters.

The Family Research Council has been the fast-rising star of the Religious Right ever since political wunderkind Ralph Reed left the Christian Coalition in 1997. Whereas the Christian Coalition openly frames its policies on biblical and religious teachings, Bauer's organization struggles to maintain the appearance of a church-and-state separation between its religious principles and the family-based government policies it supports. But the distinction is more a paper curtain than an iron one. And Bauer himself has crashed through it repeatedly.

In October 1997, for example, when the Promise Keepers convened a massive rally on the National Mall, the Family Research Council welcomed the organization of Christian men to Washington with special events, tables full of literature, lighted billboards in downtown subway stations, and a four-page advertising supplement in the *Washington Times*. Bauer was an early financial backer of the Promise Keepers, along with Dobson, Pat Robertson, and Jerry Falwell. He knew as well as anyone that the Christ-focused men's group overtly avoided both political candidates and political issues, yet he aggressively and repeatedly used Promise Keepers events to promote the Family Research Council.

To engage in direct lobbying—something that federal law restricts 501(c)(3) tax-exempt organizations such as the Family Research Council from doing—Bauer founded a sister organization that he named American Renewal. Most of American Renewal's artillery has been fired at President Clinton.

Bauer, for example, viciously attacked Clinton's plan to overhaul the nation's health-care system. In one particularly provocative newspaper ad, he published a large photograph of then-Surgeon General Joycelyn Elders, a popular punching bag for the right wing of the GOP until Clinton fired her for advocating that masturbation be addressed in high school sexual-education courses. The large headline that framed the photo read: "Bill Clinton Chose This Doctor. Now He Wants to Choose Yours."

During the Monica Lewinsky scandal, Bauer pledged to spend $250,000 on television ads that called for Clinton's resignation. The ad opened with footage of children watching TV news broadcasts about the scandal, including Clinton's now infamous "I did not have sexual relations with that woman" line and a talk show host saying, "Everyone lies about sex." Then a somber-looking Gary Bauer appeared on the screen and said: "Mr. President, it's time for you to put our country and our children first. It's time for you to resign."

Bauer is on leave from his $160,000-a-year job as the president of the Family Research Council. He is also on leave from his roles as chairman of both American Renewal and his PAC, the Campaign for Working Families. But he won't have to do without the money he would have earned running the Family Research Council: Shortly before he left to run for the White House, the organization gave him a $150,000 bonus—just about what he would have earned during the year his campaign is expected to consume.

Altogether, the kid from working-class Newport took home $784,200 in 1998 and the first five months of 1999. In addition to his salary and "bonus" from the Family Research Council, American Renewal and the Campaign for Working Families paid him a total of $105,000 in consulting fees. He made at least another $150,000 in interest, dividends, and capital gains on his stock portfolio, which is worth more than $630,000. Most of the rest of Bauer's income came in the form of speaking fees. Bauer delivered a total of forty-two paid speeches during this period, most of them to local anti-abortion groups, such as New Hope Family Services in Syracuse, New York, and New Life Pregnancy Center in Decatur, Georgia. He charged most of these small organizations $5,000 an appearance. The fees they paid went directly into Bauer's pocket—not to his organizations, his presidential campaign, or elsewhere to the cause.

Bauer took yet another bold step toward the political limelight shortly after the 1996 elections, when he created a conservative political action committee called the Campaign for Working Families. It came from nowhere and took in so much money so quickly that it blew by such long-established political big spenders as the National Rifle Association and the Teamsters union, as well as such big conservative PACs as Campaign America and the New Republican Majority Fund. By the end of 1998, Bauer had raised more than $7 million for the new organization. Only EMILY's List—a PAC for "pro-choice" Democratic female candidates—raised more that year.

Most of the money Bauer raised was from small donors who were new to the political process. The Campaign for Working Families claims a base of more than 80,000 donors. More than 90 percent of its donations were in amounts of less than $100; the average donation was only $35.

With the stated goal of electing "men and women who are Reagan Republicans," Bauer's PAC poured money into more than one hundred fifty state and federal elections in 1998. It gave $290,000 to state candidates and $470,000 to federal candidates, and it made another $710,000 in independent expenditures.

Bauer's money helped win some high-profile conservative victories. When Representative Jim Bunning of Kentucky left his seat to run for the U.S. Senate, he anointed former aide Rick Robinson to take his place. But Bauer backed conservative Gex (Jay) Williams, who upset insider Robinson in the GOP primary. And in California, Bauer helped conservative Tom Bordonaro defeat GOP moderate Brooks Firestone—even though Firestone had the support of then-House Speaker Newt Gingrich and other GOP heavyweights. Bauer hit Firestone hard, with $100,000 worth of TV ads bashing Firestone's stand on "partial-birth abortion." (Bordonaro lost the general election to Democrat Lois Capps, who succeeded her late husband, Walter Capps, in claiming the House seat.)

In addition to proving Bauer's fund-raising muscle, the Campaign for Working Families also afforded him a place to preassemble his current campaign staff. Nearly all his aides in the presidential campaign moved over from the PAC, including:

- President Jeffrey Bell, now serving as a "senior consultant" to Bauer's campaign. The head of Bauer's inner circle, Bell has been active in Republican presidential politics since he helped prepare Richard Nixon's campaign briefing book in 1968. Bell worked on Reagan's 1976 and 1980 campaigns and was second in command of Jack Kemp's 1988 campaign.

- Treasurer Frank Cannon, now Bauer's campaign manager. Cannon, who coordinated Reagan's national student campaign in 1980 and worked with Bell on the Kemp campaign, oversees the campaign's day-to-day operations.

- Executive director Connie Mackey, now the deputy manager of Bauer's campaign. Mackey, who was the national finance director of Patrick Buchanan's 1996 presidential campaign, works on political organizing and fund raising.

- Direct-mail expert Walter Lukens, now Bauer's "senior finance consultant." Lukens worked for the Reagan–Bush campaign in 1984, and is the president of Lukens-Cook Company, a direct-mail fund-raising firm in Arlington, Virginia. Bauer's campaign headquarters is in the same suburban office tower as Lukens's company.

• Robert Heckman, now a senior political consultant to the Bauer campaign. Heckman, a veteran of six presidential campaigns, directed the multimillion-dollar "Citizens for Reagan" independent-expenditure campaigns in 1980 and 1984.

With nearly its entire staff on loan to Bauer's campaign, the Campaign for Working Families is limping along through the 2000 campaign season with an interim leader: Ronald Reagan's son, Michael Reagan.

Bauer's presidential campaign has had an easier time attracting political operatives from the Campaign for Working Families than it's had attracting contributions from donors to the Family Research Council. Bauer's campaign was deep in debt even as he won his eye-catching fourth-place finish in the August 1999 Iowa straw poll, so much so that it had to delay the payment of several sizable bills.

Some of the most prominent donors to Bauer's conservative causes are sitting out his presidential bid. Dick DeVos, the president of Amway Corporation, footed much of the bill for the Family Research Council's posh new Washington headquarters. But DeVos has said that while he will continue to underwrite Bauer's causes, he will back another presidential candidate. DeVos's wife, Elisabeth (Betsy), chairs the Michigan Republican Party and could not endorse a candidate in the primary. But the DeVoses flew to Austin, Texas, for a private dinner with Governor George W. Bush and reportedly were impressed. Bauer's hard-line stance against trade with China may have cost him the couple's support; Amway does hundreds of millions of dollars worth of business in China each year and has made clear its disagreement with Bauer on this issue.

Bauer has been extremely successful, however, at attracting legions of small-dollar donors who support his church-and-family social agenda. By the fall of 1999 he had built a base of some 50,000 mostly small donors; the size of the average contribution to Bauer's campaign was $47. Through the first half of 1999, roughly 84 percent of Bauer's campaign donors had given no more than $200. By contrast, only 41 percent of Bush's donors fell into that category.

Stephen and Sylvia Slifko are Bauer's No. 1 career patrons, and they are also supporting his presidential bid. Highly visible within the national right-to-life movement, the Ohio couple has given Bauer's causes a total of at least $33,000. They are best known for their public 1993 offer to adopt a teenager who was left in a persistent vegetative state after an automobile accident. With the help of the anti-abortion group Operation Rescue, the Slifkos tried to reverse a judge's decision to allow the fifteen-year-old's food and water tubes to be disconnected.

Orville and Ruth Merillat, Bauer's No. 3 career patrons, have given at least $32,100 to Bauer-connected causes over the years. They are the founders of Merillat Industries, Inc., the nation's largest manufacturer of cabinets. They are also regular donors to conservative Republicans, including former Representative Robert Dornan of California, Senator Jesse Helms of North Carolina, and former Vice President Dan Quayle.

Members of the boards of Bauer's various not-for-profit organizations have predictably been consistent supporters of his efforts. Lee Eaton, who's been a vice chairman of the Family Research Council, has, along with members of his family, given at least $26,000; Larry Smith, a director, of the council, has, along with his wife, given more than $24,000. Eaton is a Kentucky businessman and horse breeder who backed the Bush-Quayle ticket in 1988 and Buchanan in 1996. Smith runs a family-owned investment company in Newport Beach, California.

Smith is also one of several Bauer supporters who's tackling the tough job of recruiting new money. He is assembling a committee, each member of which is charged with finding ten $250 donors. Each of those ten donors must find ten more donors, and so on. Such political newcomers are the most valuable donors in politics. They tend to contribute repeatedly, and mailing lists filled with their names fetch high prices once the campaign is over.

Among the newcomers in Bauer's column are John and Margaret Whitlock of Richmond, Virginia, who, along with other family members, have given at least $33,000 to his causes. William and

Nora Bolthouse of Bakersfield, California, the owners of Bolthouse Farms, Inc., a third-generation family firm that's one of the nation's leading carrot producers, have given $22,000 to Bauer's efforts.

Throughout the second half of 1999, Bauer adroitly maneuvered himself as the heir to Pat Buchanan's position as favorite son of the Religious Right. It's a move he's been preparing for ever since he left the White House.

At both the Family Research Council and the Campaign for Working Families, Bauer fashioned powerful communications networks that have operated below the radar of the national news media—and sometimes even of his Republican rivals. Most months, more than 400,000 Americans get a letter from Gary Bauer. "That's a lot more devoted supporters around the country than a lot of Senators have," William Kristol, a former Quayle aide who's a close friend of Bauer's and now the publisher of *The Weekly Standard*, a conservative magazine, told a reporter for the *New York Times*.

Bauer has remained close to rank-and-file Christian conservatives by staying true to the cause and by showing his sense of humor. At several campaign stops in Iowa, for example, he promised his audiences that if he were elected, they would not only receive an invitation to his inauguration, but would also be invited to stay overnight in the Lincoln Bedroom.

Bauer also has organized a network of thousands of Americans to pray for him every day. Participants in Bauer's "prayerful pursuit of the presidency" receive crib sheets suggesting what they should beseech the Lord to do for Brother Bauer. One day they prayed for Bauer to "be protected from the fiery darts of opponents, the media, and opposition groups." Another day they asked the Holy Spirit to "protect the Bauer Team from deception and misperception."

Bauer isn't alone in directing the prayers of his supporters. James Dobson, the Colorado-based radio-show host who put Bauer in charge of the Family Research Council more than a decade ago, could steer as many as a million votes in Bauer's direction. This fact has not been lost on Bauer. "I talk to Jim almost every day," Bauer told a writer for *The Washington Monthly*. "He certainly cannot endorse candidates through Focus on the Family, but he has individually endorsed candidates in the past."

But the thing that endears Bauer to the Religious Right more than any other is neither his direct-mail savvy nor his heaven-and-earth alliances. What conservative Christians love most about Bauer is the way he routinely nips at the heels of the mainstream Republican power brokers who, they feel, have sold them out time and again. The way many religious conservatives see it, President George Bush and Senator Robert Dole both wooed them during the primaries and then dumped them at the altar of the Republican National Convention. Now they believe George W. Bush is doing the date-and-ditch dance one more time.

Gary Bauer has emerged as the conservative David against the GOP Goliath. While Dole and others within the party mainstream fattened their campaign war chests with money from "sin industries" such as gambling and tobacco, Bauer blasted the party for taking tobacco money and fired back with a slingshot called the National Gambling Impact Study Commission. (Kay Coles James, a former vice president of the Family Research Council, chaired the congressionally created commission, and Dobson was one of the other eight members.) And while other would-be conservatives latched on to Malcolm "Steve" Forbes, Jr.'s flat-tax proposal, Bauer attacked it on the grounds that it would tax families while giving corporations a free ride.

And then there's China. Bauer argues that the world's most populous nation "brutalizes its own people, steals American nuclear secrets, threatens America, Taiwan, and its own Asian neighbors with ballistic missiles, and represses free expression and religious liberty." While most other Republicans support the party's free-trade orientation, Bauer would refuse to renew China's most-favored-nation status and would deny it membership in the World Trade Organization.

Bauer frequently likens his stance against China to Reagan's notoriously rigid stand against the "Evil Empire." Yet in lobbying for religious freedom and human rights in China, Bauer has dined with Richard Gere and the Kennedys, held a press conference with leaders of the AFL-CIO, strategized with House Democratic Leader Richard Gephardt, and teamed up with former California governor and Democratic presidential candidate Edmund G. (Jerry) Brown, Jr.—now the mayor of Oakland, California—to debate GOP bigwigs. "[Brown] was quite eloquent about the religious persecution issue," Bauer told *Mother Jones* magazine. "I'm looking across the table at Henry Kissinger, Trent Lott, and William F. Buckley, Jr., and thinking, 'What's wrong with this picture?'"

Nothing, say Bauer's supporters. They know his candidacy is a long shot at best. But he's doing exactly what they expect of him: He's just doing his conservative thing until someone tells him to stop.

GARY BAUER
Top Ten Career Patrons

Ranking	Company/Individual/Family Name	Total
1	Stephen and Sylvia Slifko family, Barberton, Ohio	$33,000
1	Whitlock family, Richmond and Mineral, Virginia	$33,000
3	Merillat family, Adrian, Michigan	$32,100
4	Eaton family, Fort Lauderdale, Florida and Lexington, Kentucky	$26,000
5	Larry and Margie Smith, Newport Beach, California	$24,172
6	Miller Energy, Inc., Portage, Michigan	$24,000
6	John and Carolyn Saeman, Denver	$24,000
8	William and Nora Bolthouse, Bakersfield, California	$22,000
9	John and Nancy Gordon, Grand Rapids, Michigan	$20,000
10	Bagnoli family, New Providence, New Jersey	$18,500

This list is based on individual and PAC contributions to Campaign for Working Families PAC from 1995–1998; individual and PAC contributions to Bauer's presidential campaign through June 30, 1999, and all contributions to the Campaign for Working Families PAC Virginia account.

Sources: Federal Election Commission; Center for Responsive Politics; Virginia State Board of Elections.

George W. Bush

||||||||||

On January 30, 1990, *Platt's Oilgram News,* a respected trade journal of the petroleum industry, reported that a subsidiary of a small, Dallas-based independent oil company, Harken Energy Corporation, had just signed an agreement with the government of Bahrain. "Harken Bahrain Oil Company signed a production sharing contract today," the article announced, "that gave the company exclusive rights to carry out exploration, development, production, transportation, and marketing of petroleum throughout most of Bahrain's Gulf offshore areas."

That the government of Bahrain, and its state-owned petroleum franchise, Bahrain National Oil Company, or Banoco, should choose tiny Harken Energy to explore for oil off its coast came as something of a surprise to industry experts. Amoco, the global oil giant, had also wanted the contract, and Chevron Corporation, another multinational, had advised the Bahraini government on choosing an American company for the venture.

Harken Energy had fewer than a thousand employees, and no experience whatsoever in international oil production. The company had confined its activities entirely to the domestic production of oil, and to expanding itself through the acquisition of troubled oil U.S. produces at bargain-basement prices. And it was so cash poor that it didn't even have enough capital to drill for oil without bringing in well-heeled partners to finance the exploration.

Even more surprising, Harken hadn't even actively sought the deal.

"It was not our intention to seek out international opportunities," Monte Swetnam, the president of Harken Exploration Company, the Bahrain-based subsidiary of Harken, told *World Oil,* another industry trade publication. "However, we were introduced to officials in Bahrain and were able to present our credentials to them. And from that, a relationship developed . . . that has evolved into one of mutual respect, ultimately resulting in signing the production-sharing contract."

The relationship promised Harken more than respect. The offshore fields were bordered on one side by a Saudi Arabian deposit with proven reserves of about 7 billion barrels, and a field belonging to Qatar with 2 billion barrels. The Bahraini offshore reserves had the potential to be enormous.

Harken Energy was in the right place at the right time. But it had something else—the right name. In January 1991 a global coalition led by President George Bush had mobilized an enormous military force to drive Saddam Hussein and the Iraqi army out of Kuwait. Another George Bush—the son of the President of the United States—was a director and shareholder of Harken Energy.

The few press reports about the deal questioned the motives of the government of Bahrain for making the deal with Harken Energy. Even the *Wall Street Journal,* customarily reserved on such matters, reported in a page-one analysis of the contract in December 1991 that it "raises the question of . . . an effort to cozy up to a presidential son."

Bush says that he pulled no strings to win the contract, and that he in fact opposed the deal, but his presence may have been enough. According to Swetnam, the Bahrainis knew that Bush was on the company's board of directors and "were clearly aware he was the President's son."

Alas for Harken, the Bush name wasn't magical enough to ensure a strike off the coast of Bahrain. The company drilled two dry holes. Bush himself fared better. He sold off two-thirds of his holdings in Harken for nearly a million dollars, and bought a small share of the Texas Rangers, a deal that ultimately netted him—with a helping hand from Texas taxpayers—some $15 million.

Which is all par for the course for the front-runner for the Republican presidential nomination. Whenever he's struck a dry hole, someone has always been willing to fill it with money for him. Throughout his long business career and in his six years as governor of Texas, Bush has relied on family connections, sweet-heart deals, and the inside track to build a fortune. And Bush, both in private life and since he became governor of Texas, has always been willing to return the favors.

Governor George W. Bush makes a lot of his Texas childhood. He proudly boasts of his tenure at San Jacinto Junior High School in Midland, Texas. But the first place he ever lived was next door to the president of Yale University.

Yale was like a second home for the Bushes of Greenwich. Bush's grandfather, Senator Prescott Bush, graduated from Yale. So did his uncles Prescott Jr. and Jonathan. When Bush was born in New Haven on July 6, 1946, his father, George H.W. Bush, was finishing his college degree there.

Bush returned to Yale himself in 1964. He wasn't quite the all-around scholar-athlete his father had been, but he was elected the president of his fraternity and invited to join the exclusive and secretive Skull & Bones Society.

When Bush graduated in 1968, he faced the prospect of being sent to Vietnam, but avoided combat by joining the National Guard. At the time, the Guard had 100,000 applicants on its wait-ing list. But Bush was sworn in as a member of the 147th unit of the Texas Air National Guard the same day he applied. Ben Barnes, who was then the Speaker of the Texas House of Representatives, recently said under oath that he secured a spot in the guard for the young Bush at the urging of Sid Adger, a Houston businessman and close friend of Bush's father, then a U.S. Representative from Houston. Bush wasn't the only son of a prominent Texan in his unit. Others included the sons of Senators Lloyd Bentsen (a Demo-crat) and John Tower (a Republican), and at least seven members of the Dallas Cowboys football team.

The only battle Bush fought during those years was on the

home front. He says that he struggled to establish an identity separate from his famous father, who went on to become the chairman of the Republican National Committee, chief of the U.S. Liaison Office in China, and director of the Central Intelligence Agency under President Ford. Young George's identity crisis reportedly reached its climax one night in Midland when he was confronted by his father for taking his brother Neil, then fifteen, out drinking. Bush, the story goes, challenged his father with the words, "Do you want to go mano a mano right here?"

But there was never really any doubt that Bush would hew to the family path. At that point, he was already talking to friends about running for the Texas statehouse. After being rejected from the University of Texas law school, he enrolled in Harvard Business School. Two years later, MBA in hand, he returned to Midland to find his own fortune in the oil fields, just as his father had done twenty-seven years earlier. Bush had no experience, but he had $13,000 in seed money from his parents and a network of well-heeled family friends, who became the principal financiers of his oil ventures.

Before going into business, however, Bush took a quick detour into politics. In 1978 he ran for a seat in the U.S. House of Representatives from Midland after hurriedly assembling all the trappings of a candidate. In one year he started a business, Arbusto Energy, Inc. (Arbusto is Spanish for Bush); married Laura Welch, a librarian who grew up in Midland; and bought a house in the district of retiring Representative George Mahon. Don Evans, his best friend and fellow Texas oil man ran the campaign.

Bush lost the election, but won the confidence of relatives and family friends who agreed to gamble on Arbusto. Owing to the huge losses its limited partners sustained, Bush's wildcat operation doubled as a tax shelter.

From 1979 to 1983 some fifty individuals pumped at least $4.7 million into Arbusto and its successor, Bush Exploration. Among them were some of his father's most durable political supporters, who guaranteed that the shaky company stayed afloat. John Macomber, the chief executive officer of Celanese Corporation, invested $79,500, and William Draper III, a venture capitalist, put in $93,000. Macomber, a friend of Bush's uncle Jonathan

Bush, would go on to serve as the president of the Export-Import Bank of the United States under President Reagan, and Draper would land the same job under President Bush.

George Ohrstrom and his wife invested $100,000 in Arbusto. Ohrstrom had attended Greenwich Country Day in Connecticut with Bush's father. Ohrstrom was a business partner of Philip Uzielli, a wealthy investor and the owner of Executive Resources, a company based first in the Dutch West Indies and later in Panama. Uzielli put $50,000 into one of the early Arbusto partnerships. In January 1982, his company bought ten percent of Arbusto's stock for a cool $1 million. The investment made Uzielli Arbusto's largest benefactor, a privilege he paid well for. The million-dollar purchase price was at least three times more than the stock he bought was worth. Uzielli, incidentally, had another connection to the Bush clan besides Ohrstrom. He'd been a close friend of James Baker III, who was intimately involved in the elder Bush's political career, ever since the two had been classmates at Princeton University. Baker managed Bush's presidential campaign in 1980 and was Secretary of State during Bush's sole term as President.

Russell Reynolds, Jr., the founder of his own executive search firm, Russell Reynolds Associates, put up $23,250. H. Leland Getz, who co-founded the firm, invested twice as much—$46,500. "These are all the Bushes' pals," Reynolds once said of Arbusto's backers. "This is the A-Team."

Reynolds knew whereof he spoke. He'd gone to Yale with George W.'s uncle Jonathan Bush, an investment manager and New York Republican Party official who lined up most of Arbusto's backers. Many of them were already clients of his, and he charged his usual commission for recruiting them. Jonathan Bush, who tapped Reynolds for a turn with Yale's a capella group, the Wiffenpoofs, would later take a turn on the board of directors of Russell Reynolds Associates. Reynolds, a former finance chairman of the Connecticut Republican Party, also raised $4 million for Vice President Bush's 1988 presidential campaign. "In Greenwich," he told an interviewer last year, "the Bush family are absolute tops."

Investing in Arbusto, however, turned out to be the absolute pits. By April 1984, Arbusto had drilled ninety-five holes, with forty-seven yielding oil, three yielding natural gas, and forty-five that were dry. The company had returned only $1.5 million to its investors. "The bottom line is it didn't work out very well with Arbusto," Russell recalled. "I think we got maybe twenty cents on the dollar."

Philip Uzielli tried to shore things up by buying another ten percent stake for $150,000, but to no avail. "We lost a lot of money in the oil business," Uzielli told a reporter for the *Wall Street Journal* in 1991. "We had a lot of dry wells. . . . Things were terrible. It was dreadful."

But the A-Team was willing to take a bath to help out a Bush. "We wrote the money off the minute we invested," said Stephen Kass, a classmate of Bush's at Harvard Business School. Trying to capitalize on that sentiment, Bush changed the name of the company from Arbusto to Bush Exploration in 1982. His father had been Vice President for more than a year at the time.

But the name change didn't help. The world price of oil was collapsing, and even the savviest of the independent oil companies were hard hit. The less savvy were going bankrupt. By 1984 the only way Bush could save his business was to find yet another well-heeled partner. This time he turned to an old Yale classmate of his, William DeWitt, Jr., who owned Spectrum 7 Energy Corporation, an Ohio oil exploration company. DeWitt came from a wealthy background; his father once owned the Cincinnati Reds baseball club. DeWitt and his investment partner, Mercer Reynolds, later became donors to the elder Bush's 1988 presidential campaign and to the Republican National Committee.

The two men also took care of the son. Rather than invest in Bush Exploration, they bought it out. And they didn't just pay for the office furniture. As part of the deal, Bush became Spectrum 7's chief executive officer, at an annual salary of $75,000, and got 1.1 million shares of the company's stock. Unfortunately for DeWitt and Reynolds, Bush turned Spectrum 7 into a money-losing enterprise. Two years after the merger, in 1986, world oil prices fell even further. Bush needed another bailout, and fast. He found a willing savior in Harken Oil and Gas, an oil exploration company based in Dallas.

Despite the fact that Spectrum 7 had posted losses of $400,000 just six months earlier and carried $3 million in debt, Bush and his partners received $2 million worth of Harken stock. Bush's cut was worth about $500,000. Bush also became a director, and he was paid as much as $120,000 in consulting fees plus $131,250 in stock options even though he spent much of 1987 and 1988 working on his father's presidential campaign. That was fine with Harken; unlike DeWitt, Bush's new benefactor wasn't interested in having him run the company.

"His name was George Bush," Phil Kendrick, Harken's founder, said. "That was worth the money they paid him."

Stuart Watson, who was a member of Harken's board of directors at the time of the Spectrum deal, echoed that view in a 1994 interview with a reporter for the *Dallas Morning News*. "George was very useful to Harken," Watson said. "He would have been more so if he had had funds, but as far as contacts were concerned, he was terrific."

Indeed, once Bush signed on, business at Harken began to pick up.

When Harken bought out Spectrum 7, the company was broke and desperately needed a cash infusion. As the talks with Spectrum 7 progressed, Harken officials were lining up a major new financial backer: Harvard Management Company, Inc. The investment firm's only client is Harvard University; it manages the school's multibillion-dollar endowment.

A month after Bush came on board, Harvard Management agreed to invest at least $20 million in Harken. It would eventually come to own some ten million shares of Harken's stock, making it one of the company's largest investors.

The Bush name may have helped seal the deal.

Michael Eisenson, a partner in Harvard Management Company who sat on Harken's board of directors, said that he and other Harvard officials picked Harken after reviewing several proposals from energy companies. "Harken management seemed capable and honest," Eisenson said.

The Bush name certainly would have made an impression on Eisenson's boss, Robert Stone, Jr., who was one of Harvard Management's directors. Stone was "the driving force" behind Harvard's Southwest oil and gas investments, according to Scott Sperling, who worked with Eisenson at Harvard. Stone himself was a player in the Texas oil and gas industry; at the time, he was the chairman of Kirby Exploration, an oil and gas transportation company based in Houston. As a longtime resident of Greenwich, Connecticut, he also knew the Bushes. His father-in-law, Godfrey Rockefeller, had invested in George Bush's oil drilling ventures in the late 1940s. Stone's brother, Galen L. Stone, was the U.S. envoy to Cyprus during the first Reagan-Bush Administration. In 1980 and 1988 he contributed to the elder Bush's presidential campaigns. And like Bush's uncle Jonathan, Stone had been on the board of directors of Russell Reynolds Associates. (Stone did not return the Center's phone calls)

In a recent interview, Scott Sperling told the Center that he doesn't recall Harken as "an investment that had come specifically recommended by any board member."

But according to Bing Sung, who was an investment manager at Harvard Management Company until 1986, "You just don't knock on the door of a major endowment, which Harvard certainly was, and say, 'Listen, I've got a great idea and I want to present it to the board,' . . . unless you have an in."

Harken was Harvard Management's first major investment in Texas wildcat operations, a part of the university's investment history it would rather forget. The investments in oil and gas would eventually generate nearly $200 million in losses for the endowment.

The university's commitment to Harken was surprising in view of the bad shape the company was in. "I took some time and looked at it and I went, God, I don't want to be anywhere near this," a prospective investor in Harken from the late 1980s told the Center. "This thing looks like a train wreck."

By Harken executives' own accounts, the company's financial statements were "a mess" and "a fast numbers game." But insiders insist that Harvard's money managers wouldn't have kept pumping money into Harken if they didn't think it would become profitable.

For a time, they had reason to believe it would.

The Bahrain agreement, announced on January 30, 1990, seemed to justify Harvard's enthusiasm for Harken. While Bush said he had no role in securing the deal, and added that he had argued against it, his wealthy patrons certainly ensured that Harken could pull it off.

Bass Enterprises Production Company put up $25 million to finance the drilling. After Bass Enterprises invested in the Bahrain operation, paying for the exploration that would eventually produce two dry wells, Harvard Management upped its stake in Harken to 30 percent.

Bass Enterprises is part of the financial empire of the Bass brothers of Fort Worth, two of whom became members of Team 100, an elite club of big donors to the Republican National Committee, during the elder Bush's 1988 presidential campaign. The Bass family has been generous to the son as well; it ranks No. 5 among Bush's career patrons, having contributed more than $273,000 to him. All four Bass brothers—Sid, Robert, Edward, and Lee—attended Yale, as did their father, Perry Bass. Edward was enrolled at the Ivy League school at the same time as George W. Bush.

In August 1990, Harken posted a $23 million loss from its consolidated operations, sending its share price down from $3 to a year-end low of $2.37. Bush, however, avoided the downturn in the company's fortunes. Two months earlier, on June 22, 1990, he had unloaded 212,140 shares, or about two-thirds of his holdings, for $848,560.

As a director of the company, Bush was required to promptly report the stock sale to the Securities and Exchange Commission. He did—eight months late. Bush later claimed he had indeed reported the transaction in a timely manner, but that somehow the paperwork had been lost. Whatever the case, the eight-month delay attracted the attention of SEC investigators. The timing of the transaction seemed too good to be true.

As a member of Harken's audit committee, Bush was familiar with the company's finances and was aware that it was about to restructure its debt—a move that would depress its share price. In addition, he may have been alerted that the company was about to post a huge loss. In April 1991 the SEC launched an insider-trading investigation of Bush. The outcome of the probe raised more questions than it answered.

When the investigation began, the chairman of the SEC was

Richard Breeden, who had been appointed by President Bush. Before joining the SEC, Breeden had for several years been the President's economic policy adviser. Bush even thanked Breeden by name in several speeches. Breeden's office at the SEC was adorned with so many pictures of President and Mrs. Bush that a reporter for the *New York Times* observed, "George Bush is Breeden's Mao." Before going to the White House, Breeden had been a partner in Baker & Botts, the law firm started by the grandfather of James A. Baker III, President Bush's Secretary of State.

The SEC's general counsel at the time, who would be ultimately responsible for any litigation the commission would initiate, was James Doty. Doty had also worked at Baker & Botts, where he represented the younger Bush in business related to his stake in the Texas Rangers baseball team.

In addition to collecting reams of documents, investigators for the SEC interviewed Harken's lawyer as well as the broker who'd sold Bush's stock. Then, in 1993, the agency dropped the investigation. William McLucas, the director of the SEC's enforcement division, said "there was no case there." (McLucas had been promoted to the job of being the SEC's top cop by Breeden.) But in a letter to George W. Bush announcing the agency's decision, McLucas's deputy, Bruce Hiler, wrote that the end of the probe "must in no way be construed as indicating that the party has been exonerated or that no action may ultimately result from the staff's investigation."

Bush, who by then was running for governor of Texas, gave the letter his own spin. "The SEC fully investigated the stock deal," he said in October 1994. "I was exonerated." Since 1993, Breeden, Doty, and other lawyers at Baker & Botts have given Bush $182,050, making the firm his No. 13 career patron.

One of the questions the SEC didn't answer was who bought Bush's stock.

In his statement of intent to sell, which Bush also had to file with the SEC, he said he was putting his 212,140 shares on the open market. That was nearly twenty times the daily volume of stock that traded on average during June 1990; without a buyer willing to absorb such a large block of stock, the share price would have plummeted.

Under questioning by SEC investigators, Ralph Smith, a Los Angeles broker with Sutro & Company, who handled the sale, said that he solicited the shares at the behest of an institutional investor, which he didn't name.

The available evidence suggests that the investor was Harvard. The university increased its holdings in Harken around that time. No new institutional investors appeared on the scene. At the bottom of a spreadsheet Smith used to record his calls to Bush was the name of Michael Eisenson, along with the telephone number of Harvard Management. (Eisenson did not return the Center's telephone calls.)

If Harvard was the institutional investor that bought Bush's stock, it would be the second time in his career that Bush was bailed out by his alma mater. Bush needed the money from the sale to secure his stake in the Texas Rangers baseball team, an investment he believed would propel him into politics, and that would ultimately bring him $15 million.

When Bush first embarked on the deal to buy the Texas Rangers in 1988, he already had his eye on the governor's mansion in Austin. But he knew that to have a shot at winning, he would need better credentials than a string of unsuccessful oil companies and a failed bid for a seat in the U.S. House of Representatives. In 1989 he told *Time* magazine, "My biggest liability in Texas is the question, 'What's the boy ever done?' He could be riding on Daddy's name."

But his father's connections were instrumental in helping Bush overcome that perception. Back in 1973, when his father was the chairman of the RNC, Bush befriended one of his father's assistants, Karl Rove. Rove cut his teeth alongside the senior Bush's chief political strategist, Lee Atwater. Rove would become George W.'s own Atwater, helping to run his 1978 bid for Congress and laying the groundwork for his 1994 run for governor. As the Rangers deal got underway, Rove told Bush that baseball was his ticket to the big-time. "It gives him . . . exposure and gives him something that will be easily recalled by people," Rove said.

Rove's calculation turned out to be right on the money.

It all began in the fall of 1988, when William DeWitt, Jr.,

Bush's partner in Spectrum 7, called to let him know that Eddie Chiles, the owner of the Texas Rangers, was looking for a buyer. Chiles, a family friend who called Bush "Young Pup" when he was a kid, was eager to sell to Bush. And so Bush and DeWitt quickly assembled a team of investors. They hit a snag when Peter Ueberroth, the commissioner of Major League Baseball, told them he wouldn't approve the sale without more investors from Texas. Ueberroth believed that local owners would be less likely to relocate the team. The commissioner, a GOP donor himself, wanted the deal approved before his term expired at the end of 1989, and so he and American League president Bobby Brown took it on themselves to line up Fort Worth financier Richard E. Rainwater.

Rainwater and Bush weren't exactly strangers. Rainwater was a contributor to his father's presidential campaigns and, later, an overnight guest in the Bush White House. Until 1986 he was the chief money manager for the Bass brothers, the Fort Worth billionaires who financed Harken's drilling in Bahrain. By 1988, Rainwater was managing his own fortune. He agreed to put money in the Rangers, but only if his trusted associate, Edward "Rusty" Rose, was installed as general managing partner along with Bush.

With this arrangement in place, Bush and his partners bought the team from Chiles on April 21, 1989, for $86 million. To scrape together his $500,000 stake in the Rangers, Bush borrowed the money from a bank in Midland where he once was a director. He owned 1.8 percent of the Rangers. (He later invested an additional $106,302).

Bush made up for his minor stake by taking more than his share of credit for bringing the owners together. "I wasn't going to let this deal fail," he said last year. "I wanted to put together the group. I was tenacious."

Others close to the deal paint a different picture.

"George W. Bush deserves great credit for the development of the franchise," Ueberroth said. "However, the bringing together of the buying group was the result of Richard Rainwater, Rusty Rose, Dr. Bobby Brown, and the commissioner."

Nonetheless, Bush's partners rewarded him by upping his ownership stake in the Rangers, giving him another ten percent of the team.

"He had a well-known name, and that created interest in the franchise," Tom Schieffer, the Rangers president, said last year. "It gave us a little celebrity."

Usually parked in a front-row seat by the dugout, with his feet up and a bag of peanuts perched in his lap, Bush put a congenial face on a crooked deal, at the heart of which lay a complicated land play.

When they bought the team, the Rangers were playing in an old minor-league stadium. It didn't have the fancy sky boxes and other amenities that helped make other franchises much more profitable. As a result the team couldn't compete with other big-city teams for good players. But the new owners weren't willing to finance the construction of a new ballpark. They decided to hit up taxpayers for the money.

First, the new owners threatened to move the team out of Arlington, Texas, sending local officials scurrying to put together a deal they couldn't refuse. Under the resulting agreement, the taxpayers of Arlington would raise $135 million, the bulk of the cost of construction, through a hike in sales taxes. During a campaign to sell the sales tax increase to Arlington voters, Mayor Richard Greene said the team owners would put $50 million of their own money into the deal up front. It didn't quite work out that way; the owners raised a hefty portion of their down payment from fans, through a one dollar surcharge on tickets.

The city spent $150,000 on an advertising campaign to persuade voters. Opponents of the deal couldn't compete with glossy brochures, telemarketing calls, and a "Hands Around Arlington Day." On January 19, 1991, citizens of Arlington voted two-to-one to approve a sales-tax increase dedicated to building the new park.

Between the sales-tax revenue, state tax exemptions, and other financial incentives, Texas taxpayers handed the privately owned Rangers more than $200 million in public subsidies. Taxpayers didn't get a return from the stadium's surging new revenues, either. The profits went almost exclusively to the team's already wealthy owners.

The stadium's lease is a case in point. Unlike an apartment tenant, the rent that the team's owners pay is applied toward purchasing the stadium. The maximum yearly rent and maintenance fees for the Rangers are $5 million; the total purchase price for the Ballpark at Arlington is $60 million. Thus, after twelve years the owners will have bought the stadium for less than half of what taxpayers spent on it.

But Bush and his partners weren't satisfied lining their pockets with average Texans' hard-earned cash. They wanted land around the stadium to further boost its value. To that end, they orchestrated a land grab that shortchanged local landowners by several million dollars.

As part of the deal, the city created a separate corporation, the Arlington Sports Facilities Development Authority (ASFDA), to manage construction. Using authority granted to it by the city, ASFDA seized several tracts of land around the stadium site for parking and future development.

While on paper ASFDA was a public entity, in practice it was merely a puppet for Bush and his partners. According to documents obtained by the Center, the owners would identify the land they wanted to acquire. A Rangers owner, realtor Mike Reilly, would then offer to buy the parcels for prices he set, which in several cases were well below what the owners believed their property was worth. If the landowners refused to sell to the Rangers at the offered price, ASFDA could take possession of their land and leave the price to be determined in court.

Several of the landowners took ASFDA to court over the seizures and won settlements totaling $11 million. In a final insult to taxpayers, the Rangers resisted paying the settlements, trying to pass off yet another cost to Arlington residents. (In 1999 the Rangers, under new ownership, finally agreed to pay up.)

When confronted with the seamy details of the land grab, Bush professed ignorance. But Tom Schieffer, the team's president, has testified that he kept Bush aware of the land transfers. In October 1990, Bush also let slip to a reporter for the *Fort Worth Star Telegram,* "The idea of making a land play, absolutely, to plunk the field down in the middle of a big piece of land, that's kind of always been the strategy."

It was a strategy that would have an enormous payoff for Bush personally.

After he became governor of Texas, Bush put all of his assets into a blind trust, with one notable exception: his stake in the Rangers. Schieffer kept Bush apprised of the owner's efforts to sell the team to Thomas Hicks, the chairman of Hicks, Muse, Tate and Furst, Inc., a firm that specializes in leveraged buyouts and owns AMFM, Inc., the nation's largest chain of radio stations. Hicks and employees of his companies are Bush's No. 4 career patron, having given him at least $290,400.

In 1998, Hicks helped provide Bush with an even greater windfall. He bought the Texas Rangers for $250 million, three times what Bush and his partners had paid ten years earlier. The new stadium and the real estate around it greatly boosted the final sale price. And, since his partners had upped Bush's stake in the team from 1.8 to 11.8 percent, his cut from the proceeds of the sale was $14.9 million, a twenty-five-fold return on his investment of $606,302. Rainwater, who had put far more money into the team than Bush, made $25 million.

Just as important as the cash, however, was the cachet that came with the deal's success. The Ballpark at Arlington finally opened in April 1994, just as Bush was running for governor. He touted the new stadium as a win-win proposition for taxpayers and the team. "Am I going to benefit off it financially?" he asked reporters. He answered his own question: "I hope so." Four years later, everyone would know by how much.

In his first race for political office in sixteen years, Bush showed that he had learned a lot all those years on the sidelines of his father's campaigns. He went up against Governor Ann Richards, a sharp-tongued Texas Democrat who, at the 1988 Democratic National Convention, took a shot at his father by saying, "Poor George, he can't help it, he was born with a silver foot in his mouth." She gave the younger George much the same treatment with nicknames like "shrub" (little Bush). But Bush didn't respond. Instead he stayed on four themes: frivolous lawsuits, welfare reform, juvenile justice, and education. His focus prompted Richards to comment years later, "If you said to George, 'What time is it?' he would say, 'We must teach our children to read.' " But his message reached voters, and in November they elected him with nearly 54 percent of the vote.

When Bush moved into the governor's mansion in January 1995, he arrived indebted to dozens of industries and wealthy patrons. He repaid some of his supporters with choice political appointments.

One of the most prestigious of political appointments in Texas is a seat on the University of Texas Board of Regents. The board is filled with Bush's top-dollar donors. The chair of the U.T. Regents is Donald Evans, Bush's old friend and longtime fund-raiser who, as the finance chairman for Bush's presidential bid, has overseen the campaign's record-shattering fund-raising drive.

Evans is the chief executive officer of Tom Brown, Inc., an oil and gas company based in Midland, Texas. In 1989, Bush joined the board as an outside director. He received $12,000 a year plus stock options for attending several meetings and participating in conference calls. He also sat on the compensation committee that boosted Evans's salary by $75,000 and awarded him a bonus of $35,000 before Bush left the company in 1994. Shortly after he was elected governor of Texas, Bush sold his Tom Brown holdings for a profit of $297,550.

Another regent and top Bush patron is A.R. "Tony" Sanchez, the chairman and chief executive officer of Sanchez-O'Brien Oil and Gas Corporation. Sanchez started the company with his father and his father's business partner in 1974, after they discovered a major natural-gas source. Sanchez and his mother also own a controlling stake in International Bancshares Corporation, the holding company of International Bank of Commerce, a Texas banking chain founded by his father in 1966. Over Bush's career, Sanchez, members of his family, and employees of his companies have given him at least $320,150, making them his No. 2 career patron.

But Bush owed few people more than Richard Rainwater, the Fort Worth financier. "[Rainwater] just loves to make people rich," observed Alfred Checci, the former chairman of Northwest Airlines, who worked with Rainwater in the early 1980s. That's a passion Rainwater has had ample opportunity to indulge. When Rainwater started with the Bass brothers in 1970, they had an inheritance of $50 million. When he left in 1986, the family fortune had grown to at least $4 billion.

Rainwater provided much the same service for Bush. He was

the man behind the Rangers deal that would ultimately net Bush a profit of more than $15 million. And when Bush was first elected governor, more than 60 percent of his income came from businesses in which he and Rainwater were partners, according to his 1994 financial disclosure statement.

Rainwater himself hails from modest roots. His father was a wholesale grocer and his mother worked at JCPenney to put him through school. At fifty-five, he still likes to cut million-dollar deals in faded jeans, tasseled loafers, and a baseball cap rather than a business suit.

Getting his name on a plaque wasn't going to cut it for the governor's personal rainmaker. With Bush in Austin, Rainwater soon found himself awash in potential windfalls. While some never materialized, many did.

One of Rainwater's first ventures after leaving Bass Enterprises was the creation of Columbia/HCA, Inc., which is now the nation's largest for-profit hospital chain. Columbia/HCA's operations were controversial from the start. Physicians at the hospital chain have a financial stake in the operation, which critics say carries the risk that they will put their own profits ahead of patient care. In 1997, federal agents raided Columbia/HCA facilities in Florida, Texas, and other states as part of an investigation, still ongoing, into whether the company had defrauded the federal government out of millions of dollars in Medicare reimbursements. The FBI, the Internal Revenue Service, and the Department of Health and Human Services are all involved in the probe.

In 1995, Bush vetoed a Patient Protection Act that, among other things, spelled out the obligations hospitals and health-care providers have to those who need medical care. In a written statement explaining his veto decision, the governor argued that the bill "unfairly impacts some health care providers while exempting others." He ultimately instructed his Insurance Commissioner to implement many of the bill's provisions as new state regulations. One notable exception was a provision that would have cut into the profits of Columbia/HCA.

The provision in question would have required health maintenance organizations to let patients see doctors outside their own networks. Giving patients this choice would undermine Columbia/

HCA's ability to hammer out agreements with hospital maintenance organizations (HMOs) and preferred provider organizations (PPOs).

In 1997, Bush proposed in his biannual budget that the state look into privatizing Texas's mental-health hospitals, just as Rainwater was in the midst of building a mental-health-care chain. Rainwater launched an investment company in 1994, Crescent Real Estate Equities Company. Besides Rainwater, Crescent's management team included Bush's fellow Rangers owners Gerald Haddock and John Goff and Rangers lawyer William Miller. In 1997, Crescent purchased ninety-five mental-health hospitals from Magellan Health Care Services of Atlanta, and also became a fifty-fifty partner in Magellan's Charter Behavioral Health Systems. It quickly became the nation's largest provider of private mental-health-care services. The governor's proposal was never enacted. Charter Behavioral struggled for profitability, and Crescent's plan to buy out Magellan for sole ownership of the chain soon collapsed.

In 1997, Bush backed a plan to cut state property taxes that would have saved Crescent some $2.5 million in state taxes. Though the Texas House passed the proposal, the Texas Senate ended up scuttling it and passing a scaled-back version.

Later that year, however, Bush signed a bill into law that produced a $10 million windfall for Crescent, and millions more for Ross Perot, Jr., and Thomas Hicks, the leveraged buyout expert who bought the Rangers from Bush and his partners in 1998. Perot, who owns the Dallas Mavericks basketball team, and Hicks, who owns the Dallas Stars hockey team, wanted to build a new stadium to enhance the value of their teams.

Just as with the Rangers deal, Dallas taxpayers were to foot most of the bill for the new sports arena. But before city officials could negotiate with the team's owners, the state legislature had to pass a bill allowing cities to raise taxes to finance the project. While the bill wended its way through the Texas Legislature, Rainwater, through Crescent, bought a 12 percent stake in the Mavericks. Under the purchase agreement, Crescent will get $10 million when the arena is completed in the fall of 2001. Then the legislature passed the bill allowing the sales-tax hike and Bush signed it in June 1997.

When it comes to taxpayer money, Bush has been more than willing to use it to repay the largesse he's received over the years from his patrons. The Texas Teachers Retirement System, which manages the pension fund for the state's 800,000 public school teachers, sold two office buildings and a mortgage on a third to Crescent in 1996 and 1997 at a $70.4 million loss. As first reported by R.G. Ratcliffe of the *Houston Chronicle,* two of the sales were done without public bids, and the Teachers Retirement System refused to disclose what the initial bids were on the third. At the time of at least one of the sales, Bush owned about $100,000 worth of Crescent stock.

The University of Texas Investment Management Company (UTIMCO), which manages the state university system's $12 billion worth of assets, sank at least $8.9 million into Crescent Real Estate. The company's chairman is none other than Hicks. Under Hicks's watch, UTIMCO has steered close to $1.7 billion of its assets into private investments; a third of that money has gone into funds run either by his business partners or by Bush patrons.

In July 1998, a month after Hicks purchased the Rangers from Bush and his partners, he led a meeting of UTIMCO directors hundreds of miles away from UTIMCO's office, in the boardroom of the Ballpark at Arlington. There they approved a $96 million investment into Maverick Capital Fund of Dallas, a hedge fund run by Sam and Charles Wyly of Dallas. The Wyly brothers are ninth on Bush's list of career patrons.

Finally, nine years after its investment in Harken helped save Bush from financial ruin, Harvard Management Company got a deal on a piece of real estate it bought from the Texas Teachers Retirement System. In 1995 the TRS sold the Anatole Hotel in Dallas to a partnership that included the Crow family, which owns a controlling interest in Trammell Crow Company, one of the nation's top real estate management companies, and Harvard Management. Without taking bids, the TRS reportedly sold the hotel for $27 million less than it had spent to make improvements on the structure.

Harvard, Rainwater, and Hicks are not alone among Bush patrons who have received favors from the governor. Industries that have provided the bulk of Bush's campaign contributions have gotten his help in a variety of endeavors, from staving off pesky environmental regulations and shielding themselves from consumer lawsuits to driving off meddlesome investigators.

For three decades now, hundreds of electrical power, oil refining, and chemical plants have been pumping toxic particles into the air over Texas. These plants produce as much smog-forming nitrogen oxides as 18 million cars, making Texas the state with the largest volume of air pollution in the nation. The Texas Legislature passed the Texas Clean Air Act in 1971, but plants built before the law was passed don't have to comply with its rules.

In December 1996, staff members of the Texas Natural Resources and Conservation Commission (TNRCC), the state environmental agency, began meeting with representatives from eleven companies to talk about reducing the emissions of the plants that benefited from the grandfather clause. But when it looked like the commission was moving toward eliminating the exemption for those plants, energy-industry executives balked and headed straight for the governor's office.

On January 14, 1997, Bush's environmental director, John Howard, told his boss in a memo: "Industry has expressed concern that the TNRCC is moving too quickly and may rashly seek legislation this session."

In early March, Bush tapped Vic Beghini, an executive with Marathon Oil Company, and Ansel Condray, an executive with Exxon Corporation, to come up with a plan to let the industry comply voluntarily with the state's clean-air regulations.

According to documents obtained by the Sustainable Energy and Economic Development Coalition, an environmental group based in Austin, Beghini and Condray then presented the finished proposal at a June 19, 1997 meeting of about forty industry executives. In his notes of the meeting, James Kennedy of E.I. du Pont de Nemours and Company, the giant chemical manufacturer, wrote, "Amoco presented the paper to the group at the meeting as something that has been agreed to at high levels and was not subject to change."

If Kennedy felt a little left out of the process, the plan drafted by Beghini and Condray, and backed by Governor Bush, would shaft the public even more so. "The concept put forward was that the industry group and the Governor's Office would develop the program, then take it to some broad-based group, including public representatives, who would then tweak it a little bit and approve it," Kennedy noted.

Sure enough, on September 10, 1997, the TNRCC announced the formation of the Clean Air Responsibility Enterprise committee. The CARE committee's job was to come up with a voluntary program to reduce emissions from grandfathered facilities. But the CARE committee simply rubber-stamped the proposal that Exxon, Amoco, and Bush had already signed off on.

The smoke and mirrors weren't over yet. A list of incentives for companies that participated in the governor's plan sent to TNRCC commissioner Ralph Marquez from Howard suggested that "a recognition program for participants may be appropriate to encourage participation." Thus, industry would be rewarded with free publicity for complying with the new regulations that they had proposed.

On March 31, 1998, Bush appeared at a press conference flanked by executives of Exxon, Amoco, and Texas Utilities, among others, to announce that twenty-six companies—representing sixty of the 831 pollution-producing plants in the state, had pledged to reduce emissions by 15,000 tons a year. "We're committed," Bush said, "to clean air in the state of Texas."

But whether companies cut back on emissions didn't really matter to the governor or to the industry. Du Pont's Jim Kennedy had realized that way back at the June 19, 1997 meeting, where the plan was first presented. "The concept paper has no 'meat' with respect to actual emissions reductions," Kennedy wrote. "One of the leaders actually stated that emissions reductions was not a primary driver for the program."

As far as Bush was concerned, his voluntary compliance plan was already a rousing success, a model of public-private partnership good enough to take on the road to the presidential primaries. Three weeks after Bush announced that he was a candidate for President, his spokesman, Scott McClellan, boasted: "Governor Bush was the first governor in Texas to tell grandfathered industries, 'It's time to clean up.' Voluntary programs are working in Texas."

Well, not really. A study by the Environmental Defense Fund published six months after Bush's press conference found that only three of the twenty-six companies had actually scaled back their emissions. (In 1999, under increasing public pressure, Bush finally signed a bill that forces power plants to cut their emissions in half by 2003.)

The energy industry was still grateful for Bush's efforts. According to a study by Public Research Works, Bush raised $566,000 from the grandfathered polluters for his two gubernatorial campaigns. And from March 4, 1999, to March 31, 1999 Bush raised $316,300 from PACs, employees, lobbyists, and lawyers for grandfathered companies for his presidential campaign. They included: Enron (Bush's No. 1 career patron); Vinson & Elkins (Bush's No. 3 career patron), a law firm that represents Enron and Alcoa, a grandfathered polluter; and companies owned by the Bass family (Bush's No. 5 career patron). Another such company with grandfathered plants is Sterling Chemicals, Inc., a subsidiary of Sterling Group (Bush's No. 6 career patron). All told, the four patrons have given Bush at least $1.4 million over the course of his career.

Calling Texas "litigious heaven," Bush promised during his first campaign for governor that, if elected, he would push legislation to limit frivolous lawsuits. He argued that fewer lawsuits would lead to lower insurance rates for average Texans. Of course, limiting the right to sue would also benefit insurers with deep pockets who end up footing the bill for many multimillion-dollar settlements.

Bush has raised millions from companies that have pushed "tort reform." Farmers Insurance Group, Inc., based in Los Angeles, is Bush's No. 8 career patron. During his two gubernatorial races, Bush also collected $4.5 million from officers and board members of Texans for Lawsuit Reform and the Texas Civil Justice League.

In June 1995, Bush followed through on his campaign promise and signed a series of bills that limit the access of victims to the court system and the amount of damage awards they can receive. Bush also signed into law measures that make it harder for consumers to sue real estate agents and that make it more difficult for them to collect damages when they're injured by more than one party.

Limiting personal-injury lawsuits did produce savings for insurance companies, but that money went straight to the industry. From 1996 to 1998, insurance companies made a $3 billion profit while the average Texan's auto insurance rates continued to climb.

Texans have paid the price in other ways, too. When a jury in San Antonio found that an oil company's lax safety measures had caused the death of a refinery worker, it wanted to send a message by ordering the company to pay $42.5 million in damages to the worker's widow. But thanks to the laws Bush signed, the company walked away paying only $200,000. "Two hundred thousand dollars is just pocket change," Wilda Hosch, a juror in the case told the *New York Times*. "They'll just write it off."

On May 18, 1998, Eliza May, the executive director of the Texas Funeral Service Commission, was summoned to the office of Joe Allbaugh, Governor Bush's chief of staff. Waiting for her were Allbaugh, Margaret Wilson, the governor's general counsel, and State Senator John Whitmire of Houston. Whitmire pressed May for details of her agency's investigation into the embalming practices of Service Corporation International (SCI), the world's largest "death care" company, which is based in Whitmire's district. The only trouble was that Robert Waltrip, the founder and chairman of SCI, and Johnnie B. Rogers, Jr., the company's lawyer, were also in the room.

May said later that the meeting was "clearly designed to intimidate me."

The meeting was prompted by a six-page complaint that Waltrip wrote and hand-delivered a month earlier to May and Governor Bush.

Waltrip is not in the habit of delivering his own mail, but he had a lot at stake in the investigation. He is SCI's largest individual shareholder, and his mother and children are on the company's board of directors.

In recent years, Waltrip and his company have given more money to Bush than to any other politician. Waltrip is also a longtime supporter of Bush's father. He contributed to the elder Bush's congressional campaigns in the 1960s, donated more than $100,000 to the Bush Presidential Library, and paid the former president to speak before a funeral directors association.

The day Waltrip dropped off his complaint to Allbaugh, Bush reportedly spotted him and said, "Hey Bobby, are those people still messing with you?" Waltrip replied yes.

May alleges that during the funeral agency's investigation, Governor Bush allowed two men who work for SCI to serve on the Texas Funeral Service Commission, even though state law prohibits a single funeral company from having more than one seat on the commission. The two commissioners, Leo Metcalf and Robert Duncan, made several attempts to slow the agency's investigation.

"SCI poured money in all the right places and kicked our butts," Kenneth Hughes, a member of the Texas Funeral Service Commission, said. "They told us, 'We'll go to the governor and get this thing thrown out.' I didn't think they were that strong."

Despite the mounting political pressure, May and her staff pressed on, and in August 1998 the commission's complaint review committee fined SCI $450,000. The company appealed the fine. But the agency's actions did not go unpunished.

In January 1999 the Texas Funeral Service Commissioners put May on administrative leave. In March, the House Appropriations Committee of the Texas Legislature voted to eliminate the agency's budget. In the end, the agency survived, but May did not. The commissioners fired her on February 8, 1999. May filed a wrongful termination suit against the agency and SCI, which is still pending. Bush has refused to testify in her case.

Since then, the company's embalming practices have become the subject of a lawsuit filed by the family of North Texas TV anchor Frank "Tres" Hood. After the thirty-one-year-old died of colon cancer in July 1998, his family took his body to an SCI-owned funeral home in Wichita Falls, Texas, which in turn sent it to an SCI-owned funeral home in Dallas—one of the facilities that May and her staff had investigated—without the family's knowledge. After Hood's body was entombed in the family crypt, it leaked so much fluid that his wooden casket broke, and his relatives had to foot the bill to clean it up. The case is still pending.

*   *   *

Bush denies pulling strings for anyone.

"Any insinuation that I have used my office to help my friends is simply not true," Bush told a reporter for the *Houston Chronicle* in August 1998. "I don't talk to my business associates about doing business with state government one way or another."

But Bush's own words and actions prove that he mastered the art of greasing the wheels of politics with favors long ago.

After his father was elected in 1988, Bush was tapped to head what was known around the White House as the Silent Committee, an informal group of about fifteen hard-core Bush supporters. Bush's assignment: to see that members of the Silent Committee landed jobs in the administration. Long after his father was sworn in and he returned to Texas, Bush continued to intervene on behalf of his father's backers. According to Chase Untermeyer, a former director of personnel in the Bush Administration, the President's son would "call to say someone on the Silent Committee list was being jerked around by a Cabinet officer. I'd frequently get calls asking that I see someone or not forget someone." In 1994, Bush lobbied on behalf of catalog baron Roger Horchow, who unsuccessfully sought the chairmanship of the National Endowment for the Arts. Asked by reporters why he pushed so hard for Horchow, Bush replied, "He gave money to my father."

If Bush is elected, he already has a long list of contenders for his own Silent Committee. The only question left would be who gets to be chairman.

GEORGE W. BUSH
Top Ten Career Patrons

Ranking	Company/Individual/Family Name	Total
1	Enron Corporation, Houston	$550,025
2	Sanchez family and related business interests, Laredo, Texas	$320,150
3	Vinson & Elkins, Austin, Texas	$316,700
4	Hicks, Muse, Tate and Furst, Inc., and affiliated companies, Dallas	$290,400
5	Bass family and business interests, Fort Worth, Texas	$273,927
6	The Sterling Group and related companies	$259,000
7	Pilgrim's Pride Corporation, Dallas/Lonnie "Bo" Pilgrim	$231,750
8	Farmers Group, Inc., Los Angeles	$223,500
9	Sam and Charles Wyly, Jr., and business interests, Dallas	$222,773
10	Arter & Hadden, Cleveland/Tom Loeffler	$210,700

This list is based on individual contributions to Bush's House campaign from 1977–1978; individual and PAC contributions to Bush's gubernatorial campaign from 1993–1998; individual and corporate contributions toward the 1995 renovation of the governor's office; individual and corporate sponsors of the 1995 and 1999 Bush inaugurals; and individual and PAC contributions to Bush's presidential campaign through June 30, 1999.

Sources: Federal Election Commission; Center for Responsive Politics; Texas Ethics Commission; Governor Bush Committee; State Preservation Board.

1. Includes contributions from employees of Enron and its subsidiaries, including Enron Energy Services; Enron Capital and Trade Resources; Enron Europe; Enron Gas Pipeline Group; and Enron Export Services. Also includes contributions from employees of Azurix, which was formed by Enron and is 69 percent owned by Enron.

2. Includes contributions from Antonio R. Sanchez, Jr., of Laredo and his family members. Also includes contributions from International Bancshares Corporation, which is 9.66 percent owned by Tony Sanchez and 17.92 percent owned by his mother, Alicia. Also includes contributions from employees of its subsidiaries, chiefly the International Bank of Commerce and Commerce Bank.

4. Includes contributions from employees of Hicks, Muse et al, and employees of two media firms founded by Hicks, Muse: Chancellor Media (FKA Chancellor Broadcasting) and Capstar Broadcasting. Chancellor Media, which was recently renamed AMFM, Inc., now owns Capstar.

5. Includes contributions from Perry Bass; his sons Sid, Edward, and Lee; and their family members. Also includes contributions from employees of their businesses, including Bass Companies; Bass Brothers Enterprises; Bass Enterprises Productions Co.; and Lee M. Bass, Inc. Also includes contributions from two PACs primarily funded by the Bass family: the Good Government Fund and the PSEL PAC.

6. Includes contributions from Gordon Cain, founder of the Sterling Group. Also includes contributions from executives of several companies formed by the Sterling Group, including Sterling Chemicals Holdings (FKA Sterling Chemicals) and Arcadian Corporation.

8. Farmers Group, Inc., is now part of Zurich Financial Services.

9. Includes contributions from the Wyly brothers and their family members. Also includes contributions from employees of their business interests, including Maverick Capital; Michaels Stores, Inc.; and Sterling Software.

10. More than half of this money came from Arter & Hadden partner Tom Loeffler and his wife.

Elizabeth Dole

||||||||||

Not long after graduating from Duke University, Elizabeth Hanford applied for a job at the *Charlotte Observer,* the largest newspaper in her home state of North Carolina. She'd never worked as a reporter, not even on her college newspaper. What's more, she'd never studied journalism or even evinced much interest in the field. But she figured that she was ready for the influential newspaper—and vice versa.

"I went in assuming that if you wore the right dress and nodded at appropriate moments," she later wrote, "your credentials would speak for you."

The editors, however, figured otherwise. Hanford was not hired. Instead of pursuing a career in journalism, she went to Harvard Law School and became the only woman in U.S. history to hold two separate Cabinet posts in two different administrations. Nonetheless, she recounted the *Charlotte Observer* story in *Unlimited Partners,* the 1988 political biography she co-authored with her husband, former Senator Robert Dole. The incident taught her an important lesson: "If you couldn't, or wouldn't, make the case for why you should get the job," she wrote, "you could hardly expect a prospective boss to make it for you."

After two decades of toil in her husband's political campaigns,

Elizabeth Hanford Dole spent most of 1999 making the case for why she should be the forty-third President of the United States. Her strongest assets were her popularity and name recognition. For years, Gallup polls listed her as one of the world's most admired women, and early in 1999 she ranked close behind front-runner George W. Bush in most polls.

But Dole, who dropped out of the race on October 20, 1999, apparently didn't learn the lesson she laid claim to in Charlotte. Her presidential campaign—like her long career as a Washington insider—consisted primarily of wearing the right dress, nodding at the right moments, and letting her credentials speak for her.

Within Washington, Dole has a reputation as someone obsessed with her own public image. When she was Transportation Secretary, her aides marveled as she reironed her skirts after helicopter trips. Before her nationally televised speech at the 1996 Republican National Convention—where she roamed the floor with a microphone—she meticulously coordinated her bright red dress to match the color of the convention hall carpet. Such attention to detail was evident even on her campaign's Web site. Ranked at the very top of her most "frequently asked questions" was: "What is Elizabeth's favorite color?" (Answer: "All bright colors, especially yellow.")

Dole flip-flopped on major political issues so many times that the *Washington Monthly* dubbed her "the Wallenda of Washington's big top." During her political career, she changed her party affiliation from Democrat to Independent to Republican. She went from being a Nader-style consumer advocate to a Reaganesque defender of corporate rights. And while she billed herself as a women's candidate—appealing to what she called "an invisible army" of female political neophytes—her positions on such issues as abortion and the Equal Rights Amendment were always in flux.

Dole avoided discussing these and other issues on the campaign trail by repeatedly reminding audiences "that the candidate with the most experience is more qualified than the candidate with the most money." This was her way of lashing out at rivals George W. Bush, who had raised ten times more than Dole by the summer of 1999, and Malcolm "Steve" Forbes, Jr., whose vast personal wealth permits him to spend however much he is willing to spend.

"The bottom line is money," she said in announcing her exit from the presidential race. "It would be futile to continue."

Dole's reliance on her résumé suggested that she'd learned only half the lesson presented to her in Charlotte all those years ago. There's no doubt that she learned how to make a persuasive case— she made a mountain of money as a motivational speaker—but she appeared oblivious to the fact that she had no journalism credentials back then and had only meager political and executive credentials as a presidential candidate. She had never run for or been elected to any public office. And during her tenures as a Cabinet Secretary and as the president of the American Red Cross, she proved herself an aloof manager who was obsessed with her own public image.

Elizabeth Dole tells the same joke dozens of times a year. It goes like this:

"*People* magazine published a photograph of Bob and I making the bed together in our Watergate apartment. A few days after the magazine hit the newsstands, Bob got a letter from an irate California Republican. The man wrote that he had nothing against a female Cabinet officer. His complaint was personal. 'Senator Dole,' he wrote, 'my wife saw that picture of you making the bed, and now she has me helping make the bed. Please, Senator, you've got to stop doing all that work around the house. You're causing problems for men all across America.' Well, Bob wrote back to the man. 'You don't know the half of it,' my husband replied. 'The only reason she was helping make the bed was because they were taking pictures.'"

Crowds love it. And pleasing crowds has made Dole a multimillionaire in her own right. She raked in $1.6 million in speaking fees in 1998 and the first half of 1999, usually netting $40,000 per appearance. She delivered the making-the-bed icebreaker so often that when Bob Dole was scheduled to speak to a group she had addressed the previous day, she left him a handwritten note on their bathroom mirror that said, "Don't use the joke about the bed—I already used it."

One reason the joke went over so well is that Elizabeth Dole inherited many of her lucrative speaking engagements directly from Bob. At least five of the forty-three organizations she spoke to in 1998 and the first half of 1999 were groups her husband had been speaking to for years. Senator Dole was no stranger to the speaking circuit. He collected $1.4 million in appearance fees from 1981 to 1991—even though throughout that time Senate rules prevented him from accepting more than $2,000 per speech. In 1993 new rules went into effect that barred senators from keeping such fees. Elizabeth Dole picked up the slack, and began speaking to some of the same groups. From 1991 to 1994—while her husband was still Senate Minority Leader—she spoke to at least sixteen high-paying organizations that had business pending before the government.

Senator Dole temporarily ceased making paid appearances during each of his presidential campaigns. Democratic presidential candidate Bill Bradley, who collected more than $1.6 million from personal appearances in 1998, took himself off the speaking circuit when he launched his campaign. But Elizabeth Dole didn't. In the first seven weeks after she formed her "exploratory committee," Dole made nine paid appearances before various organizations and audiences. Through 1998, she averaged two paid appearances a month; in March and April of 1999, she doubled her speak-for-pay pace even with the added demands of a presidential campaign.

Likewise, Dole used her tenure as the president of the American Red Cross to boost her profile—and fees—as a speaker. Although she was president of the charity through the end of 1998, none of the money for the twenty-nine speeches she made that year went to the American Red Cross. (Dole was prohibited from accepting speaking fees while she served as a Cabinet secretary, though she did take in $100,000 in fees during the year between her stints at the Transportation and Labor departments.) While Dole took large fees for her speeches, her predecessor rarely charged anything. "Most of the time, I didn't get remuneration," Richard Schubert, who was the president of the American Red Cross from 1983 to 1990, told the Center for Public Integrity. "If I did, it was in the form of a donation to the Red Cross."

Throughout the early 1990s, Dole tried to deflect criticism of her seemingly mercenary speaking habits by repeatedly promising to donate the money to charity. But of the $875,000 in speaking fees she earned from 1991 to 1994, only $405,513—or just 46 percent—went to charitable organizations. The rest went to cover her personal expenses, and to her substantial retirement fund. (In response to heavy criticism in the wake of a January 1996 story in the *Los Angeles Times* about her tight-fisted giving, Dole blamed her accountant for the errors and made an additional charitable contribution of $75,000.) And the charity to which Dole donated less than half her speaking fees was none other than the American Red Cross, which under her leadership was facing one of the most severe financial crises of its hundred-plus-year history.

Dole, apparently, no longer gives to the Red Cross. The proceeds from her speaking engagements in 1998 went into the Elizabeth Dole Charitable Foundation, about which her campaign would provide no information.

Of the $1,136,000 in speaking fees that Dole received in 1998, only $602,458 went to the Elizabeth Dole Charitable Foundation, the Center's comparison of her financial disclosure form with her foundation's tax return shows. The rest of the money went to taxes and to another generous contribution to her retirement plan, according to Robert Davis, Dole's longtime lawyer and another of the foundation's three directors. The Dole Foundation is a creation of a Cleveland-based accounting firm called Investment Advisors International, Inc., itself a subsidiary of the renowned celebrity agency International Management Group, which is best known for its representation of such sports superstars as Tiger Woods, Joe Montana, Wayne Gretzky, Andre Agassi, and Arnold Palmer. (The agency has also represented violinist Itzhak Perlman, supermodel Tyra Banks, Margaret Thatcher, and Pope John Paul II.) The Elizabeth Dole Charitable Foundation is controlled by Elizabeth Dole. In 1998 it gave away only $29,157 out of more than $1 million in assets, the minimum required by law to maintain its foundation status.

The Doles are no strangers to the kinds of services that IMG provides. In early 1997 the firm set up a for-profit operation, Bob Dole Enterprises, Inc., to capitalize on the Senator's name. Dole became a TV pitchman for everything from Visa check cards to

Viagra, proving that even if there are no second acts in American politics, there are still commercials after the first one.

After he lost the presidential race in 1996, Bob the Bedmaker became an overnight celebrity. He filmed commercials for Pentax cameras and Air France, appeared on the network TV program "Suddenly Susan," and popped in on several late-night talk shows. Elizabeth Dole's connection with IMG suggests that she may have been less interested in moving into the White House than in further feathering her nest at the Watergate. (In the summer of 1999, the Doles purchased the place next door—most recently occupied by Monica Lewinsky—to expand their apartment.) As soon as Dole got out of the presidential race, IMG was poised to help her cash in on her heightened celebrity status and her campaign-financed mailing lists—and, of course, to put her back on the road telling bedroom jokes for a million dollars a year.

Mary Elizabeth Alexander Hanford grew up in the small city of Salisbury, North Carolina, but it may as well have been called "Mayberry." Her childhood home came complete with a large attic and an imaginary friend named "Denaw." Her backyard was shaded by a towering magnolia tree, beneath which she ceremoniously buried a cat named Beauty and a Chihuahua named Penny.

She gave herself the nickname "Liddy" —a name she now, by all accounts, detests. Her father, an affluent florist, gave her just about everything else: summer houses and debutante balls, ballet and horseback riding lessons.

Her most fearsome childhood demons were within herself. She was a perfectionist from the start, obsessed with making a good impression on everyone she met. "When my second-grade teacher sent me home to fetch a forgotten book," she wrote, "I considered myself such a total failure that I cried all the way down South Fulton Street."

She followed her much older brother to Duke University, where she joined a sorority. Poised and pretty, she was elected Queen of May and invited into "White Duchy," an elitist secret society. She was elected president of the student body, and graduated in 1958 with a degree in political science.

Hanford turned down a chance to work in the family business

and spent the next few years exploring her options. "A diploma is not a compass," she wrote, "and the end of my college days found me groping for direction." She studied education at Harvard University and traveled to England and the former Soviet Union before landing a summer job in Washington, D.C. There, she was impressed by Senator Margaret Chase Smith, a popular Republican from Maine and one of only two women in the Senate at the time. In a brief meeting, the aging Yankee advised the young Hanford to go to law school.

Hanford soon enrolled as one of two dozen women in Harvard Law School's class of 1965. Among them was Patricia Schroeder, who would later be elected to the House of Representatives from Colorado. (They met after Hanford smashed her car into Schroeder's.) Hanford viewed herself as something of a female pioneer at Harvard, bucking against a male-dominated system. But she relished even more the sense of entitlement that Harvard nurtured. In her own words: "Harvard had come to be known, only half in jest, as the fourth branch of American government."

In 1960, Hanford worked briefly as a greeter on the Kennedy-Johnson campaign's whistle-stop tour of the South, a job that required little more than wearing the right dress and nodding at the appropriate moments. She also worked briefly at the United Nations in New York City and the headquarters of the Peace Corps in Washington.

After graduating from Harvard Law School, Hanford worked at the Department of Education and briefly in private practice before she landed a job in 1968 on President Johnson's Committee on Consumer Interests.

Hanford threw herself into the fledgling consumer movement, wearing her newfound activism on her sleeve. Once, when she had a hot-off-the-press copy of a Ralph Nader report, she brought it along on a date. To the dismay of her suitor, she ignored the Washington Redskins game he had taken her to and spent her stadium time engrossed in the report.

Ten months after she went to work in the Johnson Administration, Richard Nixon took over the White House. The consumer office quietly backed off from its activism to focus instead on distributing product information and mediating conflicts with manufacturers. Hanford dropped her Naderite loyalties and switched her party affiliation from Democrat to Independent. She was rewarded with several promotions; in 1973 Nixon nominated her to the Federal Trade Commission.

In the early 1970s the solidly Democratic Congress wanted an activist FTC that would bust up monopolies and wage war against the excesses of corporate America. Hanford complied. During her time as an FTC commissioner, she opposed nearly every proposed corporate merger that came across her desk.

Hanford was introduced to Senator Dole in the spring of 1972. She was involved with someone else at the time, and had already turned down several marriage proposals. Dole was then the chairman of the Republican National Committee and had recently divorced his first wife. Their first date was at a Watergate restaurant. Three years later, on December 6, 1975, they were married. She was thirty-nine; he was fifty-two. She rehearsed her vows again and again. He just winged it.

"Elizabeth comes from a family of perfectionists, so she has a natural tendency to dwell on what she sees as her own imperfections," Senator Dole wrote of his wife. "Over the years I've tried to convince her that life is too short to worry about yesterday, and perfection is an impossible standard."

About the same time she changed her name to Dole, she also changed her party registration from Independent to Republican. Her conversion came not a season too soon. The following summer, President Gerald Ford chose Senator Dole to be his running mate. Even while retaining her post at the FTC, Elizabeth Dole went on the campaign trail, charming crowds with her polished style and North Carolina drawl. Ford lost the White House to Jimmy Carter. But the Doles were anointed Washington's new power couple; *Newsweek* compared them to Tracy and Hepburn.

Over the course of the Senator's many presidential campaigns, the U.S. Secret Service—not an organization generally noted for its sense of humor—gave the Doles their most apt and durable nicknames: Ramrod and Rainbow.

With her husband's help, she lobbied for a Cabinet job in 1980 but was reportedly blackballed by Joseph Coors, the patriarch of Adolph Coors Company, who considered her to be insufficiently conservative. Instead, President Reagan gave her a job running the White House public-liaison office. It was during this time that Dole abandoned her commitment to the Equal Rights Amendment and became one of the most visible defenders of Reagan's anti-ERA stance.

On a crisp autumn morning in 1986, a well-coiffed Elizabeth Dole stood at the entrance to the parking garage of the U.S. Department of Transportation. Alongside her stood an aide dressed as a crash-test dummy. With a small metal Stop sign in her gloved hand, she waved arriving Transportation Department employees over for an inspection. Those who didn't have their seat belts buckled got a safety lecture from Dole and a handout from the dummy.

The Dole-and-dummy shtick was but one of hundreds of safety-related photo opportunities Elizabeth Dole staged during her four years as Transportation Secretary. After a formidable lobbying effort by her husband, President Reagan appointed Dole to the post in 1983. (Her White Duchy pals congratulated her by sending white carnations.) She quickly dubbed herself the "Safety Secretary."

On the campaign trail, Dole liked to brag about how she "forced" the automobile industry to begin installing air bags and other passive restraints. She has called the air bag battle the toughest fight of her career. But the truth is that Dole rarely stood up to her famously antiregulatory boss over air bags or any other safety issue. She simply complied with a Supreme Court ruling that directed her agency to enforce the air bag regulations that had been developed by the Carter Administration.

Reagan, who complained that industry was "regulated to death," had no appetite for new safety rules. And without the Supreme Court behind her, Dole crumpled like a cheap bumper. She exempted light trucks and sport-utility vehicles from several existing safety standards. She delayed setting a side-impact crash standard for automobiles. And she opposed releasing the results of government crash tests to the public. (Ironically, the crash-test results represented precisely the type of objective consumer data she had fought for during her years at the FTC.)

Compared with these missed opportunities, Dole's list of accomplishments is short. She deserves credit for the 1983 rule ordering automobile manufacturers to install third brake lights, which don't save many lives but do prevent thousands of minor collisions each year. She campaigned vigorously for higher drinking ages, an effort led by Mothers Against Drunk Driving. And she pushed rules aimed at improving airline service. "I was a frequent flier myself and had experienced my share of cancelled flights, misplaced garment bags and nervous checking of my watch," she wrote. "One of the worst hours of my life was spent at Dulles Airport."

But it was airline safety—not airport convenience—that became the defining issue of Dole's Transportation Department. Reagan had fired all 11,400 of the nation's striking air traffic controllers in 1981, and the nation's airways were in shambles by the time Dole took the helm. To get the crippled airlines back to their 1981 levels of service, Dole worked Federal Aviation Administration supervisors and their newly hired trainees to the bone. Vacation and sick leave was cancelled; six-day work weeks were mandatory. When the controllers complained, she ridiculed them in public—and openly dismissed the idea that theirs were uniquely stressful jobs.

By 1987, public confidence in airline safety had crashed. Commercial airliners were reporting near-midair collisions at the rate of more than one a day. In May the National Transportation Safety Board warned that the overburdened and understaffed air traffic control system was headed for disaster. *Newsweek* magazine dubbed 1987 "The Year of the Near Miss."

Congress begged the FAA to hire more air traffic controllers, but Reagan refused. His "Safety Secretary" never challenged him. "The skies are safe," Dole repeatedly told reporters. "We have the safest system in the world."

Management-by-photo-opportunity quickly became the hallmark of Dole's leadership style. She showed little interest in—and less knowledge of—the agency she headed, leaving the big decisions to her superiors and the rest to her staff.

Her remarkable talent was (and is) her ability to turn an incident that would have been an embarrassing gaffe for a male politician into a cute photo opportunity. Her first steps aboard a U.S. Coast Guard cutter provided a case in point. Although she often boasts that she was the first woman to head a branch of the armed forces—the Coast Guard is part of the Department of Transportation—hers was hardly a disciplined command: She teetered up the grated gangplank of a Coast Guard cutter in three-inch heels. And rather than politely returning the rigid salute of the rank officer at the end of the ramp, she handed him her purse.

Dole repeated this pattern during her 1989-90 stint as Secretary of Labor. She had little impact on policy, even on legislative issues she claimed to support—such as raising the minimum wage, parental leave, and child-care issues.

On at least one occasion, however, the Dole-and-dummy shtick crashed and burned—literally. In December 1984, Dole invited a crowd of six hundred reporters and industry executives to the California desert to promote a new airplane fuel that was designed to prevent deadly explosions during aviation mishaps. Dole and the other VIPs watched from a nearby rooftop as the FAA intentionally crashed a remote-controlled Boeing 720 carrying seventy-five crash-test dummies, twelve high-speed cameras, and 350 electronic sensors in the cabin. After slamming into the Mojave Desert near Edwards Air Force Base in California, the old Boeing was engulfed in a fireball three times the height of the plane. The fire burned ferociously for another nineteen minutes, until a radio call for help came from technicians closer to the crash site: "We're having some problems putting this fire out."

By the time the startled reporters turned to her for comment on the miserably failed test, Dole had vanished. FAA Administrator Donald Engen was left to field the embarrassing questions. Dole's office said later that she had another appointment that conflicted with the $11.8 million FAA demonstration.

Elizabeth Dole has never lacked for money. She and her husband are worth at least $7 million, a large part of which is invested in the stocks of such blue-chip U.S. companies as Microsoft Corporation and Walt Disney Company. She has always had considerable personal wealth independent of her husband's, especially after she received her family inheritance following her father's death in

1981. In spite of these advantages, her financial life has been peppered with questionable business dealings, several of them engineered by longtime friend David Owen.

Owen stepped into the center of Dole's life in 1974, when Bob's first Senate reelection campaign was faltering. The retired rodeo-star-turned-politician didn't seek reelection as Kansas's lieutenant governor, took over the Dole campaign and rustled up a narrow victory. Owen remained Dole's main fund-raiser throughout the 1980s, and he was the national finance co-chairman of Dole's 1988 presidential campaign. He once estimated that he had raised more than $10 million for the Senator.

Owen did far more than raise money. After joining the Reagan Cabinet, Dole put her money into a blind trust. In 1985, Owen was hired as the trust's investment advisor. He had power—indeed, the responsibility—to make investment decisions without apprising Dole of them. Owen's stewardship of the trust followed a familiar pattern for the Doles: time and time again, their personal fortune would either provide benefits to, or directly benefit from, their political careers.

In 1982 Elizabeth and her brother were on the receiving end. They bought a beach home at the exclusive Seaview condominium development in Bal Harbour, Florida. Although neighbors such as television newsman David Brinkley and former Senate Republican Leader Howard Baker, Jr., paid full price, Elizabeth Dole got her condo for only $150,000—tens of thousands of dollars below market value. The seller in this sweetheart deal was another Seaview neighbor, Dwayne Andreas, then the chairman of Archer Daniels Midland Company, an international agribusiness giant that has received billions of dollars of government subsidies as a result of programs pushed by Senator Dole. The "frequently asked questions" page on Dole's campaign website listed Bal Harbour as her favorite vacation spot.

In 1979, when Bob Dole was running for the Republican presidential nomination, their personal fortune came to his political rescue—though through a circuitous route. Dole's campaign was running out of cash. Owen wanted to loan money to his old friend through a Kansas bank he controlled, but the campaign most likely didn't have the assets to support such a loan. So Owen arranged for Elizabeth to use her personal assets as collateral for a low-interest $50,000 loan, the proceeds of which she immediately loaned to her husband's campaign. The Federal Election Commission investigated the loan in 1980. Lawyers at the FEC believed that the transaction violated federal campaign-finance laws, which limit contributions (and loans) from individuals to $1,000. But the agency's politically appointed commissioners later voted not to pursue the case.

Early in 1986, Dole's blind trust, under the direction of Owen, paid $1,350,000 for a drab, two-story office building in Overland Park, Kansas, a well-to-do suburb of Kansas City. Before the year was out she sold the building—to herself and a partner—for a $63,000 profit. Her partner in the purchase was a company owned by John Palmer, a former aide to Senator Dole. To facilitate the transaction, the Dole trust had loaned Palmer part of the money. With the Senator's help, Palmer received a no-bid contract to provide $26 million worth of food service at a U.S. Army base in nearby Missouri. (The chairman of the House Small Business Committee later branded the contract "replete with appearances of improper activities.")

Of course, such sweetheart deals have added to Dole's considerable wealth. Like many of the well-to-do, she's been willing to shield some of the investment income she's received by taking advantage of tax loopholes. In 1983 she invested in a tax shelter called Altenn Associates Limited Partnership. (Altenn's name was derived from its ownership of real estate in Alabama and Tennessee.) Altenn was set up to lose money for fifteen years, thereby enabling its forty-nine limited partners to reap far more in tax breaks than the investment they risked. The Doles, for example, received more than $300,000 in tax write-offs over five years, for an investment of $14,651 in cash and $156,780 in the form of a note. In 1996, the Center reported that the shelter had reduced the Doles' taxes by $150,000. They would have received even more in subsequent years, but Congress cracked down on such loopholes in 1986. Ironically, Senator Dole was one of the most outspoken critics of such tax shelters.

Ever since news stories about these and other questionable investments began surfacing during Senator Dole's 1988 presidential campaign, Elizabeth Dole has repeatedly said that she had no knowledge of Owen's investments on her behalf.

Owen was forced to resign from both the trust and from the Senator's 1988 campaign after his handling of the couple's finances led to a minor scandal. After lengthy state and federal investigations, Owen was convicted on two counts of tax fraud. He served a one-year sentence, and then went back into the investment business in Overland Park.

Dole's tenure as the president of the American Red Cross echoed her performance at the Transportation and Labor departments. She remained uninvolved in the day-to-day operations of the $1.9 billion-a-year charitable organization, and attempted to manage a staff of 31,000 primarily through pronouncements to the press.

When she took over the century-old charity, the world's attention was focused on the crisis in Kuwait and the ensuing Persian Gulf War. In March 1991, as soon as the fighting was over, she flew to the front to be photographed with Red Cross staff and the troops they were supporting. After touring an understaffed children's hospital in Kuwait City, she told the cameras that her organization would send doctors and supplies. Her unilateral gesture offended Muslim factions within the fragile coalition of organizations that makes up the international Red Cross and Red Crescent movement. On the job barely three months, Dole's May Queen style of diplomacy had already initiated a minor international incident.

Dole's stump speeches were filled with references to her proudest achievement at the Red Cross: "a seven-year, $287 million transformation of the way the organization collects, tests, and distributes half of the nation's blood supply," or almost six million units of blood a year. But as was the case with air bags, it took a court order to force the action for which Dole now takes credit.

During the 1980s, the Red Cross and other organizations had been slow to begin testing for new blood-borne diseases—including AIDS—and the public was losing confidence in the blood supply. By the time Dole was hired, testing costs were climbing, donations were falling, and the organization was slipping behind on reforms promised in a 1988 agreement with the Food and Drug Administration. Congressional hearings were focusing national attention on the Red Cross's failures.

Dole responded with a press conference. On May 20, 1991, she announced a two-year "transformation program" that would rebuild the Red Cross blood-supply system from the ground up. Twenty-eight separate computer systems would be replaced by one national computer, which would contain the medical histories and test results of every donor. Dole called her plan "the most dramatic and far-reaching public safety step the Red Cross has taken in its history."

Congress and the media responded warmly to Dole's pronouncement. But much of her own staff was shocked. Few of them heard anything about her plan until they read it in the newspapers. And many feared her sweeping reorganization—which called for temporarily shutting down every Red Cross blood center in the country—would risk leaving too many patients high and dry.

By 1993—nearly two years after Dole's sweeping pronouncement—the Red Cross had consolidated some of its testing laboratories, upgraded its computer systems, and begun providing better training at its blood banks. But the FDA still wasn't satisfied. So the Justice Department sued the charity on behalf of the FDA. The lawsuit, *United States* v. *American National Red Cross,* accused the charity of distributing "adulterated" and "misbranded" blood and blood products. The government promised to file criminal charges against Red Cross executives—including Dole—if the organization failed to meet a new set of deadlines.

Dole wasted no time in responding. First, she sent her lawyers back to the FDA to negotiate a new consent decree that didn't hold her personally responsible. Then, in a move perceived by many to be the ultimate expression of how distant she was from her own senior staff, she assigned two longtime associates to investigate what her people were doing and report back directly to her.

The blood-supply system was eventually rebuilt. But Dole's leadership style remained unreformed. She continued to insulate herself from the organization through an inner circle with deeper connections to Republican politics than to the work of the Red Cross. The members of Dole's palace guard included: Jennifer

Dorn, her top aide at the Transportation and Labor Departments; John Heubusch, who went on to become the executive director of the National Republican Senatorial Committee; Mari Maseng Will, a speechwriter for Presidents Reagan and Bush who had worked in all of Senator Dole's campaigns; and Robert Davis, her private attorney. Her reliance on this shadow staff of consultants was singled out for criticism in a 1996 review of the charity by the auditing firm KPMG Peat Marwick.

At times this inner circle put its own interests ahead of the Red Cross's. In 1995, for example, the Red Cross was putting the finishing touches on a pamphlet, posters, leaflets, and videotapes to be used by instructors in its AIDS-awareness education program. Funded by a $5 million grant from the Centers for Disease Control and Prevention, the Red Cross program sends trained instructors to schools, churches, and civic organizations to teach people how to protect themselves from HIV, the virus associated with AIDS. The carefully edited materials advise sexual abstinence but also illustrate the safe use of condoms. It is the largest AIDS education program in the United States, reaching two million people a year— half of them youth.

But release of the AIDS awareness supplies to the charity's 1,300 local chapters was delayed for months so that the language—which had already been carefully reviewed by the Red Cross staff—could be further scrutinized. Dole's husband was running for President, and her political advisers feared that the materials' frank discussions of sex might upset the Senator's delicate courtship of Christian conservatives. Dole's allies reedited the materials, playing down the use of condoms and instead stressing abstinence. Never before had there been such high-level interference in the AIDS program.

Dole's final act in her $185,000-a-year job was her most transparent use of the charity for her own political ends. She gave herself the starring role in "The American Red Cross Celebrates Real Life Miracles," a nationally televised Christmas Eve extravaganza produced by Dole's media adviser and paid for by the Red Cross. The 1998 special featured long scenes of Elizabeth Dole glowingly describing the Red Cross's accomplishments, as well as shots of its Washington, D.C., headquarters, which bears a remarkable architectural resemblance to the White House. An estimated 3.6 million viewers watched the show, which urged viewers to call and donate to the Red Cross via a toll-free telephone number. The show raised $25,000 in pledges—at a production cost of $1.3 million.

Dole's 2000 presidential campaign was a continuation of her long-standing management style. She breathlessly delivered her standard twenty-minute stump speech, ticking off one-liners as if racing through a checklist. She referred to "the Republican nominee, whoever she may be" and concluded many talks by appealing to her supporters: "Let's make history."

At least a dozen women, however, sought the White House before Dole. Among them were Democratic Representative Patricia Schroeder, her Harvard classmate, who ran in the 1988 contest but dropped out in frustration after reporters repeatedly ignored her positions on issues to ask her what it was like to run as a woman.

Throughout her speeches and public appearances, Dole repeatedly promised to "tell it like it is." Her stump speech was basically a long list of "important issues" that she told her audience she wanted to talk about.

She avoided reporters whenever possible, scheduling few in-depth interviews and waving off most in-the-field questions with a joke and a smile. When cornered—as she was by NBC News's Tim Russert on the morning after her impressive third-place showing at the August 1999 Iowa straw poll—she answered in nonspecific platitudes. When Russert, the host of "Meet the Press," asked how she would keep her promise to shut down illegal drug traffic from Mexico, she said only that "there are a number of options" a President could consider. Russert asked whether she agreed with the Kansas Board of Education's decision to strike evolution from the school curriculum. Dole replied she would leave that important decision to the states.

Dole raised only $3.5 million through the first half of 1999. Her husband's prestigious Washington law firm, Verner, Liipfert, Bernhard, McPherson, and Hand, is the top patron of her current campaign, with $38,750 in contributions from its partners and their spouses during the first half of 1999.

Dole also tapped into the connections she made at the American Red Cross. The Andreas family and executives at Archer Daniels Midland were among her top patrons. So were Red Cross directors Charles Heimbold, Jr., the chairman and chief executive officer of Bristol-Myers Squibb Company, the pharmaceutical giant, and Jon Huntsman, the chairman and chief executive officer of Huntsman Corporation, which manufactures chemicals, plastics, and packaging products. Heimbold and Huntsman, in fact, co-hosted a Washington fund-raiser for Dole that brought in $500,000.

But even Dole's supporters didn't seem to take her candidacy seriously. Her campaign listed Earle Mack of New Jersey and Howard Wilkins of Washington as members of her finance committee. Mack's office has said that he's supporting Bush. Wilkins has said that he's raising money for Dole and Bush, but mostly for Bush. Many of her husband's generous law partners also gave money to the campaign of Democrat Albert Gore, Jr.

Even her husband raised doubts about Dole's candidacy, telling a reporter for the *New York Times* that he was thinking of contributing to the presidential campaign of Republican Senator John McCain of Arizona. As her campaign boasted about her third-place finish in the electorally insignificant Iowa straw poll, her husband pooh-poohed the event. "Only one-tenth of one percent of the Iowa Republicans are voting here," he told reporters. "I don't think it will determine the outcome."

Dole repeatedly denied that she was really running for Vice President. But the fact that she had to do so at campaign stop after campaign stop suggested that even her supporters saw her as a candidate for the No. 2 job. That job, after all, would allow Dole to do what she's always done best: wear the right dress, nod at the right moments, and let her credentials speak for her.

ELIZABETH DOLE
Top Ten Career Patrons

Ranking	Company/Individual/Family Name	Total
1	Verner, Liipfert, Bernhard, McPherson, and Hand, Washington	$38,750
2	Galpin Motors, Inc., North Hills, California	$22,500
3	American Financial Group, Inc., Cincinnati/ Lindner family	$15,000
3	Tiger Management, New York	$15,000
5	Kirk Kerkorian and business interests, Las Vegas, Nevada	$13,000
5	NJK Holding Company, Bloomington, Minnesota	$13,000
7	Archer Daniels Midland Company, Decatur, Illinois	$11,000
8	Reppert family, Saint Petersburg, Florida	$10,000
8	Ruan family and business interests, Des Moines, Iowa	$10,000
10	Wachovia Corporation, Winston-Salem, North Carolina	$9,500

This list is based on individual and PAC contributions to Dole's presidential campaign through June 30, 1999.
Sources: Federal Election Commission; Center for Responsive Politics.

5. Includes contributions from Kerkorian; employees of his Tracinda Corporation; and PACs associated with Metro-Goldwyn-Mayer, Inc.; and MGM Grand, Inc.
8. Includes family member contributions from Florida, Illinois, Massachusetts, and Missouri.
9. Includes contributions from employees of Ruan Corporation, Iowa Import-Export, and the PACEG PAC, which is supported by employees of these two companies.

Malcolm "Steve" Forbes, Jr.

||||||||||||

"Contrary to what some people would have you believe, there really is no difference between values and economics," Steve Forbes told a crowd of 150 supporters in Sioux City, Iowa, in January 1996. "They're one and the same."

The line came from Forbes's standard stump speech; he used the same words in appearances across Iowa and New Hampshire in his first run for the White House. For Republican-primary voters who were concerned about family values, abortion, and social decay, Forbes had a simple message: America was poised on the brink of the greatest "economic boom and spiritual renewal" in its history.

All the nation had to do was seize the golden ring.

"We have to start not by being timid, but by being bold, by tackling and getting rid of one of the major obstacles on family life today and the major source of power in Washington, the major resource for the Washington culture, and that is the tax code," Forbes told voters, in this case those hearing him in Portsmouth, New Hampshire. He called the tax code a monstrosity, a dead weight on family life, and blamed it for the rise in the number of families with both parents at work.

"No one outside of Washington could have consciously devised something more incomprehensible, more corrupting," he said. "You can't reform it. You can't trim it. The only thing you can do with this monstrosity is to scrap it, kill it, drive a stake through the heart, bury it, and hope that it never rises again to terrorize the American people. And contrary to what certain Washington politicians say, we should replace it with a simple flat tax."

Every four years, it seems, at least one candidate emerges in the presidential primaries with the latest political elixir to cure America's ills. In 1980, Ronald Reagan pushed supply-side economics—"voodoo economics," in the words of his primary rival, George Bush—all the way to the White House. In 1984, Gary Hart proposed scrapping the income tax in favor of a national consumption tax. In 1988, Pierre S. "Pete" Du Pont IV called for privatizing Social Security; George Bush called that one "a nutty idéa." Ross Perot changed the formula somewhat in 1992—he offered himself, the independent candidate and man of means, as the solution to the problems he spelled out in his signature charts and graphs. And in 1996 it was the turn of a bespectacled, millionaire publisher from New Jersey to sell the latest quick fix to the electorate.

Forbes bears more than a superficial resemblance to those before him who built presidential candidacies on big ideas. His flat tax was backed by the same economists who were behind Reagan's low-tax, high-growth platform. Like Hart's national sales tax, Forbes's proposal would scrap the Internal Revenue Code. Both Forbes and Du Pont are independently wealthy heirs who favor privatizing Social Security. And Forbes is the second major candidate in the 1990s who views the presidency as an entry-level position in politics—Perot, in 1992, was the first.

While Forbes has never held elective office, he's done as much as any other candidate running to change the rules of campaign finance. By the time Forbes finally dropped out of the 1996 presidential race in March, he'd spent more money than anyone else: $35.5 million. Fully 90 percent of the money came out of his own pocket. Forbes, with a personal fortune at his disposal, chose to refuse federal matching funds, which allowed him to ignore the state-by-state spending limits established by the Federal Election

Campaign Act. As a result, his 1996 campaign shattered federal campaign-spending ceilings, highlighting the weakness of the laws.

The hefty bankroll he brings to the 2000 primaries has already made itself felt. His chief rival for the nomination, Texas Governor George W. Bush, has broken all fund-raising records and eschewed spending limits to prepare for the expected Forbes onslaught, which is likely to reprise the strategy that catapulted Forbes into the position of Robert Dole's chief rival in 1996.

Forbes may not have won the nomination, but he proved he was willing to open his wallet to get his message out. He pushed his vision of tax reform—a radical, untested scheme that would dramatically alter the sources of federal revenue. He saturated the airwaves in early primary states with commercials that relentlessly attacked Dole's record in the Senate on taxes. He finished as the runner-up to Dole in the primaries, and even forced the Republican nominee to make a tax cut part of his presidential campaign.

All of which is quite a surprise for someone who wasn't even expected to run in the early days of the 1996 election season. When The Center for Public Integrity prepared its first edition of *The Buying of the President* in 1995, Forbes's name hadn't yet surfaced as a potential candidate; all the other candidates who ran had already thrown their hats into the ring.

When Steve Forbes announced his candidacy in September 1995, he was the editor-in-chief of *Forbes* magazine, the linchpin of the family business he inherited from his father. The son followed in his father's footsteps in more ways than one: Forbes recalled his father, Malcolm, Sr., describing the presidency as "the Holy Grail; the gold at the end of the rainbow." The elder Forbes, after graduating from college, moved to Ohio, partly because of the number of presidents the state had produced. Forbes's father never made a run for the White House.

In 1917, B. C. Forbes quit his job as a financial reporter in New York City and started his own magazine to report on business "doers and doings." In his March 2, 1918, issue, for example, the fledgling publisher offered an early precursor of the magazine's famed list of the 400 wealthiest Americans. B. C. Forbes listed the thirty richest people in the United States, along with an article that tried to put their holdings into some sort of perspective.

"John D. Rockefeller's fortune passed the billion-dollar mark, I am told, three or four years ago, at the time Standard Oil Securities more than doubled the price ruling before the dissolution of the Oil Trust," Forbes wrote of the robber baron who topped his 1918 list. "He is now credited with $1.2 billion. His income is estimated to work out at $2,739,726.02 a day, $114,155.25 an hour, $1,902.58 a minute, and $31.70 a second." (As astounding as those figures are, bear in mind that a dollar in 1918 had more purchasing power than ten dollars does today.)

Lest anyone think he was fanning the flames of class envy, Forbes added, "Mr. Rockefeller's wealth, if it could be turned into cash and distributed equally—which it couldn't—would give every man, woman and child in the U.S. $10 each." Rather, the founder of the magazine set a tone to which it remains faithful to the present day: the celebration of wealth.

B.C.'s son, Malcolm, joined the business in 1947 after fighting in World War II, where he received a Bronze Star and a Purple Heart for his bravery at the Battle of Aachen. His son, Malcolm Stevenson Forbes, Jr., was born on July 18, 1947.

Although his father was already involved with the family's magazine by the time he was born, Steve spent much of his early years following his father's on-again, off-again pursuit of political office. When Steve was four he was already on the campaign trail with his father's 1952 race for a Republican seat in the New Jersey state senate. Forbes won and wasted no time in looking beyond. He captured the Republican nomination for governor in 1957, but lost in the general election to Democrat Robert Meyner.

Politics rubbed off on young Steve. During his father's campaigns, Steve developed an interest in politics, although it was more an affinity for numbers and statistics than for meeting people and pressing the flesh.

"He used to flip me out," Forbes's father once said of his son. "When I was running for governor and state senate, Steve could tell me county by county what they had done in past years."

Malcolm Sr. took control of *Forbes* magazine in 1957, the same year his political career ended. He was far more successful as a publisher; he built the publication into one of the most successful business magazines in the world. In 1961 he hired James Michaels as editor, and, under Michaels's stewardship, *Forbes* gained a reputation as a magazine with a skeptical, contrary perspective that didn't base its reporting on business hype or trends. Meanwhile, Malcolm spent his time courting advertisers for the magazine, an activity he made into a family affair.

On autumn Saturday mornings in the 1960s, the elder Forbes required that the boy entertain corporate executives on *The Highlander,* the company yacht. Young Steve and his brothers spent their weekends memorizing the names of guests, fetching drinks, and awkwardly attempting small talk. Occasionally he and his brothers were obliged to put on kilts and play the bagpipes.

"My father made sure that we knew that there's nothing wrong with salesmanship," Forbes told *Fortune* magazine in 1996 in reference to the yacht parties. "At a very early age, we were expected to know, as my father put it, where our bread was buttered."

He attended Princeton University in the tumultuous 1960s, but it was business, certainly not protest, that he saw "Blowin' in the Wind." He founded a student business magazine and mocked the counterculture, antiwar movement when he had the chance. After a local altercation between student protesters and the police, he wrote: "We found it a refreshing sight to see the cops, their clubs a swingin', disrupt a band of willful ruffians disrupting an entire university."

In 1970, Forbes graduated from Princeton as had his father before him, and wrote a telling entry in his senior yearbook. He said that he wanted to attend business school, get involved in publishing, and "dabble in politics." Forbes skipped business school, but still managed to fulfill the two other goals.

Upon graduation, Forbes won a coveted place in the New Jersey National Guard, which kept him away from possible military service in Vietnam. His military obligation dispensed with, Forbes moved back to New Jersey, near Timberfield, the family's estate, and set right off to work with his father. There was no question that he would take over the business. He started as a research assistant at the magazine in 1970, and became associate editor in 1976.

In the 1970s, Forbes's father drew attention to himself by pursuing an extraordinarily extravagant lifestyle. He drove Harley-Davidson motorcycles, collected Fabergé eggs, dated actress Elizabeth Taylor, and on his seventieth birthday threw a $2 million birthday bash for himself in Tangiers. The self-promotion brought a higher profile for *Forbes* magazine and bigger profits.

By 1982, Steve Forbes was the magazine's deputy editor-in-chief and heir apparent to the Forbes throne. Forbes still jokes about his rise. In 1996 he told a reporter: "As my father liked to say, there is nothing wrong with nepotism so long as you keep it in the family."

Forbes inherited the business in 1990 when his father died. By that time, the flagship family publication was among the top business magazines in revenue. Today the magazine takes in about $315 million a year and employs about 600 people. Besides *Forbes* magazine, Forbes Inc. now owns and operates a host of publications, including *American Heritage*; *American Legacy,* which covers African-American history and culture; *Forbes Global Business & Finance*; *Forbes FYI,* a lifestyle magazine for corporate executives; four magazines on trends in technology—*Forbes ASAP, The Gilder Technology Report, Invention & Technology,* and *Executive Edge*—as well as *Forbes Digital Tool,* a Web business magazine.

Forbes also inherited Timberfield, a ranch in Colorado, a castle in France, a palace in Morocco, a Boeing 727 jet called *Capitalist Tool,* and a total worth estimated at $439 million.

Forbes's long-shot campaign for the presidency has everything to do with his acquired wealth—he was born to money, sheltered by it, taught to worship at its altar. Today, the presidential candidate makes no apologies for where money has taken him in life. He dismissed questions about the propriety of using his own fortune to bankroll his presidential ambitions, telling reporters in the 1996 campaign that the criticism "has been there since day one, but the key is the message."

But ever since he first arrived on the political scene as an adviser to Christine Todd Whitman in her first gubernatorial campaign in New Jersey, that message has been inextricably entwined with wealth.

*　　*　　*

In the summer of 1993 it appeared that Christine Todd Whitman had had her moment in the sun. In November 1990, Whitman, then a little-known county official, had shocked Senator Bill Bradley, and much of the national political establishment, by capturing 47 percent of the vote and nearly unseating him. Whitman rode on a wave of voter discontent created by Governor James Florio's massive tax hike; she had bumper stickers printed that read, "Get Florio, Dump Bradley."

Three years later, she would take on Florio directly, but an unfocused message and a series of gaffes set her back in the polls. She turned to some of her top advisers and friends for help.

Steve Forbes had known Whitman since the two attended the exclusive Far Hills Country School. In 1952, as children, they presented a pair of dolls to Richard Nixon's daughters when the vice-presidential candidate made a campaign swing through New Jersey. Their estates are both located in Somerset County, and the two both sent children to the same private school where they had been classmates. So when Whitman asked Forbes to aid her campaign, he was happy to oblige, and served as her chief economic adviser.

Forbes's economic philosophy derives largely from the supply-side economists who provided the intellectual argument for Ronald Reagan's tax policies. In 1978, Jude Wanniski, a former editorial writer for the *Wall Street Journal,* published a political and economic treatise titled *The Way the World Works.* Wanniski argued that broad, across-the-board tax cuts, limited government spending, and a stable currency would unleash an entrepreneurial golden age in the United States. As part of an effort to popularize his ideas, Wanniski organized meetings with a loosely connected group of New York investment bankers, politicians, and Washington insiders. Among the participants were economist Arthur Laffer and Representatives David Stockman of Michigan and Jack Kemp of New York. Conservative Washington journalist Robert Novak was a sometime participant in the talks. Occasionally, Forbes—who by then was working as an editor at *Forbes*—would attend meetings and listen attentively.

Rather than being a vocal participant, Forbes sat awkwardly on the fringes of the group as "an interested observer," Wanniski told the Center. "He showed up to meetings and scribbled notes in his notebook."

The emerging philosophy became known as "supply-side economics," and Forbes—despite his awkward reticence—became a disciple of the cause. Wanniski's treatise "could do for the Republican Party what Marx's manifesto did for communism," he wrote in the magazine after attending several sessions.

Forbes dusted off the supply-side theories for Whitman. With some help from Lawrence Kudlow, a former official in the Reagan Administration, he drew up a plan for a 30 percent across-the-board tax cut that became the centerpiece of Whitman's campaign against Florio. Politically, the plan played well with New Jersey voters, reminding them of the tax increases that Florio had championed in his first year of office. Whitman argued that the tax cuts would create hundreds of thousands of new jobs and pave the way for a revival of the state's economy. She hammered away at the tax issue and won the election.

For Forbes, his old friend's victory proved that the appeal of tax cuts as a political platform had outlived the Reagan Administration. It also did something else. Late in 1994, with Whitman's economic program already in effect, New Jersey was on the upswing. While there were other factors in the state's improving fortunes—1994 was a good year for the nation's economy generally—New Jersey companies spent $1 million on a thirty-seven-page glossy magazine promotional spread touting the state, the tax cuts, and the governor who pushed for them.

The publication that landed that million dollars in advertising revenue? *Forbes*.

In 1995, Jude Wanniski was distressed. Jack Kemp, whom he hoped would carry the torch for supply-side economics, had announced early in the year that he would not seek the Republican nomination for President. Bob Dole, the party's front-runner, had a mixed record at best on the issue of taxes. Senator Phil Gramm of Texas, who had hoped to run as the true conservative, had already lost a straw poll in Louisiana to Pat Buchanan, whose protectionist views on trade put him at odds with supply-side dogma. None of the other candidates seemed viable.

If not most, certainly many Americans who are registered as Republicans or Democrats find themselves in the same situation when looking at the candidates for the White House. The wish that someone else was running is one that goes unfulfilled. Unless one happens to have a friend like Steve Forbes.

Wanniski urged Forbes to run as Kemp's replacement to promote his tax-cutting agenda. Before he pushed the idea in earnest, he called three members of the Political Club for Growth, a group of Wall Street brokers and investment bankers who used to meet informally with Wanniski in the late 1970s. All three—Ted Forstmann, the millionaire leveraged-buyout financier; Lawrence Kudlow, who'd helped Forbes design Christine Todd Whitman's tax-cutting plan; and Dick Fox, a Philadelphia real estate developer—were enthusiastic and offered their financial support. Wanniski tracked down Forbes on summer vacation with his family and set out the reasons he should run.

Forbes was at first reluctant. *Business Week* reported that he visited Gramm in his Senate office to see if his views matched those of the supply-siders but came away disappointed. Forbes also asked Kemp's former chief of staff, William Dal Col, to help him decide whether he should run. Dal Col, who at the time was the president of Empower America, a conservative advocacy organization, didn't discourage him. Later that spring Forbes started to put together his own organization with Dal Col as the campaign manager.

In the fall, members of the Political Club for Growth gathered in the Manhattan office of Richard Gilder, a partner in the investment firm Gilder, Gagnon and Howe and a charter member of the group, to hear Forbes speak.

"Steve made a terrific presentation and really got people excited," Daniel Gressel, the manager of Teleos Asset Management, a hedge fund, said at the time in an interview with the *Wall Street Journal*. "We think of ourselves as the growth wing of the party, and Steve's message really resonates with us."

Forbes formally declared his candidacy for the presidency on September 22, 1995.

* * *

Given that the centerpiece of Forbes's 1996 campaign was a radical overhaul of the tax system that would have benefited individuals like Gressel the most, it's little wonder that the candidate's message resonated with him.

Forbes's version of the flat tax, which he's still pushing in his second run for the White House, is a tax only on wages and salaries. Income from dividends, capital gains from the sale of stocks and other assets, pensions, Social Security benefits, interest from savings and the like, all would be exempt from taxation. At the same time, high-income earners would be taxed at the same rate as lower income earners—a flat 17 percent. Itemized deductions would be eliminated, including those for charitable contributions and interest on home mortgages. Instead, individuals would get a standard deduction of $13,000; for married couples, the deduction would total $26,000. For each dependent, a taxpayer could claim another $5,000 deduction. Thus, Forbes trumpets his plan by noting that for a husband and wife with two children, the first $36,000 in income would be tax-free.

Steve Forbes has not made his own tax returns public, so to understand how his flat tax would benefit the wealthy, consider his rival for the Republican nomination, George W. Bush. In March 1999, Bush announced that the year before, he had taxable income of $18.4 million. Most of that amount came from capital gains when he sold his share of the Texas Rangers for $14.9 million. (Bush had bought into the baseball team in 1989 for $500,000.) Much of the rest of his money came from various trusts and investments he owns; his salary as governor totaled $97,890. Bush ended up writing a check to the Internal Revenue Service for $3.8 million.

Under Forbes's flat tax, none of the profit from selling the Rangers would be taxable. None of the millions his other investment trusts earned would be, either. Bush's total income would be $97,830. After taking the deduction for himself and his wife and his two dependent children, he would pay the flat 17 percent tax on what remained.

Bush would have owed the IRS just $10,521.

Forbe's signature line in his 2000 campaign is "Steve Forbes: He wants you to win." But who's the "you" in his slogan?

Of Forbes's top ten patrons, six are Wall Street investment bankers, who earn the lion's share of their income speculating in the stock market. All that income would be tax-free.

Heirs to large fortunes, on the other hand, would see the estate tax eliminated. That would be particularly beneficial to millionaires like Forbes: Since his father died in 1990, the family has been paying off the estate-tax bill in installments, according to an August 1999 article in the *Washington Post*. Perhaps that's why Forbes is so adamant about eliminating the estate tax. His campaign's Web site says that estate taxes are "regressive taxes that hurt working families, small-business owners, and especially farmers who want to pass their farms on to their children."

As for corporations, Forbes would slash their income tax rate from 35 to 17 percent. As with the flat tax for individuals, many deductions that are important to the middle class would disappear. For example, the write-offs that corporations can take for offering fringe benefits like health insurance would disappear, which might tempt employers to stop offering medical coverage for their employees. Similarly, the share of Social Security and Medicare taxes that employers pay could no longer be written off.

Forbes's flat tax would also eliminate the unlimited write-off for interest; while the deduction helped fuel the leveraged-buyout craze of the 1980s, eliminating it wholesale would hammer companies that are carrying a lot of debt. Similarly, it would abolish tax breaks for research-and-development costs, which would hurt high-technology companies.

While those deductions would disappear, others would be added to the code. Depreciation would disappear, allowing corporations to immediately write off the entire cost of capital investments in land, construction, and machinery. Business expenses, including travel and entertainment costs (even three-martini lunches), would be fully deductible.

As *Fortune* magazine pointed out in a 1996 article, one of the companies that would benefit most from rewriting the corporate tax rules would be none other than Forbes, Inc. The closely held firm carries little debt, has relatively few employees, and no research-and-development expenses. What's more, Forbes could write off the entire cost of entertaining wealthy advertisers on board his yacht. As advantageous as the tax would be to Forbes, he nonetheless has to live under the rules of the current system. He's proven to be quite adept at that as well.

Forbes attacks the current tax code on the grounds that it allows the rich and powerful to carve out loopholes for themselves while average Americans bear the brunt of the tax burden. He speaks from personal experience.

To encourage family farms, federal tax law allows cattle farmers to enjoy substantial write-offs on their business expenses. On top of the federal tax break, New Jersey cattle farmers get a property tax break if they own at least five acres of land and generate at least $500 in revenue a year. Which helps explain why Forbes is in the cattle business. His New Jersey farm meets the state's revenue test, with about $5,500 in yearly income, and he gets the federal write-offs for raising cattle, too.

Forbes raises three different breeds of show cows: Polled Herefords, Galloways, and belted Galloways. "You don't make money selling hamburger meat," Forbes told *Fortune* magazine in 1996. "You make money breeding show cows; that's the name of the game."

If Forbes did not stock his land with show cows, his property would be valued for tax purposes at $9 million according to a local land assessor. The assessor estimated that, with the cows, Forbes's land is assessed at only $160,531. On the 449 acres of his land with cows grazing, Forbes pays just $2,215 in real-estate taxes. On the smaller 70.5-acre plot without cattle, Forbes pays $50,000.

Forbes's bending of the tax code isn't limited to cattle. Just months after the 1996 election, when he failed in his attempt to "bury the tax code," he brought in tax attorneys to figure out a way to keep his ad campaign running on a year-round basis.

The resulting nonprofit organization, Americans for Hope, Growth, and Opportunity (AHGO), was designed to continue broadcasting his message and seek a broader base through television, radio, and the Internet. It solicited money, bankrolled ads featuring Forbes, and sent out press releases detailing the candidate's political views on issues of the day. William Dal Col was the president of Americans for Hope, Growth, and Opportunity; he switched over in 1999 to serve as manager of the 2000 campaign, the same post he held in 1996.

Forbes launched and operated AHGO in near-total secrecy. Because it has not applied for tax-exempt status, AHGO is shielded from the scrutiny that a tax-exempt organization receives. Tax-exempt organizations, for example, must make significant portions of their tax returns public; Forbes's not-for-profit corporation is under no such legal obligation.

Al Olsen, the accountant who prepared the tax return for AHGO in 1997, said he thought that Forbes's intent was indeed to avoid disclosing the organization's finances. "They told me I had to file a Form 1120," Olsen said in an interview with the Center for Public Integrity. "They used their own lawyer."

Had AHGO filed Form 990, as required for tax-exempt organizations, he would have been required to include all of its sources of revenue. AHGO listed its donors (by last name and first initial) on its Website, but when the Center asked Dal Col to provide the full names and the amounts and dates of their contributions, he refused.

The Forbes campaign was no more eager to release AHGO's tax returns than it was to disclose Forbes's own returns. Paul Sullivan, an attorney for Forbes, did not respond to the Center's request for a copy of the most recent tax forms filed by Americans for Hope, Government, and Opportunity.

In the 1996 presidential campaign, Forbes was coy about more than just his tax returns. He avoided talking about social issues altogether. He hardly ever mentioned abortion, saying only that he opposed a constitutional amendment to outlaw the procedure and that before abortions could be restricted, the hearts and minds of the American people would need to be changed. Forbes even antagonized one of the Republican Party's strongest grassroots groups. After learning that the Christian Coalition had attacked his position on abortion, he snapped that the group "doesn't speak for all Christians." While his statement was certainly accurate, it was hardly the best way to drum up support in the Iowa primary, where the organization that Pat Robertson founded still has considerable clout among voters. In 1988, incidentally, Forbes dismissed Robertson as a "toothy flake" in a column he wrote.

While the flat-tax plan in 1996 was undeniably popular among the financial elite (Patrick Buchanan memorably dismissed them as the "Chablis and Brie" wing of the GOP), it didn't draw the social conservatives to Forbes's campaign. They listened for the core issues: abortion, family values, and school prayer. Forbes did not give them what they wanted to hear, and his campaign ultimately suffered for it. He was determined not to let that happen in 2000.

A year after the 1996 election, Forbes addressed a convention of the Christian Coalition, where he declared that "life begins at conception." Early on in his 2000 campaign he changed his stump speeches to include a plug for a constitutional amendment that would ban abortions. He publicly promised to only appoint federal judges who passed an abortion litmus test. And on his campaign's Web site, Forbes now describes himself as an advocate of school choice and a proponent of "cultural renewal," an adaptation of the family-values theme.

"You don't succeed unless you're attentive to your customers," he said in 1998, when asked to explain the change.

The millionaire has courted social conservatives in the same way he attracted attention to his campaign in 1996: with lots of his own money. While Congress debated whether to ban "partial birth" abortions in 1997, Forbes financed radio advertisements in seven states in support of the ban. And when his old friend Christine Todd Whitman, who's drawn fire from religious conservatives for her pro-choice views, vetoed a partial-birth abortion ban in New Jersey, Forbes turned on her. He ran commercials in the state pushing for the legislature to override her veto.

In the 1996 campaign, Forbes argued that economics were inseparable from values, and that if the flat tax were implemented, everything else would fall into place. This time around, he's changed his tune. When he was asked what he would do if he had to choose between outlawing abortion and imposing a flat-tax plan, he said he would outlaw abortion.

That may be more a rhetorical nicety than a real reflection of Forbes's priorities. "If Forbes had his choice," said former adviser and confidant Jude Wanniski in 1998, "economics is all he'd want to talk about."

In any case, Forbes is getting what he wants. His 2000 campaign has received a boost of support from the Religious Right. He's hired Steve Scheffler, a former field director for the Christian Coalition, and Nancy Streck, a Christian Coalition activist who backed Buchanan in 1996, to work on his campaign. Prominent social conservative leaders such as Paul Weyrich and Richard Viguerie are now on his side, as well as former Christian Coalition chairmen from California, Georgia, and Louisiana.

Viguerie, a former aide to Barry Goldwater in 1964, helped to organize and establish the "New Right" movement in the 1970s, the precursor to today's religious conservative wing of the Republican Party. Viguerie, a pioneer in the political direct-mail business, was once dubbed the "King Midas of the Right."

Weyrich started the conservative Heritage Foundation and did his part to organize evangelical Christians into an active block of the Republican Party, a group he termed the "Moral Majority." In endorsing Forbes, Weyrich urged "pro-family conservatives" to fall in behind Forbes, who has "the financial resources to win the White House in 2000."

He has that in spades.

Despite the fact that he's never won a statewide election, let alone a national one, Forbes personifies the relationship between money and higher office. His inherited fortune, and his pledge to spend as much of it as he had to get his message out, gave him instant credibility in 1996. After winning early primary elections in Arizona and Delaware, he saw his economic agenda become the main issue of the Republican campaign. Pressured by the popularity of Forbes's candidacy, front-runner Bob Dole crafted his own plan to cut taxes and ran on that issue in the general election.

Forbes's 2000 strategy consists of more of the same: spend and spend some more. Just as he did in 1996, Forbes is refusing federal matching funds and will once again flout the spending limits. By the end of September 1999, the Forbes campaign had spent $18.9 million, more than any other candidate except for

George W. Bush, and far more than most candidates had even managed to raise by that point in the race.

That largesse fulfilled a promise that Forbes's campaign manager made early in 1999. William Dal Col pledged that Forbes would spend "whatever it takes to get the message out." While other candidates have raised money at $1,000-a-head appearances, Forbes can sell off a few assets to free up even more money to spend on the campaign. He sold the high-maintenance Boeing 727 before the 2000 race, put the family island in the South Pacific up for sale in 1997, and in 1999 was prepared to begin selling public shares in *Forbes Digital Tool,* Forbes, Inc.'s business-news Web site.

The prospect of another Forbes spending spree in 2000 sparked an historic fund-raising "arms race" with George W. Bush. Even before the formal campaign began in 1999, the Bush campaign decided that to compete with Forbes's money, it also would have to ignore the spending limits set by federal law. Forbes created a situation in which, for the first time since the campaign-finance system was erected to tame spending in 1974, two candidates were willing to raise and spend so much money that they would completely sidestep the campaign-finance system.

Forbes's campaign is remarkable not only for the amount of money he's willing to spend, but also for the way in which he spends it. While there's nothing all that original about negative advertising, Forbes has shown that he's willing to hire the best to dish out dirt on his opponents. In the 1996 campaign he hired campaign strategists Carter Wrenn and Tom Ellis—who crafted attack ads for the archconservative Senator Jesse Helms of North Carolina—and swamped Bob Dole with a torrent of negative commercials. By the end of February 1996, Forbes had spent $20 million on ads, most of which bashed Dole's record in the Senate, contrasting the front-runner's "Washington values" with his own "conservative values."

In 2000 the Forbes campaign was ready to repeat that strategy against front-runner George W. Bush. After his strong second-place showing in the Iowa straw poll, Forbes saw an opportunity to catch up with the Texas governor, and the Forbes campaign began polling Bush supporters in an apparent effort to find which stories would most damage Bush's popularity. When the Bush campaign warned Forbes against launching a mudslinging campaign, Forbes declared that if Bush did not want heat on the issues, "he should stay out of the kitchen."

In 1996, Forbes found that his checkbook could even substitute for popular support. To get on the ballot of the New York State primary, he needed tens of thousands of signatures statewide, but he didn't have the time, the campaign staff, or the grassroots support to make the deadline. The solution was to pay a consulting firm, New York Strategic Planning, Inc., of Clifton Park, New York, to do the legwork. He made the ballot and paid the firm $1.4 million for its work.

This time around Forbes has been just as willing to use his money to solve problems. As early as 1998, he needed to hire a high-impact player to jump-start his efforts on Iowa, whose crucial caucus in 2000 would solidify the front-runners of the presidential campaign. Forbes's solution was to recruit Iowa Republican Party chairman Steve Grubbs, and he did it with typical wealthy excess.

He dazzled Grubbs with the full Forbes VIP treatment: a special flight to Boston and a cruise on *The Highlander* in the company of former First Lady Nancy Reagan and former British Prime Minister Margaret Thatcher. Grubbs signed on with the campaign, a major leap for Forbes in buying his way into a race Bush already dominated.

Forbes often tells his audiences that he is "spending" his own money, but that's not entirely correct. In 1996, Forbes financed his presidential campaign almost entirely through more than $37 million in personal loans. The loans remained on the campaign's books until early 1999, when Forbes forgave them. This time around, Forbes is simply giving money to his presidential campaign, though he could switch back to lending mode—or some combination of cash and loans—whenever he chooses.

Forbes's list of top donors reads like a "Who's who" of Wall Street. Six of his top ten patrons are Wall Street investment banks or individual investment bankers. They are: the Equitable Companies and its subsidiary, Donaldson, Lufkin and Jenrette, Inc. (No. 2); Fleet Securities and its subsidiary, Quick & Reilly Group, Inc. (No. 4); Bear Stearns Company, Inc. (No. 5); Forbes's old friend and patron, Richard Gilder, and his firm, Gilder, Gagnon, Howe & Company (No. 7); Merrill Lynch & Company, Inc. (No. 8); and Castle Harlan (No. 9). John Castle, the firm's founder, used to work for Donaldson, Lufkin and Jenrette.

Richard Gilder was an early member of Jude Wanniski's group of supply-side devotees, and he helped run the Political Club for Growth. He and his firm also gave more than $360,000 to Newt Gingrich and GOPAC. In 1996 the treasurer of the Political Club for Growth, Lisa Britton Nelson, also served as GOPAC's executive director. Gilder also chaired Forbes's two most lucrative fund-raisers for the 1996 and 2000 election cycles—both held at the Waldorf-Astoria in Manhattan.

Carl Lindner, Forbes's No. 5 career patron, is the chairman and chief executive officer of American Financial Group, Inc., an Ohio-based insurance company that owns part of Chiquita Banana Brands International, Inc. Lindner has enough money to spread his campaign contributions around to both Republicans and Democrats; since 1991, Lindner and his companies have given more than $1 million in soft money to the Democratic Party, and more than $3 million in soft money to the Republican Party. He has contributed money to both Senator Jesse Helms of North Carolina and to the Democratic National Committee. In 1998, *Mother Jones* magazine ranked Lindner and his wife Edyth as the fourth biggest political donors in the United States. As in 1996 Forbes is again the beneficiary of Lindner's largesse.

Lindner is no stranger to Republican politics and to the benefits he can achieve by playing the game. In 1995, Bob Dole, a longtime recipient of Lindner's campaign contributions, tried to weigh in for Chiquita in a trade dispute with the European Union about the importation of its bananas. And Lindner served as a mentor to one of the most infamous alleged influence peddlers of all: Charles Keating, the savings-and-loan operator who turned to five U.S. Senators—later dubbed the "Keating Five"—for help when federal regulators began investigating his investments.

Another insurance provider, Conseco, Inc., is No. 10 on Forbes's patron list. Stephen Hilbert, its chairman, president, and chief executive officer, is one of the nation's highest-paid chief executives. Conseco, which has been described as "the Wal-Mart of financial-service companies," sells supplemental health, life, and group medical insurance; annuities; and other insurance products. Among its thirty insurance-related subsidiaries is Green Tree Financial Corporation, the top lender to owners of mobile homes in the United States.

Seven of Conseco's executive officers and a member of its board of directors have given either to Forbes's campaign, to Americans for Hope, Growth, and Opportunity, or both. None of them responded to inquiries from the Center about their contributions.

Forbes's two top patrons are members of the extended "Forbes, Inc., family." Employees of Forbes, Inc., and their family members are Forbes's No. 1 career patron, having given a total of at least $38,000 to his various political committees—in addition to the $44 million put in by their boss. Behind Forbes, Inc., is Fisher Investments, Inc., a money management firm based in Silicon Valley. Kenneth Fisher, the company's chairman and chief executive officer, is a columnist for *Forbes* magazine.

Former Reagan Administration officials are among his patrons as well. They include Commerce Secretary Robert Mosbacher, USIA Director Charles Wick, and Chief of Protocol Selena Roosevelt. Caspar Weinberger, the former Secretary of Defense, has also given generously. In 1993 Weinberger became the chairman of the board of Forbes, Inc., and he writes a column for *Forbes* magazine.

Forbes has also received money from thirty-five individuals listed by his magazine as among the 400 richest Americans, including John T. Walton, whose fortune consists largely of Wal-Mart stock; Leonard Lauder, the chairman and chief executive officer of Esteé Lauder, Inc., the cosmetics firm; and William Wrigley, Jr., the president and chief executive officer of the Wm. Wrigley Jr. Company, which makes Juicy Fruit and Doublemint gum. All three inherited their billion-dollar fortunes; all three would face hefty capital gains taxes if they sold off their stakes in their companies, or large estate-tax bills if they bequeath their wealth to their heirs.

Little wonder, then, that they support the bespectacled magazine editor from New Jersey, whose magazine reports on the "doers and doings" of the business world and whose tax proposals would save them hundreds of millions, perhaps billions, in taxes. After all, Steve Forbes wants them to win, too.

MALCOLM "STEVE" FORBES, JR.
Top Ten Career Patrons

Ranking	Company/Individual/Family Name	Total
1	Forbes, Inc., New York***	$44,062,787
2	The Equitable Companies, New York***	$26,000
3	Fisher Investments, Woodside, California/ Kenneth Fisher family***	$25,000
4	Fleet Securities, Inc., New York***	$20,000
5	The Bear Stearns Company, Inc., New York	$19,000
5	Lindner family, Cincinnati	$19,000
7	Gilder, Gagnon, Howe & Company, New York***	$17,500
8	Merrill Lynch & Company, Inc., New York	$15,240
9	Castle Harlan, Inc., New York/John K. Castle family***	$14,000
10	Conseco, Inc., Carmel, Indiana	$13,000

This list is based on individual and PAC contributions to Forbes's 1996 presidential campaign; individual contributions of $1,000 and above to Americans for Hope, Growth, and Opportunity, Inc.; individual contributions to the federal AHGO PAC; and individual and PAC contributions to Forbes's 2000 presidential campaign through June 30, 1999.
Sources: Federal Election Commission; Center for Responsive Politics; Americans for Hope, Growth and Opportunity.

1. Includes loans by Steve Forbes to the 1996 campaign that have since been forgiven; candidate contributions by Steve Forbes to the 2000 campaign; and contributions from Forbes family members and employees of Forbes, Inc.
2. Most of these contributions came from employees of Donaldson, Lufkin & Jenrette, a 73 percent owned subsidiary of Equitable.
4. Most of these contributions come from employees of Quick & Reilly, a subsidiary of Fleet Securities.

***NOTE: Donors marked by (***) have given $1,000 or more to AHGO. The Forbes campaign has thus far refused to disclose exactly how much each donor gave to AHGO. The above figures attribute $1,000 to each AHGO donor; however, such donors could have given far more than the amounts listed.

Orrin Hatch

||||||||||

During the unprecedented, raucous—at times even surreal—Senate hearings investigating the sexual harassment allegations Anita Hill made against Supreme Court nominee Clarence Thomas, Orrin Hatch accused the University of Oklahoma law professor of having words put in her mouth. He claimed that Hill, in collusion with "slick lawyers" bent on derailing Thomas's nomination, had concocted the whole tale. And on October 12, 1991, Hatch accused Hill of fabricating charges against Thomas by subconsciously drawing on works of fiction she had read. Waving a copy of William Peter Blatty's novel, *The Exorcist,* Hatch suggested that she'd stolen the by-then-infamous "pubic-hair" anecdote from the book by quoting the following line: "There appeared to be an alien pubic hair floating around in my gin."

Hatch knew all about having words put in his mouth. The Senator from Utah, once crowned the "Golden Throat" for the large number of paid speaking engagements he accepted, delivered a speech on the Senate floor on February 22, 1990, in which he defended the Bank of Credit and Commerce International. BCCI, known in some quarters as the "Bank of Crooks and Criminals International," was then under investigation by the Justice Department, the New York City district attorney's office, and dozens of law enforcement authorities in places ranging from Great Britain to Lebanon.

"The BCCI case in Tampa was a very serious matter," Hatch said of one of the many trials involving the Middle Eastern financial institution and its executives, "but the charges ought to be viewed in their proper perspective. The case arose from the conduct of a small number of BCCI's more than 14,000 employees." Hatch further downplayed the dimensions of the scandal: "No member of the bank's senior management or its board of directors was alleged in the indictment even to have been aware of any of the laundering transactions—much less to have approved them."

Once known as one of the sharpest lawyers in Pittsburgh, Hatch said he based his defense of the bank on a briefing by officials of the Justice Department. He failed to mention that he'd also met with the defendants' lawyers, one of whom, Robert Altman, was a close friend. A memo written by Altman disclosed that Hatch's speech defending BCCI and its top management wasn't his own work; BCCI's lawyers had drafted it.

Shortly after he delivered his remarks, Hatch telephoned Swaleh Naqvi, the bank's chief executive officer, and sought a loan for a business partner and campaign contributor of his, Houston developer Monzer Hourani. When the local news media got wind of the call, Hatch denied wrongdoing, and requested that the Senate Select Committee on Ethics investigate his relationship with BCCI.

That relationship was tangled. One of Hatch's top aides, Michael Pillsbury, had a financial relationship with Mohammed Hammoud, a large stockholder in BCCI. Pillsbury advised Hatch on his dealings with BCCI; in 1989, the Senator and his aide attempted to help the bank settle federal money-laundering charges.

On November 20, 1993, the committee cleared Hatch of any wrongdoing.

As for BCCI's top management, they didn't get off as lightly as Hatch. Swaleh Naqvi, for example, was indicted on fraud charges in New York related to BCCI's collapse. And Hourani, Hatch's old business partner, was fined $10,000 in 1995 for conspiring to evade contribution limits by using his employees to funnel $7,000 to Hatch's 1988 reelection campaign.

After he was cleared by the Senate Ethics Committee, Hatch released a statement saying that he was "confident my fellow Utahans understand that those who, like myself, will never be part of the Washington establishment and who stand up for what they believe is right, are sometimes wrongfully smeared."

Hatch may not have started life as part of the Washington establishment, but by the time he announced his candidacy for President in the summer of 1999, he had certainly learned to play by its lax rules.

Hatch was born in Pittsburgh, Pennsylvania, in 1934, during the darkest days of the depression. His father, Jesse Hatch, was a metal lather while his mother, Helen, took care of Orrin and his siblings. Once, when the Hatches lost their home, Jesse Hatch borrowed $50 to buy second-hand building materials to put another roof over their heads. Hatch's life was hardly privileged. He worked as a janitor, an all-night desk clerk, and, like his father, as a metal lather.

Hatch attended Brigham Young University, but interrupted his studies for two stints as a missionary—one for himself and the other for a brother who was killed in combat during World War II. Hatch returned to school and received his bachelor's degree in history in 1959. After that, he put himself through law school at the University of Pittsburgh partly by mopping dormitory floors. He earned his law degree in 1962.

Hatch, whose great-grandfather helped to settle Utah, set up his own home there in 1969. He became a successful tax-fraud attorney, but left a prestigious law firm and substantial salary to pursue a career in politics, taking on an entrenched three-term Democrat, Frank Moss, in 1976. Hatch was virtually unknown at the time he declared for the race. He attracted some measure of national attention by delivering the nominating speech for Ronald Reagan at the 1976 Republican National Convention in Kansas City, Missouri. While Reagan would have to wait four years to be his party's nominee, Hatch upset Moss. The son of two New Deal Democrats was sworn in as the Republican Senator from Utah in 1977.

Hatch made his Washington debut as an especially audacious

freshman Senator. By his own admission, he was initially perceived as pushy, arrogant, and sometimes irritating in his zeal to impress Senate veterans. Dissatisfied with this perception, Hatch heeded the advice of Senator James Allen, a courtly Republican from Alabama, who urged him to learn the lay of the land before alienating himself from his more-experienced colleagues.

Hatch's first target was the Labor Law Reform Bill of 1978, which would have made it much easier for labor unions to organize and recruit new members. Hatch's history as a card-carrying member of the Wood, Wire and Metal Lathers Union didn't thwart his resolve to make a big mark as a Senate conservative. Hatch took on the legendary Hubert Humphrey—the labor bill was the Minnesota Senator's last major legislative initiative—and won, chiefly by introducing nearly 1,200 amendments to the bill as part of his filibuster, earning him the nickname "Borin' Orrin" for talking the bill to death.

Hatch certainly learned to use the rules of the Senate to partisan advantage quickly; he also learned how to make them benefit the fat cats who supported his campaigns. In 1982, Hatch introduced an amendment to the Tax Equity and Fiscal Responsibility Act that allowed companies to deduct "construction period interest and taxes for construction projects that were planned by July 1, 1982; for which governmental approval has been requested in writing; and on which construction will begin before January 1, 1984."

A member of the House Ways and Means Committee told the *Washington Post* in 1982, "That description was drawn up to fit Marriott." Marriott International is the second-largest lodging company in the world; the giant hotelier's revenues neared the $8 billion mark in 1998, making it No. 206 on the *Fortune* 500. In 1982, the company hired then–Speaker Thomas "Tip" O'Neill's son, Christopher "Kip" O'Neill, to lobby House Democrats for its special tax break. Among Republicans, the company had an even better lobbyist: Orrin Hatch.

The owners of the corporation, the Marriott family of Bethesda, Maryland, are Hatch's No. 2 career patron, having given him $82,000 over the years. Members of the Marriott family (which now includes one of Hatch's sons) were particularly generous to Hatch when his involvement with BCCI led to a Senate ethics investigation; they contributed some $50,000 to his legal defense fund, almost one-sixth of the total amount Hatch raised to pay his attorneys at Miller, Cassidy, Larroca & Lewin. That was small change compared to the service Hatch had already provided to Marriott: The amendment he sponsored saved the company upward of $55 million.

But then, Hatch has never been shy about using his power in the Senate to push for legislation that benefits his most durable and deep-pocketed supporters. In 1990, R. Earl Holding, a wealthy real-estate developer, wanted to open a ski resort in the Wasatch Mountains in Utah. The land Holding sought was owned by the federal government and administered by the U.S. Forest Service. Holding offered to swap other land he owned in Utah for the Wasatch Mountain property. Reluctantly, the Forest Service agreed, and granted him 220 acres.

At a community meeting in Ogden, Utah, Hatch called the grant to Holding, considerably less than the developer sought, "a dumb-assed, boneheaded decision." When Hatch asked if anyone at the meeting supported it, there was no response. "Well, if you do hear of someone, I want to know," he said. "I'll kill them." Hatch then put his arm around Stan Tixier, the Forest Service's regional forester whose job included managing federal lands in Utah and said: "I've never asked Stan to help us yet that he hasn't done it. I hope that puts you on the spot, Stan."

Indeed it did. Holding wound up with 1,320 acres of land in the Wasatch Mountains. The property, now known as the Snowbasin Ski Area, will host some of the events of the 2002 Winter Olympic Games. Holding, who sat on the committee that lured the games to Utah, also landed $13.8 million in contracts for the use of his resort in the games.

Holding and his family, who also own Sinclair Oil Corporation, Little America Hotel Company, and Sun Valley Corporation, are Hatch's No. 8 career patron. The developer also helped Hatch's personal bank balance. Thanks to the development of the Snowbasin Ski Area, a parcel of adjacent land that Hatch owned—he declared its value to be no more than $15,000 on his Senate financial disclosure forms—netted him $140,000 when he put it up for sale in 1999.

Pushing the land deal for Holding was just one of many favors Hatch has done for his wealthy contributors, many of which have benefited the Senator personally. Consider Hatch's relationship with the dietary supplements industry. When the Food and Drug Administration sought to tighten labeling laws for vitamins and other dietary supplements in 1991, the industry fought back hard, with Hatch leading the charge. (Hatch's state is home to so many supplement companies that Wall Street analysts have dubbed it "Vitamin Valley.")

On September 18, 1992, as the Senate considered a major drug bill, Hatch introduced an amendment that prohibited the FDA from monitoring and evaluating health claims for dietary supplements until the end of the following year. Hatch's amendment passed, and then-President Bush signed the drug bill into law.

At the time, Hatch owned nearly 72,000 shares of Pharmics, Inc., a Utah company that sold prenatal vitamins and vitamin C additives. Walter J. Plumb III, the company's president, is Hatch's former law partner. Hatch maintained that there was no conflict of interest because he was unaware of the company's nutritional supplements business at the time he introduced the legislation.

But Hatch, apparently, was just warming up. In 1994, he introduced the Dietary Supplement Health and Education Act, which was aimed at even further restricting the FDA's jurisdiction over vitamins and other dietary supplements. At a fund-raising brunch in Las Vegas in 1993, eighty or so leaders of the industry gathered to pay tribute to Hatch—and his 1994 re-election fund. Hatch's legislative beneficence gave the industry a big boost, contributing to a multibillion-dollar-a-year surge in sales.

"My bottom-line goal," Hatch said in 1998, "is to allow the one hundred million Americans who regularly consume dietary supplements to continue to reap the ever-growing body of science indicating that dietary supplements can promote health." Hatch has pushed a wide array of legislation to benefit firms that manufacture and market dietary supplements—chief among them Herbalife International, the Los Angeles-based company that is Hatch's

No. 3 career patron. His son, Scott, used to lobby for Herbalife. Now, he works for Parry, Romani, DeConcini, Inc., a Washington lobbying firm that counts Herbalife among its clients.

Thomas Parry, Hatch's former chief of staff and chief counsel, is one of the firm's founders. One of three former aides to Hatch who now lobby for the dietary supplements industry, Parry also raises money for Hatch and runs his annual charity golf event.

Hatch has been equally generous to more traditional medications. Eli Lilly & Company, the pharmaceutical giant, is No. 10 on Hatch's career patron list. The Indianapolis-based firm has reaped significant rewards from the Waxman-Hatch Act of 1984, which gave many of its products up to five years of additional patent protection. Among them is Prozac, the world's best-selling antidepressant medication. Thanks to the Waxman-Hatch Act, Eli Lilly still holds exclusive rights to Prozac, which accounts for nearly 30 percent of the company's total revenues.

Hatch did much the same favor for Glaxo Wellcome, another pharmaceutical manufacturer. In the fall of 1995, Hatch brokered a compromise bill that let Glaxo, which produces Zantac, an ulcer medication, keep its nineteen-month patent extension on the world's top-selling drug. Glaxo Wellcome is Hatch's No. 7 career patron.

Hatch's leadership role on the Judiciary Committee has proved beneficial to the Seagram Company, one of the world's largest distillers and the owner of Universal Studios, and Hatch's No. 6 career patron. The committee has jurisdiction over the copyrights of musical recordings—an issue of dire importance to PolyGram, the largest music company in the world, which Universal Studios acquired in 1998.

In 1995, Hatch and Democrat Dianne Feinstein of California proposed a bill to protect the copyrights of recorded music—and the interests of large royalty owners like PolyGram—from digital distribution in black market mediums, including the Internet. Hatch had something of a personal interest in the legislation; over the years, he's handsomely supplemented his Senate salary with royalties from his recorded Scripture readings, and from two compact discs for which he composed inspirational lyrics in 1998.

Hatch owes thanks for some of the royalties to Marilyn Bergman, the president of the American Society of Composers, Authors, and Publishers. In 1997, she encouraged the aspiring songwriter to try his hand at writing lyrics—just at the time when the legislation Hatch and Feinstein had proposed was pending before the Judiciary Committee. Bergman forwarded Hatch's work to Sony Music Entertainment, Inc. in Nashville.

Hatch was also instrumental in protecting PolyGram's interests in 1997, when he sponsored legislation to close a loophole in the copyright laws opened by two federal court rulings. At issue were songs recorded before the 1978 copyright law took effect; federal judges in Nashville and San Francisco held that unless royalty owners placed a copyright notice on them, the songs would enter the public domain. Most songs had no such notice. The bill sponsored by Hatch—and passed by the Senate unanimously—provided them with copyright protection, worth some $1 billion a year to the major record companies.

Wealthy industries form the branches of Hatch's money tree. When Hatch shakes it, whether to launch another reelection campaign or to continue paying the lawyers who represented him in BCCI-related matters, green paper leaves come floating down. And Hatch seems eager to push legislation that will serve the interests of his biggest donors.

With perhaps one glaring exception.

In August 1988, Hatch stood hand in hand in Salt Lake City with one of the great American icons of the twentieth century: Muhammad Ali. The heavyweight boxer was there to endorse Hatch, running for his third term in the Senate, over Brian Moss, his liberal Democratic challenger and the son of former Senator Frank Moss, whom Hatch had defeated some twelve years earlier. Although Hatch and Ali seemed every bit the political odd couple, there was at least one tie to bind: Both men had been boxers.

It was on the campaign trail that year that the mysterious relationship between Hatch, the former amateur welterweight, and Ali, the three-time heavyweight champion, came to light. Hatch seemed to delight in referring to Ali as "a dear friend," though in truth he had known Ali for little more than a year. The two men had met in 1987, when Ali visited Hatch's Senate office in Washington to thank him for helping one of his associates obtain an appointment from the Justice Department. As the highest-ranking Republican on the Senate Judiciary Committee, which reviews such appointments, Hatch's endorsement carried a lot of weight. (Since 1995, when Republicans took control of the Senate, Hatch has been the committee's chairman.) Ali expressed his thanks by giving Hatch an autographed punching bag.

In the summer of 1988, Hatch sent a memo to his favorite reporters in which he said that he planned to introduce legislation that would allow Ali to refile a $50 million lawsuit against the federal government over his draft-evasion conviction during the Vietnam War. Rather than go to Vietnam, Ali had made a principled stand, fought the validity of the draft in court, and lost both his case and his heavyweight title in the process. His act of conscience cost him three prime years of his boxing career; the Supreme Court ultimately overturned his conviction in 1971.

A few months after Hatch announced that he would help the fighter in his bid to seek compensation from the federal government for the lost years of his career, Ali gave Hatch one of only two championship rings he'd won in bouts for the heavyweight title. Hatch listed the ring as a gift on his 1988 personal financial disclosure report, which he filed with the Secretary of the Senate's office on May 15, 1989, and assigned it a value of $6,500. Hatch's report also included this brief notation about the ring: "Is considered priceless to the recipient."

As well it may have been. The ring—engraved with the inscription, "With love from Muhammad Ali"—was almost certainly unique and undoubtedly could have fetched plenty more than $6,500 from a private collector. But the far more significant issue was the glaring appearance of a conflict of interest—and, in particular, the proximity of the gift to the legislation that Hatch was pushing to help Ali.

"Everyone on Capitol Hill knew this was Muhammad Ali's bill," a spokesman for Congress Watch told Rick Shenkman, a reporter for KUTV in Salt Lake City. "The fact that it's Muhammad Ali, whom a lot of us admire and respect, can't change the fact that Senator Hatch shouldn't be taking huge gifts from people with direct interests in legislation."

When Shenkman, with cameras rolling, asked Hatch if Ali had a direct interest in the legislation, the Senator replied only indirectly. "I can't say that *he* did . . . his attorney did and others did, sure." Soon, however, Hatch yielded under the torrent of negative publicity. He reneged on his promise to sponsor legislation to help Ali.

Many years later, however, Hatch paid homage to Ali in a way that did not require the consent of his colleagues on Capitol Hill. He wrote a musical tribute to Ali titled "The Difference Makes the Difference," which Gladys Knight recorded and performed on a cable-television network in February 1998.

ORRIN HATCH
Top Ten Career Patrons

Ranking	Company/Individual/Family Name	Total
1	AFLAC, Inc., Columbus, Georgia	$92,580
2	Marriott family/Marriott International, Inc., Bethesda, Maryland	$82,000
3	Herbalife International, Inc., Los Angeles	$74,684
4	Fluor Corporation, Aliso Viejo, California	$57,500
5	Contran Corporation/Harold Simmons family, Dallas	$56,000
6	The Seagram Company, Ltd., and affiliated companies, Montreal, Quebec	$55,994
7	Glaxo Wellcome, Inc., Greenford, Middlesex, United Kingdom	$46,999
8	Holding family/Sinclair Oil Corporation, Salt Lake City	$44,250
9	Baker & Hostetler, Cleveland	$38,160
10	Eli Lilly & Company, Indianapolis	$37,000

This list is based on individual and PAC contributions to Hatch's Senate campaigns from 1979 through June 30, 1999; all contributions to the Capitol Committee from 1995–1998; and all contributions to the Hatch Legal Expense Trust from 1993–1998. Contributions to Hatch's presidential exploratory committee had not been disclosed as of this writing.
Sources: Federal Election Commission; Center for Responsive Politics; Secretary of the Senate.

---

5. Includes contributions from employees of Contran Corporation; its 90 percent controlled subsidiary Valhi, Inc.; Valhi subsidiary NL Industries, Inc.; and members of Contran founder Harold Simmons's family.
6. Includes contributions from employees of Joseph E. Seagram & Sons, and from employees of Universal Studios/MCA, which Seagram acquired in 1995. Contributions come from employees of the U.S. subsidiaries.
7. Includes contributions from employees of Glaxo, Inc.; Burroughs Wellcome (which Glaxo acquired in 1995); and Glaxo Wellcome. Contributions come from employees of the U.S. subsidiaries.

Alan Keyes

In a burst of candor, Robert Dole took to the Senate floor on April 10, 1989 and told his colleagues: "PACs give to incumbents, and that is me and the other incumbents in this chamber, because access to an officeholder is more important than a Member [of Congress]'s party, ideology, or even voting record on the issues."

Therein lies the problem for Alan Keyes. Although the Republican has ideology to spare, he's never held elective office. He lost two bids for a seat in the U.S. Senate from Maryland, and in his previous presidential campaign he was never able to win more than seven percent of the vote in any primary.

So the question for Keyes in 2000 is much the same as it was in 1996: not whether he has a shot at his party's nomination, but whether he has a chance to mount a serious effort as an also-ran. If the past is any guide, Keyes doesn't have much of a chance.

The August 23, 1999 edition of *Newsweek* magazine featured a brief story on the Republican straw poll results out of Ames, Iowa. It mentioned all but one of the challengers for the Republican nomination, including front-runner George W. Bush, who won the event; Lamar Alexander, who dropped out of the race after his poor showing; and even John McCain, who didn't even bother to show up in Ames. Only Alan Keyes's name was nowhere to be read. The photograph that accompanied the piece showed all the candidates who competed in the straw poll on the stage; Keyes was hidden behind a waving Dan Quayle, barely visible.

Much like his cash-poor campaign.

For Keyes, the Iowa straw poll was a step up from some of his experiences in 1996. Keyes was arrested and hauled away in handcuffs when he tried to crash a televised debate for Republican candidates at an Atlanta television station on March 3, 1996. WSB-TV invited only the top four GOP candidates: Dole, Buchanan, Forbes, and Alexander. Keyes, who was still an active candidate at the time, screamed, "I have a right to speak," as his hands were cuffed behind his back and he was led to a waiting police car.

Oddly enough, Keyes was never charged or even booked after his arrest. He was driven around Atlanta for about twenty minutes and then dropped off in a parking lot by a City Hall annex. In essence, he'd been abducted from the steps of WSB-TV's headquarters on Peachtree Street, driven far enough away that he couldn't cause any further trouble, and let go. William Campbell, the mayor of Atlanta, drove to the parking lot and offered Keyes a ride. Keyes accepted the mayor's offer and promised him he wouldn't blame the police for the incident. Keyes threatened to sue WSB-TV for barring him from the debate. (Keyes, however, didn't follow through on his threat.)

The non-arrest may have marked the high point in Keyes's campaign—he was invited to participate in two subsequent debates, one in Dallas and another in Miami, shortly after the Atlanta incident—even as it underscored the bizarreness of his campaign.

Keyes is a black conservative whose most ardent supporters are Christian anti-abortion activists and hard-line Jewish supporters of Israel. He protested the advantages of incumbency by paying himself a salary with contributions to his 1992 Senate campaign. He attacks the corrosive role of money in politics, yet his own campaigns have been plagued by financial and ethical irregularities.

Despite his problems with campaign money, the detention in Atlanta, his low name recognition, and his lack of a strong organization, Keyes managed to get himself on the ballot for thirty-two Republican primaries in 1996. His best showing was not in a primary, however, but in the Iowa caucuses, where he drew seven percent of the vote.

Keyes was an Army brat, the youngest of five children in a family that moved frequently from base to base. Neither of his parents graduated from college, but they stressed to their children the importance of higher education. During Keyes's junior year in high school, he won the American Legion's national oratorical contest with a speech titled "The Blessings of Liberty, the Blessings of Life."

In an interview with a reporter for the *Washington Post* in 1992, Keyes said the speech "was about being proactive in defending freedom and the principles of justice," adding, "It's actually very much like the speech I give now."

Keyes was a good student, won college scholarships, and enrolled in Cornell University, but he left for Paris after a year. On his return to the United States, he transferred to Harvard University, where he finished his undergraduate education in 1972 and went on to get a Ph.D. in government in 1979.

After finishing his doctoral work, Keyes joined the foreign service. There, he attracted the attention of Jeane Kirkpatrick, the U.S. Representative to the United Nations, and Keyes soon found himself elevated to the post of U.S. Representative to the U.N. Economic and Social Council.

While there, he managed to infuriate some civil rights organizations. While nearly all Democrats and many Republicans on Capitol Hill were calling for sanctions against the apartheid regime in South Africa, the Reagan Administration opposed them. Keyes publicly supported the administration's position.

"I think it is racist to suggest that my mind should somehow be bound by black instead of reason," Keyes later explained in a January 1996 interview with a reporter for the *Philadelphia Inquirer*. "I will follow reason, and reason has no color. It doesn't have a skin."

In 1988, he defended the Bush campaign's use of the infamous "Willie Horton" ad, calling the furor that it caused "disingenuous." But Keyes has been willing to play the racism card when it suits his political ambitions. In an article he wrote after his first losing

Senate campaign, he charged the news media with both liberal bias and racism, saying that they had portrayed his candidacy as tokenism and not as a serious campaign. And in 1992 he accused the Republican Party of abandoning him because of his race. "I do not believe there is a sincere commitment on the part of the Republican Party leadership," he said, "to reach out to the black community."

Keyes served at the United Nations from 1983 until 1985, when he became Assistant Secretary of State for International Organizations. After leaving the State Department, Keyes spent a short time in residence at the American Enterprise Institute for Public Policy Research, a conservative Washington think tank. He was already being mentioned as a possible Republican candidate for Congress.

In 1988 a fortuitous series of circumstances led Keyes to run for the U.S. Senate from Maryland. In June the Republican nominee abruptly pulled out of the race, and Kirkpatrick, Keyes's former boss at the United Nations, recommended him to officials of the Maryland Republican Party. Neither of the state's two Republican House Members, Helen Bentley and Constance Morella, was interested in challenging Paul Sarbanes, the popular Democratic incumbent. The door was left open for Keyes, who handily won the party's nomination at a special convention.

In the general election Keyes was no match for Sarbanes. He managed to raise only $662,000, an unimpressive sum for a Senate race, and less than half of what Sarbanes raised. Keyes's message of moralistic conservatism didn't play particularly well in Maryland, a state where Democrats outnumbered Republicans by more than two-to-one. In the end he garnered 38 percent of the vote.

After losing in 1988, Keyes established the Campaign for Maryland's Future. The PAC's ostensible aim was to support Republican candidates in Maryland. It soon became apparent, however, that the group served to support only one candidate: Alan Keyes. In fact, in 1992 it donated $5,000 to Keyes, then became his official campaign committee. Keyes also spent time between his campaigns as the president of Citizens Against Government Waste.

When Keyes ran for the Senate again in 1992—this time against Barbara Mikulski, another popular incumbent—he was given even less of a chance than he had the first time. His campaign was especially hurt by the revelation that he was using campaign contributions to pay himself a salary.

Candidates hardly ever receive salaries from their campaigns. When they do, the pay is not usually very high. When Alan Keyes was asked about why he was drawing a salary of $8,463 a month from his U.S. Senate campaign in 1992, his response was: "I am a successful person. You want me to come work for you, you have got to pay me a certain minimum. That's where I'm established in life. If I don't breathe, eat, and live comfortably, I won't be able to function."

Even now, aides in Keyes's presidential campaign defend his decision to pay himself from his Senate campaign coffers. Mary Lewis, the chief of staff of Keyes's campaign, pointed out that those in office still draw their taxpayer-funded salaries while running for reelection. "They all know how fundamentally unfairly they've stacked the deck," Lewis told the Center for Public Integrity. "Alan thought he would be able to make a strong public case against the disproportionate advantages and featherbedding that the laws the incumbents wrote themselves allow."

Unfortunately for Keyes, he wasn't able to make the public case in 1992, and lost to Mikulski in a landslide. He received just 29 percent of the vote.

Given Keyes's electoral track record—0 for 2—it surprised many when he announced in 1995 that he would seek the Republican nomination for President. When the idea was first suggested to Keyes, in fact, he was surprised as well. In 1994, Arthur Rocker, a political consultant from Georgia, met with Keyes in Nashville, Tennessee, to urge him to run. "My reaction was, 'Excuse me? This doesn't make a whole lot of sense. I just got through losing two Senate races and you're coming and asking me to run for President?'" Keyes told the *Baltimore Sun* in a July 1995 interview.

Others echoed Keyes's initial surprise, including those who had supported him in the past. On hearing that he planned to run for President, Susan Saum-Wicklein, the manager of his 1992 Senate campaign, said incredulously, "He's doing what?" Saum-Wicklein, a former chairman of the Maryland Republican Party, added, "I think this shows that in the United States of America, anyone can run for President."

Keyes ran, but not necessarily gracefully. In the summer of 1995, Rocker, who had joined the campaign as its finance director, had an ugly falling out with the man he'd urged to enter the race. In June he quit the campaign, accusing Keyes of running merely to raise his profile so he could command higher speaking fees. The Keyes campaign countercharged that Rocker was the source of "serious, still-unresolved discrepancies in the finances" of the campaign and that some $58,000 was unaccounted for. Rocker denied the charges. Then he refused to turn his files over to the campaign. Then he sued Keyes, claiming he was owed $30,000 in back pay and expenses.

The lawsuit was resolved out of court; neither party would discuss the terms of the settlement, although Rocker told the Center that he was unhappy with the amount of money he received. "Surely it wasn't what I asked for," he said, "but the lawyer just went ahead [and settled]."

Michael Tarone, who represented Keyes in the lawsuit and still represents the presidential hopeful's campaign committee, dismissed the Rocker story. "It was settled way back," he told the Center. "It's old news."

While Rocker and Keyes's campaign staff were issuing charges and countercharges in the summer of 1995, the *Baltimore Sun* obtained internal memos suggesting that Keyes was again getting paid by his campaign, albeit indirectly. In a memo dated June 28, 1995, George F. Lynch, Jr., the campaign's accountant, warned that there was a "possible commingling of personal and campaign monies . . . If the situation which has been reported is not remedied immediately, all of the other efforts to elect Alan Keyes for President could be in jeopardy."

In a memo written a week earlier, Tarone had urged Keyes to "erect a Chinese Wall between the run for office and your other life."

Keyes raised money at churches, not for his campaign, but for his personal living expenses. His campaign staff arranged for his personal speaking appearances, from which he also derived an income. And he allegedly used campaign contributions to pay for a limousine to drive him to and from WCBM-AM, the Baltimore station that aired his call-in radio show.

Keyes was unapologetic. "The distinction between the campaign and my personal life is an absurd distinction," he told the *Baltimore Sun,* "because I've got no personal life and haven't had one for months."

Dan Godzich, who's managing Keyes's 2000 presidential campaign, called the idea that Keyes is running for his personal enrichment laughable. "To tell you the truth, every time Alan runs for office he hurts himself financially very badly," Godzich told the Center. "It's a big sacrifice for his family. He doesn't come from a wealthy background, so he doesn't have the resources of many of the people running. He's certainly not a Forbes. A lot of people don't realize that John McCain is worth about $80 million through his marriage. And on top of that he's getting a Senate salary anyway. For Alan, it's a big sacrifice."

Compared with the other candidates, Keyes is a man of relatively modest means, although his income, well into six figures, is far more than that of a middle-class American. He owns a house in suburban Maryland that he purchased in 1989 for $490,000. As of this writing, Keyes had yet to file the required financial disclosure form listing his assets and income with the Federal Election Commission, so it is unclear how much he earned in 1998 or how much he is worth. In his 1996 bid, Keyes filed an incomplete disclosure form several months late and after repeated requests from the FEC for the information. In his 1992 Senate race he disclosed that in 1991 his income was $300,000.

A look at Keyes's individual campaign donors does not reveal any well-known fat cats or scions of traditional American wealth. Among his most notable contributors: entertainer Pat Boone, foreign-policy experts Jeane Kirkpatrick and Constantine Menges (a former official of the National Security Council), and conservative intellectuals Allan Bloom, Irving Kristol, and Paul Weyrich. Keyes has connections in the Republican intelligentsia, but the economic elite has not been supportive.

"Right now we're right around 40,000 donors," Godzich said of Keyes's fund-raising efforts. "Our average donation is around $25. I think total we've maybe gotten one or two PAC donations.

And one of them was from the Kansas Republican Assembly. He went and spoke for their group and they were so appreciative that they voted on sending us like a $300 check or something. I remember when that came in the mail we all were at the office and said, 'We got a PAC check? Oh, I feel so tainted.' "

The National Rifle Association, which hasn't given a dime to Keyes since his 1992 Senate campaign, is nonetheless his No. 1 career patron, mostly because of an independent expenditure for communications it made on his behalf back then. During his first run in 1988, Maryland passed a significant gun-control law, which Keyes vigorously opposed. To avoid the appearance that his opposition to the law was a result of the NRA's financial support, Keyes held a press conference and announced that he was refusing to accept any contributions from the NRA. In Keyes's 1992 race, however, the NRA came through for him. The NRA gave him $7,306 and made another $14,903 in independent communications expenditures, making it far and away Keyes's top giver.

No other PAC has made significant contributions to Keyes. The National Right to Life PAC rewarded his ardent pro-life position with an $8,530 independent expenditure in 1992, but no other interests have made similar infusions. The reason is clear: When PACs give money to a politician, they assume the favor will be returned in some way. Keyes has simply not been in a position to return any such favors.

Godzich acknowledges this. "I think that's one of the reasons why we don't get the big-money people," he told the Center, "because the big money people want some kind of quid pro quo. He'll say, 'If you want to give me a check, that's fine, but don't expect anything.' "

And that, in a nutshell, sums up Keyes's long-shot presidential campaign. With almost no prospect of being in a position of having quos to sell for quids, Keyes has been ignored by those who do expect something for their money.

ALAN KEYES
Top Ten Career Patrons

Ranking	Company/Individual/Family Name	Total
1	National Rifle Association, Fairfax, Virginia	$22,209
2	National Right to Life PAC and state affiliates, Washington	$12,263
3	Gilder, Gagnon, Howe & Company, New York	$11,500
4	Coalition for American Principle, Oakview, California	$7,137
5	Campaign America, Washington	$6,000
5	Charles and Helen Hellmuth, Chevy Chase, Maryland	$6,000
5	Commercial Framing Company, Springfield, Virginia	$6,000
8	Hope for America, Temecula, California	$5,980
9	James and Claudia Holman, Coronado, California	$5,950
10	Bertsche family, Chicago	$5,000
10	Fund for America's Future, Inc., Washington	$5,000
10	Hooper family, Philadelphia	$5,000
10	United States Citizens' Alliance Federal PAC, Brooks, Oregon	$5,000

This list is based on individual and PAC contributions to Keyes's Senate campaigns from 1987–1998; individual and PAC contributions to Keyes's 1996 presidential campaign; individual and PAC contributions to the Campaign for Maryland's Future; and individual and PAC contributions to Keyes's 2000 presidential campaign through June 30, 1999. Independent expenditures are also included, where appropriate.
Sources: Federal Election Commission; Center for Responsive Politics.

1. This figure is primarily independent expenditures.
2. Includes contributions from the National Right to Life PAC, the Right to

Life of Maryland PAC, and the New Jersey Right to Life PAC. State chapters are affiliated with the national organization, but the FEC has ruled that their PACs are not coordinated or affiliated in any way. Includes independent expenditures.

4. This figure is entirely independent expenditures.

8. This figure is entirely independent expenditures.

John McCain

||||||||||||

The planners at Del Webb Corporation, the nation's seventh-largest builder of single-family homes, leave little to chance. In subdivisions with names like Copper Cove and Sienna Canyon, the company offers buyers homes with three-car garages, wall-to-wall carpeting, and landscaped yards. Retirees at Sunflower, a Del Webb "active adult" community in Tucson, Arizona, can sun by the pool, soak in a Jacuzzi, or hit the tennis court.

Del Webb communities dot seven states, including Arizona, where the company is headquartered. But to make way for its sprawling real-estate developments, Del Webb has arranged several controversial land swaps with the federal government.

In 1994, for example, Del Webb Corporation proposed exchanging some of its land for a 4,000-acre tract near the Red Rock National Conservation Area, a scenic stretch of desert featuring seasonal springs and clusters of Joshua trees fifteen miles west of Las Vegas. But the plan hit a brick wall when the U.S. House approved legislation to expand the Red Rock National Conservation Area to include the acreage the company wanted.

One of the company's lobbyists, Donald Moon, a burly former prosecutor with ties to Interior Secretary Bruce Babbitt, tried to get the bill's sponsors to exclude the land that Del Webb wanted from Red Rock, but nothing came of his efforts. He then turned to Republican Senator John McCain of Arizona. He knew McCain would help, for over the years, Del Webb had helped McCain. The company's executives and employees, in fact, have given McCain at least $56,535 in campaign contributions, making Del Webb his No. 7 career patron.

And help McCain did. He placed a "hold" on the legislation (through a letter of notification to Senate Majority Leader Robert Dole), thus stalling it indefinitely.

Having bought some time, Moon then arranged a meeting with Robert Armstrong, the assistant Interior secretary in charge of the Bureau of Land Management, which controlled the land Del Webb wanted. Moon reckoned that if he could get Armstrong to write a letter in support of an alternative swap, he could use it to force quick government approval of a new deal. But Armstrong refused.

Moon had better luck with members of Nevada's congressional delegation, all of whom signed a letter of support for Del Webb's new proposal to exchange 4,700 acres of federal land in Las Vegas Valley, south of the city.

Once Moon had the letter in hand, McCain lifted his hold. The legislation to expand the Red Rock National Conservation Area passed the Senate intact, and Moon used the Nevada delegation's letter to pressure the Bureau of Land Management into approving the Las Vegas Valley swap. When it came time to pay up, Del Webb offered the federal government $9,000 per acre for the land, based on an appraisal it had paid for. An appraisal commissioned by opponents of the deal, however, valued the land at $36,000 per acre. A March 1998 report by the Interior Department's Inspector General faulted BLM for relying on Del Webb's appraisal and concluded that taxpayers would have lost at least $9 million if the government had accepted Del Webb's $9,000-an-acre offer. But the report came too late: In 1997, the BLM accepted Del Webb's second offer of $10,900 per acre.

At stop after stop, traveling on a campaign bus that he's nicknamed the "Straight Talk Express," McCain tells his audiences that, as President, he would "take our politics and our government back from the special interests."

But as his actions on behalf of Del Webb Corporation demonstrate, it's sometimes hard to tell on which side of "the special interests" McCain actually stands. Through his eighteen years in the Senate, he's been an effective advocate for telephone carriers, railroads, real-estate developers, and mining companies, among other well-heeled interests. The portrait McCain likes is the one of the plain-talking crusader who's bucking the system; the one many others see is that of a politician who rarely breaks ranks with the special interests that finance his campaigns.

McCain's mouth has always gotten him in trouble. As a student at Episcopal High School, a private boarding school in Alexandria, Virginia, his indifference to rules and regulations earned him the nicknames "Punk" and "McNasty."

When he entered the U.S. Naval Academy in 1954, McCain didn't quietly abide the hazing routinely dished out by upper-classmen. In fact, the entire hierarchy of the Academy rankled him. "It was bullshit," he once said. "I resented the hell out of it."

For McCain, however, being something of a hothead was in keeping with family tradition. His grandfather, John Sidney "Slew" McCain, was an admiral during World War II whose acid-tongued assaults on his enemies can still make his grandson wince. McCain's father, John McCain, Jr., was a submarine skipper during World War II whose wild onshore antics and penchant for cursing earned him the nickname "Good Goddamn McCain."

McCain's stubborn feistiness cost him at Annapolis: He gradua-ted close to the bottom of his class. But the same qualities, years later, would see him through a gauntlet of harrowing experiences in Vietnam.

First there was the fire aboard USS *Forrestal*. On July 29, 1967, McCain, by then a Navy pilot, was getting ready for takeoff when a rocket from another plane on the deck of the carrier accidentally went off, hitting his plane as he sat in the cockpit. He miraculously managed to escape alive, but the ensuing explosions and fires took 134 lives. It was the worst non-combat-related disaster in U.S. Navy history.

Then there was his capture by the North Vietnamese. In the fall of 1967, McCain transferred to USS *Oriskany,* only to be shot down on a bombing run over central Hanoi. McCain ejected and landed in a lake, breaking both arms and one leg in the process. An angry mob fished him out and beat him with rifle butts before carting him off to Hoa Lo prison, which its captives sarcastically named the "Hanoi Hilton."

While McCain was imprisoned, his father became the commander-in-chief of all military forces in the Pacific. When his captors discovered who his father was, they offered to release him ahead of other prisoners who had been captured before him in an attempt to score propaganda points and crush the morale of the Americans left behind. McCain refused. After enduring repeated torture and two years in solitary confinement, he and the other U.S. POWs were finally released in 1973.

McCain's courage in the face of incredible adversity earned him a hero's welcome on his return, and, later, a springboard for a career in politics.

In 1976, McCain toyed with the idea of running for a seat in the U.S. House of Representatives in Florida, where he was stationed at the time. He ended up deciding not to run, but within a year he was on Capitol Hill as the Navy's liaison to the Senate. From his digs on the first floor of the Hart Senate Office Building, McCain handled everything from the day-to-day troubles of sailors who were facing courts-martial to the Navy's successful two-year lobbying push for a new nuclear carrier.

As his days in the liaison office were winding down, McCain grew impatient to run for office, but he lacked a base from which to launch his political career. As a Navy brat, he'd never lived anyplace long enough to call home. His marriage to Carol Shepp, whom he had wed in 1965, fell apart shortly after he returned from Vietnam. So, in 1981, a year after remarrying, he headed for Arizona, the home state of his second wife, Cindy Hensley.

Cindy Hensley is heir to a considerable family fortune. Her father, James Hensley, started a beer distributorship in 1955, just as Arizona's economy was entering a long boom period. Today, Hensley & Company, based in Phoenix, is the biggest Anheuser-Busch distributor in the state and one of the largest beer distributors in the nation.

From the moment McCain landed in Phoenix, the Hensleys were key sponsors of his political career. Being elected to Congress was "the ultimate goal," McCain recalled years later. "I just didn't know how long it would take."

In the early 1980s, Arizona was in the midst of reapportioning its congressional seats. It was clear that the state, owing to its significant population growth, would get an additional congressional district—the only question was where. While McCain waited for a chance to run, James Hensley gave him a public relations job at Hensley & Company so that he could travel around the state and build up contacts. McCain received an annual salary of $25,000 and an annual bonus of $25,000. His wife often acted as a one-woman advance team.

When all the lines were drawn, the new congressional district was in Tucson, far from McCain's new home in Phoenix. But McCain soon learned that Representative John Rhodes, then the House Minority Leader, was about to retire after fifteen terms. The only problem was that the McCains had settled just outside of Rhodes's district. The couple fixed that by quickly buying a house inside Rhodes's district (so quickly, in fact, that it was arranged within hours of his official retirement announcement).

Campaigning for the first time, McCain silenced critics who branded him a carpetbagger with the reply: "The place I lived longest in my life was Hanoi." And in sharp contrast to the maverick image he cultivates today, McCain sold himself in television ads as someone who "knows how Washington works," complete with photographs of him with President and Mrs. Reagan and Senator John Tower of Texas.

His war record and Washington experience put him over the top. In the spring of 1982, McCain came from behind to win a four-way Republican primary with 32 percent of the vote. He coasted to victory in the fall.

Once in Congress, McCain was the exact opposite of the hotheaded rebel he was at Annapolis. He was elected president of the incoming Republican class. He became a voice of tolerance within his party, championing the rights of Native Americans. When he disagreed with President Reagan, it was to oppose sending troops into Lebanon.

In 1986, after just two terms in the House, McCain moved on to the Senate and deeper into the arms of the GOP establishment.

In 1988, Vice President George Bush sent McCain across the country to attack his Democratic rival for the White House, Governor Michael Dukakis of Massachusetts. McCain even made the short list of contenders to be Bush's vice-president. Eager to climb the party ranks, he also sought the chairmanship of the Republican Senatorial Campaign Committee—a job that, ironically, would later go to Mitch McConnell of Kentucky, his future nemesis in the fight over campaign-finance reform.

The Hensleys helped a lot throughout these years. So did an Arizona real-estate developer named Charles H. Keating, Jr. For years, McCain accepted Keating's assorted forms of largesse—campaign contributions, all-expenses-paid vacations, free rides on his corporate jet—without realizing, apparently, that there might be strings attached.

The two men met at a Navy League dinner in 1981. Like McCain, Keating was a former Navy pilot and newcomer to Arizona. He'd moved to Phoenix in 1976 and started American Continental Corporation, a real-estate development company. When McCain announced that he was running for office, he sought out Keating, who arranged a fund-raiser for him. Over the course of his House and early Senate career, McCain would collect $112,000 in campaign contributions from Keating, his relatives, and his employees.

But there was a kicker. When he was asked, years later at a press conference, whether his contributions to politicians bought him influence, Keating replied, "I want to say in the most forceful way I can: I certainly hope so."

McCain got more than just campaign money from Keating. McCain, his family, and their babysitter flew on Keating-owned or -chartered jets nine times, including three trips to Cat Cay, Keating's vacation estate in the Bahamas. And in 1986, Keating cut Cindy McCain and her father into Fountain Square Shopping Center, a strip mall that American Continental Corporation built and managed, for a $359,000 investment.

It was just a matter of time before Keating called in his chits. When he did, it was over Lincoln Savings and Loan, a thrift in Irvine, California, that he'd bought in 1984. It turned out that Keating was raiding the assets of Lincoln's depositors to finance posh real-estate projects such as The Phoenician, a $300 million, 654-room hotel and spa in Scottsdale, Arizona, and his own lavish lifestyle. By 1986, Edwin Gray, the chairman of the Federal Home Loan Bank Board, grew worried that Lincoln had strayed too far from its core mortgage business, and began to clamp down. Keating turned to his friends in Washington for help.

On March 19, 1987, Keating appealed to McCain in person to meet with federal regulators on his behalf. At first McCain balked, but then, on April 2, he joined Senators Alan Cranston of California, John Glenn of Ohio, and Dennis DeConcini of Arizona in DeConcini's office to meet with Gray. On April 9 the four Senators, joined by Don Riegle of Michigan, sat down in San Francisco with four more regulators from the Federal Home Loan Bank Board. Following the meetings, the board delayed its seizure of Lincoln Savings and Loan for two more years.

When the federal government finally took over Lincoln in 1989, the bailout cost taxpayers $2.6 billion, making it the most expensive S&L bailout in U.S. history. About 17,000 small investors also lost a total of $190 million.

In November 1989, outrage over the bailout and the intervention of powerful lawmakers sparked an investigation by the Senate Ethics Committee. From then on, McCain and the other four Senators, who together accepted $1.3 million in contributions from Keating, were known as the Keating Five.

Caught neck-deep in Keating's pocket, McCain scrambled to extricate himself. He quickly paid Keating $13,433 for the flights he and his family had taken on Keating's jet years earlier. But it was too late to make up for the fact that, as a member of the House, he'd never disclosed the flights, as required under House rules. He refused to return Keating's contributions; instead he filed a complaint with the Federal Election Commission in which he charged that Keating had illegally made his campaign contributions through American Continental employees. (The FEC dropped the case a few years later.)

McCain readily admitted that he'd made a mistake by going to the meetings, but insisted, "I in no way abused my office." He crisscrossed Arizona, laying out his version of events before newspaper editorial boards and at town meetings. He even telephoned some reporters so many times to tell his side of the story that they stopped returning his calls. "It's like a campaign," he said at the time. "A campaign for credibility."

Transcripts of the meetings supported his claim that he'd been the most reticent of the bunch. At one point during the meeting, McCain told Gray that while American Continental was a large employer in his state, "I wouldn't want any special favors for them."

In February 1991 the Senate Ethics Committee cleared McCain, saying he had "exercised poor judgment" but that his actions had not been "improper nor attended with gross negligence."

"Clearly, 'no improper conduct' is what is important here," McCain said on hearing the committee's decision. "I view that as full exoneration."

In a postscript to the scandal, McCain finally contributed $112,000—the amount of money he'd gotten from Keating-related interests—to the U.S. Treasury. (Keating would otherwise rank as his No. 1 career patron.) McCain's wife and father-in-law, however, held on to their stake in the Fountain Square Shopping Center. In fact, they held on to it long after American Continental Corporation went bankrupt. Cindy McCain, her father, and the remaining owners sold the mall two years ago for $15 million, reaping a profit that McCain has reported as between $100,000 and $1 million.

McCain's career survived the Keating Five scandal. In 1992 he won reelection with 56 percent of the vote. Then he emerged as one of Congress's leading advocates of political reform. In 1995 he helped to pass a $50 limit on the gifts that Senators and members of their staffs can accept from outside interests, as well as a lobbying disclosure law that forces special interests to disclose how much they pay and whom they hire to lobby on particular issues. That year, McCain and Democratic Senator Russell Feingold of Wisconsin began pushing their proposal to overhaul the nation's campaign-finance system.

A year later, McCain was the only Republican in the Senate to vote against the 1996 Telecommunications Act. Proponents of the law insisted that massive deregulation of the telecommunications industry would bring more Americans into the information age at lower prices. But as McCain tells it, the legislation was "written by every interest in the world except consumers."

So far, McCain has been right. Cable rates are up 6.8 percent nationwide, and rates for telephone service have gone up as much as 20 percent in some states. Instead of stiffer competition, there's been speedier consolidation, with one merger after another: NYNEX and Bell Atlantic; SBC Communications, Inc., and Pacific Telesis Group; AT&T and TCI Communications, Inc.

In 1997, McCain found himself in a position to do something about the telecommunications mess. He succeeded the law's chief sponsor, Larry Pressler of South Dakota, as the chairman of the Commerce Committee, which has jurisdiction over the telecommunications, aviation, and high-tech industries, among others.

While McCain may have come to the job with a well-documented distaste for unregulated monopolies, his equally strong dislike of regulation has led him time and again to side with companies or industries he believes will make a market more competitive. The result: McCain pushes their agenda, and they finance his campaigns.

Corporate interests with business before the Commerce Committee have showered money on McCain—enough money to help him raise $4.4 million for his 1998 Senate race, more than ten times as much as his opponent, Ed Ranger, a political novice.

Today, McCain's presidential campaign is no different.

One day last March, he collected more than $120,000 at a Washington fund-raiser hosted by Kenneth Duberstein, a lobbyist for Time Warner, Inc., CSX Corporation, and many other corporate interests with business before the Commerce Committee; John Timmons, a former McCain aide who's now a lobbyist for America West Airlines, Inc.; and Vin Weber, a former Republican congressman from Minnesota who now lobbies for Boeing and AT&T.

Special interests are putting money into McCain's presidential campaign "under the theory," as J. Steven Hart, a lobbyist for Continental Airlines, put it to a reporter for the *Washington Post,* "that no matter what happens, he's still chairman of the Commerce Committee."

McCain betrays his own coziness with Washington's influence peddlers when he describes his lobbyist fund-raisers as "people I've done business with for the past seventeen years."

Take the case of U S West, Inc., based in Englewood, Colorado, which holds a virtual monopoly over local telephone service in fourteen states, including Arizona. In North Dakota, U S West's basic phone rates are set to go up more than 20 percent by July 2000. Last year, 15,000 U S West customers in Omaha, Nebraska, signed a petition opposing a rate increase in their state, arguing that they were already paying more than their counterparts in ten other states served by U S West.

U S West is McCain's No. 1 career patron.

In May 1999, McCain introduced the "Internet Regulatory Freedom Act," which would boost the company's efforts to offer high-speed Internet service over long distance phone lines. U S West has been especially eager to break into the long distance phone market since June 1998, when long distance provider AT&T bought cable giant TCI. The merger allows AT&T to offer high-speed Internet service over cable lines, on top of cable-television service and local and long distance telephone service. But under rules set up by the government when it broke up Ma Bell, the regional Bell operating companies—U S West among them—can provide service only within local calling boundaries known as local access and transport areas, or LATAs. McCain's bill would let U S West and the other "baby Bells" provide services beyond their LATAs.

U S West would stand to profit in a big way from McCain's bill. "If the Internet is deregulated in the manner Senator McCain is suggesting," Solomon Trujillo, the company's chairman, said the day McCain introduced his bill, "U S West will be able to provide high-speed Internet service to an additional two million households and businesses throughout our region during the first year alone."

News Corporation, Ltd., which owns Fox Broadcasting, the nation's fourth-largest television network, has also found a friend in McCain. (Employees of Fox-related companies gave McCain $14,050 in contributions on a single day in 1998.)

Last year McCain pushed a measure that would have increased

the number of local TV stations that major networks can own. The proposal would directly benefit Fox Broadcasting, the only network to have reached the ownership ceiling. At the same time McCain was taking his idea around Capitol Hill, his chief aide on telecommunications issues, Lauren "Pete" Belvin, was running an antiques business with Maureen O'Connell, a lobbyist for Fox who was working to raise the cap. Last summer, after *Mother Jones* broke the news of their personal business ties, Belvin and O'Connell dissolved their partnership.

In 1997, Congress awarded spectrum valued at $70 billion to the nation's broadcasters, Fox included, with the proviso that they switch from analog to digital television signals by 2006. McCain criticized it as corporate welfare. But he softened his stance after Fox's chairman, Rupert Murdoch,* flew him out to Los Angeles in February 1998 for a private demonstration of standard-definition digital television technology, a cheaper, lower-definition alternative that's being pushed by Fox and Microsoft Corporation. Andrew Butcher, a spokesman for Fox, told the Center for Public Integrity that, after the demonstration, McCain met behind closed doors with Fox executives. "I thought they made a pretty good case that the picture clarity at the lower level was pretty good," McCain said afterward. He promised hearings before his committee, and they were held in July.

Hensley & Company, the family business that McCain's wife serves as vice-president and director, is the Senator's No. 2 career patron. Since 1982, McCain has received at least $161,000 in campaign contributions from beer-related interests. That figure doesn't include the thousands of dollars in speaking fees from beer-related interests that McCain has donated to charity, nor does it include free travel provided to McCain by Anheuser-Busch, with whom McCain's father-in-law has had an exclusive business arrangement since he founded his company in 1955. Most of the personal wealth of the Hensleys and of McCain's children is in Anheuser-Busch stock.

---

*In the interests of full disclosure, Murdoch also owns the company that published this book.

McCain has publicly acknowledged the enormous potential for conflicts of interest by pledging to recuse himself from voting on legislation that affects the beer industry. To some extent, however, it is a half-empty gesture: He can't really avoid such legislation. In 1998 the National Beer Wholesalers Association listed twenty-six legislative priorities on its Web site, many of which were under the jurisdiction of the Commerce Committee. In the eighteen years he has been in Congress, McCain has rarely taken a stand against the beer industry's interests.

Despite his support for regulating tobacco advertising and violence on television, McCain conveniently sidestepped a controversy over television commercials for hard liquor. In June 1996 the liquor industry announced it would break its forty-eight-year voluntary ban on television advertising, prompting President Clinton to call on the Federal Communications Commission to study whether such advertising harms children.

A Commerce subcommittee scheduled hearings on alcohol advertising for February 1997, then postponed them. The beer industry, fearing that any restrictions placed on hard liquor would be imposed on beer as well, lobbied feverishly to have beer advertising cut from the hearing agenda. In the end, the industry got its wish: The hearings never took place.

In 1999, McCain pushed legislation that would have authorized another round of military-base closings beginning in 2001. While the move appeared to be classic pork-busting, it had the support of top military and civilian defense officials, as well as aerospace companies that had already secured large contracts to build military aircraft and missiles.

Among the big supporters of McCain's bill was Seattle-based Boeing Company. Boeing, which in 1997 bought its rival, McDonnell Douglas Corporation, manufactures commercial and military aircraft, missiles and space exploration equipment, defense electronic systems, and large-scale communications and information networks. Boeing is McCain's No. 5 career patron.

Boeing maintained that closing more military bases would save billions of dollars, providing the extra money needed for new equipment and initiatives to improve national defense efforts. Defense Secretary William Cohen lobbied all year for the measure, arguing that without the savings, the Pentagon wouldn't have the money needed in 2005 for major systems entering the production phase of development. The systems included the Army's RAH-66 Comanche helicopter, made by Sikorsky Aircraft Corporation (a subsidiary of United Technologies Corporation) and Boeing; the Navy's V-22 Tiltrotor, built by Bell Helicopter Textron and Boeing; and the F/A-18E/F Super Hornet, produced by Boeing.

But the idea of additional base closings proved to be too politically unpalatable, and on May 26, 1999, the Senate defeated McCain's legislation, 40-60.

McCain did better for Boeing within the Commerce Committee, where in April 1999 he introduced legislation to extend federal risk insurance to commercial satellite launchers for another ten years. Boeing has a satellite launch unit based in Huntington Beach, California.

Under the 1984 Commercial Space Launch Act, companies insure their launches for up to $500 million in damages, while the federal government pays for any damages from $500 million to $1.5 billion. Senator Ernest Hollings, a Democrat from South Carolina, has called federal risk insurance for satellite launchers nothing more than "a subsidy to the richest industry there is."

Boeing felt otherwise. "The legislation is critical to level the playing field with our international competition in the space launch arena," R. Gale Schluter, a vice-president of Boeing's Expendable Launch Vehicles division, told a hearing of McCain's committee on May 20, 1999.

Boeing executives dropped $4,000 into McCain's campaign in the days following the hearing. On June 23, 1999, his proposal passed the Commerce Committee, but it failed to pass the Senate.

On April 29, 1997, at 9:30 A.M., Raymond Stanley, the chairman of the San Carlos Apache Tribe of Arizona, was due at an oversight hearing on his tribe's water rights before the Senate Indian Affairs Committee. But instead of getting into a taxicab or taking his seat in the hearing room, he was in his hotel room across town, waiting for the other shoe to drop.

A messenger had just delivered a letter from the tribe to

McCain, who was to preside over the hearing. In the letter, Stanley explained that neither he nor the tribe's vice chairman, Marvin Mull, would be appearing at the hearing.

The Apaches' absence miffed McCain as well as J. Steven Whisler and Timothy Snider of Phelps Dodge Corporation, a copper mining and manufacturing company. (Phelps Dodge is McCain's No. 10 career patron.) McCain's office had invited the Phelps Dodge executives and the San Carlos Apache leaders to Washington to renegotiate a water-rights agreement that would let Phelps Dodge continue to use water from Apache lands for its mine in Morenci, Arizona.

A third of all the copper in the United States comes from the Morenci mine, making Phelps Dodge the largest copper producer in North America. In 1990 the San Carlos Apaches signed an agreement with Phelps Dodge to let the company use its water. In recent years, however, the tribe has complained that Phelps Dodge was using more water and extracting more copper than intended under the 1990 agreement.

"Like its forefathers," the tribe said in a statement, "the San Carlos Apache Tribe continues to defend its tribal homeland and water rights against outsiders who would destroy or deplete them."

By boycotting the hearing, the Apaches hoped to force McCain and Phelps Dodge to take their concerns seriously. Water is vital to one of the tribe's main sources of income: cattle ranching. The only other major provider of jobs on the San Carlos Apache reservation, which has an unemployment rate of 30 percent, is the federal government.

But McCain offered them little sympathy, calling their boycott "nonsensical."

In May the tribe reluctantly returned to the bargaining table. The resulting compromise, which required congressional approval, ensured that Phelps Dodge could continue to use the tribe's water in return for an undisclosed fee. "We were very successful," a spokesman for Phelps Dodge told the Center.

The agreement faced one last hurdle. On May 7, 1997, McCain and John Kyl, his colleague in the Senate from Arizona, cast tie-breaking votes to approve the San Carlos Apache Tribe Water Rights Settlement. A week later Douglas Yearley, the chairman of

Phelps Dodge, gave McCain a token of his appreciation: two checks for $1,000 to McCain's 1998 Senate campaign.

In March 1999, McCain made an appearance in Alexandria, Virginia, at the home of Mary McAuliffe, a lobbyist for Union Pacific Corporation. Also there to greet him were John Angus, a lobbyist for CSX Transportation, Inc.; Pamela Garvie, a lobbyist for Burlington Northern Santa Fe Corporation; and Wayne Valis, a lobbyist for Norfolk Southern Corporation. The guests had at least two things in common: All work for companies that operate railroads, and all gave at least $500 to McCain's presidential campaign. Over the years, railroad interests have been kind to McCain, collectively providing him with more than $140,000 in campaign funds.

And vice versa: In the months after the Alexandria fund-raiser, McCain protected the industry from new regulations.

After Congress effectively deregulated the nation's railroad industry in 1980, shipping rates fell, as did the number of rail accidents. But as railroad companies have merged, businesses that rely on rail transport have complained that they are increasingly at the mercy of regional monopolies. In 1980 there were sixty major rail carriers; today there are nine, and just four of them account for 90 percent of the industry's freight revenue. Union Pacific Railroad Company's acquisition of Southern Pacific Transportation Company in 1997, which made Union Pacific the nation's largest rail carrier, brought with it renewed calls for legislation to force competition on the industry.

In June 1999 several members of the Senate Commerce Committee, including John D. "Jay" Rockefeller IV of West Virginia and Kay Bailey Hutchison of Texas, introduced legislation that would force railroad companies to let competitors use their tracks, thus giving shippers a choice of carriers. Lobbyists for the shipping and railroad industries tried to work out a compromise, but the railroad companies refused to budge. They didn't have to: They had an ace in the hole.

Two months after he clinked glasses with railroad-industry lobbyists in Alexandria, McCain introduced legislation to reauthorize the Surface Transportation Board, the federal agency that oversees the railroad and trucking industries. His bill completely ignored the shippers' concerns. It was going to be that, McCain let it be known, or, as a lobbyist for the shippers later recalled, "nothing at all."

In February 1999, McCain took a testing-the-waters trip for a presidential bid. But he didn't trek through the snowy fields of Iowa or the meeting houses of New Hampshire. Instead he headed straight for Las Vegas.

Within days of his visit, Terrence Lanni, the chairman of MGM Grand, Inc., and Steve Wynn, the chairman of Mirage Resorts, Inc., each wrote out $1,000 checks, as did their wives, to McCain's presidential campaign.

It wasn't the first time the gambling industry has put money on McCain. McCain has collected more than $100,000 in contributions from gambling interests since 1993, and he's returned the financial favors in ways big and small. In June 1998, McCain voted for legislation to overhaul the Internal Revenue Service that included a tax exemption for the casino industry for free meals it gives to workers. The exemption is projected to cost the U.S. Treasury $316 million from 1998 to 2007. In 1995, McCain sponsored legislation that paved the way for gambling "cruises to nowhere." Even during his battle to pass tobacco legislation, McCain found a way to help the gambling industry: At the urging of the American Gaming Association, he agreed to exempt gambling establishments from his bill's ban on indoor smoking.

In the summer of 1999, as legislation vital to gambling interests made its way through Congress, McCain tapped into Nevada and Native American gambling interests for contributions to his presidential campaign. On June 10, for example, he returned to Las Vegas for a fund-raiser organized by Lanni, where he rubbed elbows with Peter Boynton, the chairman of Caesar's World, Inc.; Sheldon Adelson, the chairman of Las Vegas Sands, Inc.; and David J. Thompson, the chairman of Mikohn Gaming Corporation, a Las Vegas company that makes slot machines and other gambling equipment. The event netted McCain $51,150.

A few weeks later, on June 30, McCain headed for the woods of Ledyard, Connecticut, to collect another $14,650 at a fund-raiser hosted by the Mashantucket Pequot Indian Nation. The 155-member tribe runs Foxwoods Resort, the world's largest casino.

McCain has opposed legislation that would halt the further expansion of gambling on Indian reservations. Under the 1988 Indian Gaming Regulatory Act, Native American tribes have to reach an agreement with states about how to regulate their gaming operations. Today, 183 tribes run 263 gambling operations in twenty-eight states, most under tribal-state compacts. But one up-shot of the 1988 law is that states that want to keep Indian tribes from opening gambling operations can simply refuse to negotiate. Tribes used to take uncooperative states to court; then, however, the Supreme Court ruled that states are immune from such law-suits. Interior Secretary Bruce Babbitt tried to give tribes relief by proposing that his office settle tribal-state disputes over gambling compacts. Congress didn't like Babbitt's idea and imposed a one-year moratorium on any new Indian gambling operations outside of state compacts.

Nevada gambling operators, who see the tribes as competition, prefer leaving the states in charge. In October 1998, at the indus-try's behest, Senators Harry Reid of Nevada and Mike Enzi of Wyoming introduced a measure to stop Secretary Babbitt from stepping into tribal-state disputes.

The prospect of letting states keep their veto power over Indian gambling sent some tribes running straight for their checkbooks. From September 30 to October 6, 1998, the Mashantucket Pequots gave McCain $9,500. McCain opposed Reid and Enzi's effort, call-ing it "unwarranted" and "ill-advised."

On February 11, 1999, members of the Senate Commerce Committee marked up a bill to loosen restrictions on flights to and from Ronald Reagan Washington National Airport, just outside the nation's capital. "If we do not pass this legislation, it will be another clear victory for the major airlines and the special interests in Washington, which will not surprise me," the bill's sponsor, committee chairman John McCain, told his colleagues. "Nor will it be the first time or the last time. I intend to try to look out for the American consumer."

Experts disagree on whether adding flights at the National Airport would result in lower airfares, but one thing is certain: If passed, the measure would boost the fortunes of America West Airlines, which is based in Phoenix. McCain has angrily denied he is shilling for America West, but for more than a decade his efforts to increase the number of flights at National Airport have gone hand in hand with those of the airline, which employs about 9,000 Arizona residents. Over the years, the airline's executives and other employees have given McCain at least $17,150 in political contributions.

One of the few airlines to get off the ground after Congress deregulated the industry in 1978, America West grew to become the nation's ninth-largest commercial carrier in part by aggressively acquiring landing and takeoff rights, commonly known as "slots," at the nation's four busiest airports: La Guardia and John F. Kennedy International in New York City, O'Hare International Airport in Chicago, and National. Since the 1960s, a "high density rule" has limited the number of flights the four airports can handle, and a "perimeter rule" has limited nonstop flights to and from National to 1,250 miles. The purpose of the rules is to control congestion and noise levels.

The rules, however, prevented America West from expanding service to the East Coast. And so, in 1987, the airline petitioned the Federal Aviation Administration to force airlines to give up slots that they barely used.

McCain has been advancing America West's agenda on Capitol Hill ever since. In 1988 he pushed through legislation that required the FAA to redo its slot regulations. The FAA complied, and by the end of 1993, thanks to a combination of the new rule, exemptions granted by the FAA, and slots wrested from other airlines, America West had secured takeoff and landing rights at the four busiest airports.

But the additional slots didn't solve all of America West's problems. After posting poor earnings in 1996, the airline launched a two-year campaign to expand its service. But the perimeter rule still prevented America West from offering nonstop service from Phoenix to Washington, a lucrative route that attracts high-paying business customers.

On May 21, 1998, William Franke, the chairman of America West Holdings Corporation (the holding company for the airline), told a reporter for the *Arizona Republic,* "Washington National would be really significant. We've been working hard at trying to get the perimeter rule amended."

A few weeks later McCain pulled out all the stops to get a bill through the Senate to change the perimeter rule at National. He squashed opposition from the Metropolitan Washington Airports Authority by threatening to hold up the Senate's approval of three appointees to the panel. When his bill faced opposition in the House, McCain took funds for airport construction hostage. He refused to relinquish the funds even after the House version of his proposal died.

McCain's hardball tactics paid off in October 1999, when the Senate approved his proposal to open up twenty-four new slots at National Airport and to lift perimeter restrictions for half of those flights.

Through it all, McCain, who's made something of a name for himself as a "pork-buster," has insisted that his only goal is to improve competition in the airline industry. But even executives of America West acknowledge that few other carriers would benefit from McCain's bill.

"Other than America West and what we're doing, there aren't that many that qualify," Michael Conway, a co-founder of America West who recently started National Airline out of Las Vegas, told a reporter in March 1999.

Under McCain's proposal, America West could also keep exemptions to airport restrictions it already has—exemptions McCain won at the behest of John Timmons, America West's chief lobbyist. "It's hard for me to understand why McCain should get any more of a bum rap than Jim Moran or Connie Morella [two Washington-area lawmakers] should get," Timmons later told a reporter, "because they're shilling for their people as much as McCain's shilling for his people."

Timmons should know. Before he became a lobbyist in 1994, he worked for eleven years as McCain's legislative director.

JOHN McCAIN
Top Ten Career Patrons

Ranking	Company/Individual/Family Name	Total
1	U S West, Denver	$107,520
2	Hensley & Company, Phoenix, Arizona	$80,300
3	AT&T Corporation and affiliated companies, New York	$72,250
4	Viacom, Inc., and affiliated companies, New York	$61,750
5	The Boeing Company and affiliated companies, Seattle	$61,400
6	BellSouth Corporation, Atlanta	$60,000
7	Del Webb Corporation, Phoenix, Arizona	$56,535
8	Bank of America and affiliated companies, Charlotte, North Carolina	$55,218
9	Motorola, Inc., Schaumburg, Illinois	$49,045
10	Phelps Dodge Corporation, Phoenix, Arizona	$47,100

This list is based on individual and PAC contributions to McCain's House campaigns from 1981–1986; contributions to the McCain PAC from 1985–1988; individual and PAC contributions to McCain's Senate campaigns from 1985 through June 30, 1999; and individual and PAC contributions to McCain's presidential campaign through June 30, 1999.

Sources: Federal Election Commission; Center for Responsive Politics

1. Includes contributions from employees of U S West and its predecessor, Mountain Bell.
3. Includes contributions from employees of AT&T and its subsidiaries, including TCI; Liberty Media; Vanguard Cellular; and TelePort Communications.
4. Includes contributions from employees of Viacom and its subsidiaries, including Paramount Pictures (formerly Paramount Communications); Paramount Parks; Showtime Networks; MTV Networks; Nickelodeon; Spelling Entertainment; and World Vision Enterprises.
5. Includes contributions from employees of Boeing; McDonnell Douglas; and

Rockwell International. Boeing acquired the defense and aerospace units of Rockwell in 1996, and it acquired McDonnell Douglas in 1997.

6. Includes contributions from employees of BellSouth; employees of its predecessor, Southern Bell; and employees of L.M. Berry & Company, which BellSouth acquired in 1986.

7. Includes contributions from employees of Del Webb, and from employees of Coventry Homes and Sun City Grand, both of which are owned by Del Webb.

8. Includes contributions from employees of Bank of America and the companies that have contributed to its creation, including NationsBank; Security Pacific Corporation; Arizona Bank; Barnett Banks; and Boatmen's Bancshares.

NOTE: Individuals associated with Charles Keating-led companies, including American Continental Corp., Lincoln S&L, Continental American Securities, and Continental Homes, have given $112,000 to McCain, enough to place first on his career patron list. However, after the Keating Five scandal, McCain returned these contributions to the U.S. Treasury.

Dan Quayle

||||||||||

On January 17, 1992, Dan Quayle spotted something from his limousine. A Burger King restaurant in Norco, California—about sixty-five miles east of Los Angeles—had a NOW HIRING sign in its window. Quayle ordered his motorcade to pull over and, reporters in tow, went inside.

"I want to show you an optimistic sign that things are beginning to turn around," Quayle told the journalists traveling with him. At the time, the nation's economy was still in a slump; the unemployment rate had reached 7.1 percent the month before, and jobless claims had soared in the month of January. Some 2.1 million people had lost their jobs as a result of the recession. In the midst of the bleak news, Quayle seized on the help-wanted sign as a harbinger of good times to come.

Terie Roeder, the manager of the restaurant, told reporters that the jobs were part-time and paid $4.25 an hour. "Can they live on it?" she said in response to a question about the wage. "No. It's hard to find people who actually want to show up."

Quayle insisted that the wage and the hours didn't matter. "You have a part-time job, you have a job," he said. "That's better than no job at all."

A year later Quayle himself joined the ranks of the unemployed when he and his boss, President George Bush, lost to Bill Clinton and Albert Gore, Jr. It wasn't too long before the former Vice President was looking for entry-level part-time jobs himself. He found them—as a director of and a consultant to a half-dozen corporations. And they all paid a bit more than $4.25 an hour.

In August 1993, Quayle was hired as a consultant by Black Beauty Resources, Inc., a coal company based in Evansville, Indiana. By 1998, according to his financial disclosure form, Black Beauty was paying the former Vice President nearly $120,000 a year. It would take the Burger King employee in Norco, California, working twenty hours a week and earning $4.25 an hour, more than twenty-seven years to earn as much money.

In September 1993, Quayle joined the board of directors of American Standard Companies, Inc., a diversified manufacturing company based in Piscataway, New Jersey, that's best known for its plumbing fixtures. The company set up an account to buy $100,000 in American Standard stock for the former Vice President. That's equivalent to more than twenty-two years of labor for the part-time fast-food worker.

Quayle's job hunt didn't end in 1993. In March 1998 he joined the board of directors of FirstPlus Financial Group, Inc., a diversified consumer-lending company based in Dallas. He was paid $27,350 for his services over the next nine months—six years of earnings for the Burger King worker.

Quayle, of course, did have some corporate experience. He'd spent most of his career in Washington—eight years in the Senate and another four as Vice President—catering to the whims of big businesses. And he also had some familiarity with the companies he went to work for. The three companies have poured hundreds of thousands of dollars into his various political committees over the years.

But in the end—which for Quayle came early—the corporate support wasn't enough to overcome George W. Bush's seemingly insurmountable lead. "There's a time to stay and there's a time to fold," he said on September 27, 1999, in announcing his decision to bow out of the presidential race. "I was facing a campaign where the front-runner would have up to $100 million to spend."

*　　　*　　　*

Quayle was born in Indianapolis, Indiana, in 1947. He was named after his father's closest friend, an Army captain killed in World War II, James Danforth. His maternal grandfather, Eugene C. Pulliam, owned *The Indianapolis Star* and *News,* the *Arizona Republic,* and the *Phoenix Gazette.* Quayle graduated from Huntington High School in 1965, and received a bachelor's degree from DePauw University in Greencastle, Indiana, in 1969. That same year, he began six years of service in the Indiana Army National Guard.

Quayle attended Indiana University's law school, where he met Marilyn Tucker in 1972; they married ten weeks after their first date. Before he graduated from law school in 1974, Quayle was the chief investigator for the Consumer Protection Division of the Indiana Attorney General's Office. He later served as an administrative assistant to Governor Edgar Whitcomb, a Republican, and in the Indiana Department of Revenue. He then went to work for his father, who was the publisher of the *Huntington Herald-Press.*

His father was also instrumental in Quayle's entrance into politics. In the run-up to the 1976 elections, officials of the Indiana Republican Party were desperately seeking a strong candidate from the state's Fourth Congressional District to take on a well-entrenched incumbent Democrat. The search was anything but easy. It was the first presidential election since Richard Nixon had resigned in disgrace in August 1974; in mid-term elections that year, Democrats rode a wave of popular disgust with Republicans to a landslide. The incumbent in Indiana's Fourth Congressional District, Ed Roush, had a sixteen-year hold on the seat and in previous elections had defeated the most experienced and popular Republicans the region had to offer. No one wanted to run.

A small group of Republicans in the state decided that the party needed a fresh face to run for the seat. Dan Quayle's name was mentioned. By his father. He was handpicked for the job.

In March 1976, Orvas Beers, the Republican county chairman in Fort Wayne, Indiana, asked Dan Quayle to lunch. After some small talk, Beers got down to business. He said that he and a few of his friends wanted Quayle to run for Congress. Quayle, who was then just twenty-nine years old, was a bit taken aback. He had no experience in politics. He hadn't thought seriously about running for anything beyond the state legislature. But he took an instant liking to the idea, and he told Beers that he would consider a run under certain conditions. First, he said, the county chairman would have to keep other Republicans out of the race. The second condition betrayed Quayle's keen appreciation for what it takes to win elections. "Look me in the eye," Quayle said to Beers, "and guarantee me the money."

That was no trouble for Beers. Two of the men who had handpicked Quayle were, like his father, among the business elite of Indiana. James Loomis was president of Magnavox Government and Industrial Electronics Company, a defense contractor that within a dozen years would become Fort Wayne's largest employer. The other was Lester Gerig, the president of Mutual Security Life Insurance Company and head of the local chamber of commerce.

Gerig wanted to know Quayle's position on fifteen pieces of legislation pending in Congress. According to Gerig, Quayle told him what he wanted to hear, and Quayle got his endorsement. "The business community," Gerig later said of the young politician, "never had any representative that was more knowledgeable or did more for it."

During the campaign, Quayle succeeded in showing the business community that he was indeed its best friend. In return, he received the campaign cash that helped him win the election. Incumbents normally have an enormous fund-raising edge over challengers, but by Election Day 1976, just eight months after the lunch that got him into the race, Quayle had raised $130,000—twice as much as Roush had raised. Quayle went on to unseat the Democrat in a victory no one expected.

Ever since that election, Quayle has enjoyed particularly cozy relationships with corporations both within and outside of Indiana, and his political accounts have swelled with their contributions. After four years in the House of Representatives, Quayle used his alliances with business to help him upset Senator Birch Bayh.

Quayle's record in the Senate proved Gerig's faith in him. He did as much or more for the business community as anyone else in Congress. In 1987 he led the opposition to a bill that would have given workers advance notice of plant closings. Manufacturers vehemently opposed the measure, which was aimed at giving employees a few months to look for other work before management padlocked the factory doors. The plant-closings bill eventually passed, but not before Quayle proposed a weaker version, which he got the President of the Senate, George Bush, to back. That same year, Quayle also fought against legislation that would have required employers to inform workers who were exposed to toxic substances of the risks they ran from such exposure. The bill died in the Senate.

In 1988, George Bush surprised much of the political establishment by selecting Dan Quayle as his running mate. Speculation that he had chosen the junior Senator from Indiana more for his good looks than for his conservative credentials and his accomplishments gained steam after Quayle bumbled through his early press appearances. Once thought of as a political wunderkind, he quickly gained a reputation for making embarrassing gaffes.

While late night comedians and political cartoonists had a field day with the Vice President, Quayle was seriously at work in Washington doing what he had always done: taking care of the interests of business. He headed the President's Council on Competitiveness, a roundtable of Bush Administration officials that, under Quayle, gained a stranglehold over all proposed new federal regulations. The council, which met in secret and claimed to be exempt from the Freedom of Information Act, provided businesses with regulatory relief and other lucrative favors.

In 1992, Quayle's group recommended eliminating many of the recoupment fees levied on defense contractors. The fees, which were more or less a tax on arms exports, were designed to recoup the research and development costs of new weapons systems borne by taxpayers. On June 19, 1992, President Bush adopted Quayle's recommendation, saving the defense industry nearly $75 million a year.

That same year, the council recommended redefining wetlands to open up over a third of the protected ecosystems to agricultural and industrial use. Its recommendation ultimately was rejected. But it also won a battle with the Environmental Protection Agency, rewriting rules on air pollution to allow companies, without prior announcement, to increase the amount of emissions they pump into the atmosphere. When airlines complained about proposed federal regulations that would have required quieter jets to be in use by 2000, Quayle intervened to get the Federal Aviation Administration to relax the timetable.

The council was run largely by its staff, which was led by Allan Hubbard, a businessman from Indiana who is now the president of E&A Industries, Inc., a conglomerate that owns plastics and chemical companies. (In 1999, Hubbard signed on to George W. Bush's campaign as a fund-raiser and adviser.) Quayle gave Hubbard ethics waivers that allowed him to oversee the council's work while he maintained his financial interest in World Wide Chemicals, Inc., another Indiana-based chemical company. Hubbard owned more than half the company's stock, valued at more than $1 million. During Hubbard's tenure, the Council for Competitiveness recommended more than a hundred changes to the Clean Air Act regulations then being written by the Environmental Protection Agency. In 1992, Representative John Conyers, a Democrat from Michigan, accused Hubbard of a conflict of interest. By that time, Hubbard had left the council and gone to work as Vice President Quayle's chief of staff; he promised to put his World Wide Chemical stock in a blind trust.

Quayle's effective use of the Council for Competitiveness enhanced his reputation in corporate America as a man who could get things done. Richard Rahn, who was the chief economist of the U.S. Chamber of Commerce, was typical in his praise of the Vice President. "Quayle has gotten into the deregulation battle more substantively than anyone else," he told a reporter for the *Washington Post* in a 1992 interview. "He has done his homework. He's forceful. And he's made a difference in the eyes of American business."

Quayle, who was still trying to dispel his image as an intellectual lightweight, preferred nonetheless to have the accolades from big business—and the favors he did to earn them—remain in obscurity. Of the Council for Competitiveness's work, he told the *Washington Post,* "We've had sometimes more visibility than I really want."

Some of that visibility came from Congress, which launched

no fewer than seven investigations into the council's activities. When Bush and Quayle lost the 1992 election, Congress suspended the probes.

When Quayle left Washington in 1993, his political prospects seemed dim. But less than a year after Americans turned him out of office, Quayle quietly began paving the way for a presidential run. He joined the board of trustees of the Hudson Institute, a conservative think tank headquartered in Indianapolis. He wrote a pair of books that stressed the family-values theme he first enunciated in his "Murphy Brown" speech, in which he criticized Hollywood's glorification of single motherhood. He made speeches and attended Republican Party events. He stumped for other candidates. But most important, he raised money.

In 1995, Quayle opted out of the 1996 presidential race, citing Robert Dole's ability to lock up big-money donors as a major factor in his decision. Dole rewarded Quayle for his early endorsement by passing on to him the political action committee, Campaign America, that the Kansas Senator had formed in 1978. Quayle got control of a PAC with $1.7 million in the bank, an extensive mailing list of donors, and a head start on the 2000 money race.

During the 1996 campaign, and again in 1998, Quayle was free to fly around the country on Campaign America's checkbook. He attended picnics, fund-raisers, and campaign events for other candidates. Republican congressional candidates got to appear with the former Vice President, and the former Vice President got to meet and greet future Republican supporters, and perhaps more important, fund-raisers and donors. Thanks to his business career, Quayle already knew quite a few of them.

On March 19, 1999, Dan Quayle addressed the Los Angeles World Affairs Council. He outlined for the first time the foreign policy views that were central to his campaign. China was high on his agenda. "President Clinton has consistently supported granting China most-favored-nation status, no matter how egregious the human-rights abuses documented by his own State Department," Quayle charged. He also argued that the Bush Administration's emphasis on trade had been flawed. "I think it was a worthy objective, but upon reflection it is clear to me that the Chinese took advantage of that opportunity."

The Chinese weren't the only ones. Fortune 500 companies ranging from manufacturers of dishwashers and jumbo jets to insurance companies and movie producers were all eager to cash in on what they saw as the world's next big market. The late Ronald Brown, who, as the Secretary of Commerce in the early years of the Clinton Administration, was notorious for selling seats on trade missions to corporate donors, took a group to China in 1994 and hailed the $5 billion in deals that resulted from his trip. Brown got American executives in the door and in touch with the right decision-makers in the Chinese government. It's a trick that Quayle learned well.

On September 28, 1998, Xinhua News Agency, a Chinese wire service, reported the following item: "Chinese Premier Zhu Rongji met here this afternoon with former U.S. Vice President Dan Quayle and Emmanuel Kampouris, chairman of the board of American Standard Corporation, and their party. They exchanged views on Sino-U.S. relations and other issues of common interest. The American visitors have come to visit China as guests of the Chinese People's Institute of Foreign Affairs."

The Chinese news agency got the name slightly garbled; Kampouris is the chairman of American Standard Companies, Inc., the same firm that put Quayle on its board of directors in September 1993. American Standard manufactures everything from ceramic toilets and sinks to air conditioners, heaters, and truck brakes. Kampouris took the reins of the company in 1989, when American Standard was struggling with a load of debt that it had taken on soon after going private in a leveraged buyout the year before.

Rather than sell off profitable divisions to get out of debt, Kampouris expanded American Standard's global reach, taking advantage of cheap overseas labor to increase the company's profit margins. China, with its 1.2 billion consumers, is a natural market for the company's toilets and other plumbing fixtures. It operates seven factories there, six of them in joint ventures with Chinese companies. "Three companies are minting money, three have good earnings performance, and one is having a slight struggle," Horace

Whittlesey, American Standard's general manager in China, told London's *Financial Times* in March 1998.

While the Asian financial crisis and China's endemic corruption and sluggish progress toward a market economy have soured many companies that joined the Chinese gold rush in the early 1990s, American Standard has prospered there. "Our business grew by 60 percent last year," Whittlesey told the *Financial Times*. "If we grow by 60 percent again as we expect this year, then we're gonna be as happy as pigs in—well, you know."

Quayle had his own reasons to be happy. In 1998, the same year Quayle introduced Kampouris to the Chinese premier, the chairman of American Standard gave $100,000 in soft money to Quayle's Campaign America. In all, members of the Kampouris family and executives of American Standard (along with their spouses) made at least $139,000 in political contributions to Quayle in 1998 and 1999, making them his No. 3 career patron.

Quayle also personally profited from his association with Kampouris and American Standard. In addition to the initial $100,000 in stock the company gave him when he joined the board of directors, Quayle was paid $67,500 in director's fees in 1998 alone. His financial disclosure form lists holdings of American Standard stock valued at $500,000 to $1 million. The company has also been good to his family: Quayle's son Tucker works as its assistant director of marketing and sales in China.

The relationship has also been beneficial to Kampouris, who was introduced to Zhu Rongji thanks to Quayle. There is no record of what was discussed at their meeting, but considering that China will soon outstrip even the United States as a market for the company's wares, it's unlikely that Quayle repeated the criticisms he's often made of the Clinton Administration's policy of fostering trade with the Communist nation.

Dan Quayle loves golf. In 1992, after touting the turnaround of the economy on the strength of a NOW HIRING sign at Burger King, he went off to play in Bob Hope's celebrity golf tournament in Palm Springs. In 1993 he moved into a home in suburban Indianapolis that's less than a mile from Crooked Stick Golf Club, which has hosted any number of professional golf tournaments, including the PGA Championship. And in 1998, Quayle made an early commitment to play in the Roger Staubach FirstPlus Financial Celebrity Invitational, held in Dallas, at Prestonwood Country Club.

Daniel Phillips, the chief executive officer of Dallas-based FirstPlus Financial Group, loved publicity as much as Quayle loved golf. He sponsored celebrity golf tournaments. He hired Miami Dolphins quarterback Dan Marino and Dallas Cowboys special teamer and fan favorite Bill Bates to endorse his company. He gave lavishly to charities. He spent millions on a race car to carry the company's logo. And he even hired a former Vice President to be on FirstPlus's board of directors, all to raise his own profile and that of his firm, a seller of second mortgages.

FirstPlus Financial marketed its second mortgages as home improvement and debt-consolidating loans, offering borrowers up to 125 percent of a home's market value. Although FirstPlus's loans generally have low monthly payments (because terms are typically stretched out to twenty-five years), the interest rates on them are much higher than the prime rate. Usually, there is a penalty for early payments. The mortgages take longer to pay off, and in the end, borrowers pay much more than they would have with an ordinary mortgage. In May 1999, the Clinton Administration proposed legislation to make the higher risks of such loans clearer to the borrower.

FirstPlus Financial was a darling of Wall Street after its initial public offering in February 1996. The share price rose from an initial price of $10 to a peak of $56 in September 1997. Then, revelations that the company's accounting methods overstated its profitability caused the share price to nosedive. By October 1998 the firm had laid off more than 2,800 employees—half its workforce—as the share price plunged by 75 percent. In March 1999, FirstPlus filed for bankruptcy. A share of the company's stock could be had for a mere 34 cents.

It wasn't the first bust that Phillips had presided over. The *Dallas Morning News* reported in early 1999 that he had been involved in another questionable company. He'd been the president of Linco, Inc., a California-based company that sold health-club memberships and time-share condominiums. When it folded in 1993, creditors sued the company, claiming it had misrepresented its financial stability.

"He can go anywhere and convince people to give him money," Jack Jennings said of Phillips. Jennings, a dentist in Stockton, California, told the *Dallas Morning News* that he lost more than $200,000 when Linco folded.

The newspaper also reported that some fifteen different shareholder suits had been filed against FirstPlus, accusing Phillips of mismanaging the company. Phillips denied any wrongdoing. One suit cited specific allegations of Phillips's largesse with company funds, including $450,000 on a Super Bowl party in San Diego in 1998 for FirstPlus executives, $2 million a month on Phillips's expenses, a $5 million race car used for advertising, and $42 million for a pair of corporate jets. Among those who rode on the jets was Dan Quayle.

Quayle's relationship with FirstPlus seems to have started with Phillips. The banker came to a fund-raising event in Texas and then "became more and more eager to get involved" with Quayle's campaign, according to Michael Anton, the former finance director of Campaign America. Phillips hosted a fund-raiser for Quayle in September 1997. Craig Whitney, Quayle's chief fund-raiser (and also the chief fund-raiser for Campaign America), "set up the deal" to get FirstPlus contributions to Quayle, according to Anton.

The deal worked quite well. During the high times at FirstPlus, contributions from employees of the company made FirstPlus Quayle's No. 2 career donor. FirstPlus employees and their spouses contributed heavily from September 1997 through the end of 1998. Quayle joined the company's board of directors in March 1998. Phillips himself gave the jaw-dropping sum of $100,000 in July. Even company spokesman Dan Marino and his wife, Claire, chipped in $5,000 apiece. The contributions totaled more than $254,000.

For his part, Quayle rented the prestige of his name and his former office to FirstPlus until October 1998. The following month, the company had two announcements: First, that Quayle was leaving the board to pursue the Republican presidential nomination, and second, that it had posted a loss of $82 million for the previous quarter.

*   *   *

Quayle's No. 1 career patron is Wilshire Financial Services Group of Portland, Oregon. Like FirstPlus, Wilshire Financial is in the mortgage business; it specializes in lending to high-risk borrowers with poor credit histories. Like FirstPlus, it was led by a brash chief executive officer, Andrew Wiederhorn, who at the company's peak oversaw eight hundred employees around the world. And like FirstPlus, the company ended up declaring bankruptcy after its meteoric rise.

Wilshire Financial's problems mirrored those of FirstPlus as well. In the fall of 1998, after enjoying a profitable run, the company started losing millions, and by March 1999, it was forced into Chapter 11.

Wilshire emerged from bankruptcy in June after arranging to give stock to its two largest creditors, American Express Financial Advisors and Capital Research and Management Group, in return for a cancellation of its debts. The two creditors ended up with a 40 percent stake in the reorganized company, but lost millions in the deal. For every $1,000 of debt owed them, they got a little less than $37 worth of stock. By August 1999 that deal had improved somewhat—the company's stock price had gone up, improving the ratio for American Express and Capital Research to $135 of stock for every $1,000 owed them by Wilshire.

Just as it was emerging from bankruptcy in June 1999, First Bank of Beverly Hills, F.S.B., a subsidiary of Wilshire, was designated a "troubled institution" by the Office of Thrift Supervision, a federal agency that oversees savings-and-loans. A year before, the agency had slapped a cease-and-desist order on the S&L because of the risky loans it was buying.

Two months after it emerged from bankruptcy, Wilshire Financial's new board of directors—dominated by executives of American Express and Capital Financial—suspended Andrew Wiederhorn, the company's whiz-kid founder, who'd made a multimillion-dollar fortune before he was thirty. The board also suspended the company's president, Larry Mendelsohn.

Quayle met Wiederhorn at a fund-raiser. Wiederhorn was friends with several professional golfers; one of them introduced Wiederhorn to Quayle.

For Quayle, it was a valuable introduction. Around the time the company's fortunes began to plummet, in August 1998, Wilshire Financial made a $100,000 contribution to Campaign America. The following month, the company gave Quayle another $150,000. In all, Wiederhorn and Wilshire Financial contributed $257,000 to Quayle.

The Center for Public Integrity tried to find out why Wilshire Financial made the contributions. In August 1999, after Wiederhorn had been suspended by Wilshire's board of directors, Sheryl Seapy, who works for Morgan-Walke Associates, a media-relations firm that now handles publicity for Wilshire, said, "Those contributions are of a personal nature in reference to Andrew." She referred further inquiries to Wendy Gallamore, Wiederhorn's personal assistant, whom the Center had contacted on several prior occasions.

Contacted again, Gallamore would say only that she could not comment at that time. "You're welcome to check back in a month," she added. "It's a strange thing for me to say, but you're welcome to. Then we can explain a little better."

The ties between Quayle and his No. 10 patron go back far beyond his tenure as the chairman of Campaign America, or his years as Vice President, or even his Senate or House careers. In 1964, William Murphy opened a government relations office in Washington for the Indianapolis-based pharmaceutical manufacturer Eli Lilly and Company. Murphy was Quayle's uncle.

Murphy may have been the drug maker's first full-time Washington lobbyist, but he was hardly its most effective. That honor falls to his nephew, Dan Quayle.

While in Congress, Quayle backed legislation to allow U.S. pharmaceutical manufacturers to sell drugs abroad that hadn't been approved by the Food and Drug Administration. Executives of Lilly called it the most important drug-related bill of the session for the industry. It passed in 1986.

Thanks to Quayle, duty-free shopping wasn't just limited to the international departure lounges of airports. In 1985 he and Richard Lugar, the other Republican Senator from Indiana, introduced a bill to grant three of Lilly's factories in Indiana "special foreign trade sub-zone" status. The tax break passed. Consequently, Lilly pays no tariffs or customs duties on imported items it uses at the factories in the production of exports.

As Vice President, Quayle was in an even better position to help out his corporate friends in Indianapolis. His Council for Competitiveness pushed to speed up the FDA's process for approving new drugs, to promote biotechnology, and to limit liability lawsuits.

In 1991 the EPA proposed more-stringent emissions rules on chemical plants, oil refineries, factories, and power plants. Lilly fought the regulation. In a letter dated February 28, 1991, a lawyer for the company asked the EPA for more "operational flexibility" in complying with the regulation. On March 28, the EPA rejected the request along with a similar one from the Motor Vehicle Manufacturers Association. But as luck would have it, just nine days after the EPA rejected Lilly, David McIntosh, the executive director of Quayle's council (and now a Republican member of the House), sent a list of "suggested changes" to the EPA. The list included the phrase "operational flexibility"—precisely the language that Lilly had used in its letter to the EPA.

Lilly hasn't forgotten Quayle's help. The company serves as an employment agency for former Quayle aides. Mark Miles, who managed Quayle's 1980 Senate campaign, joined Lilly as its director of communications in 1982. The company's current vice president of corporate affairs, Mitch Daniels, has a long history as a political adviser to Quayle. While Quayle's council was removing regulations on Lilly's pharmaceutical plants, Daniels worked both at Lilly and as an adviser to Quayle. At the time, Daniels said that he and Quayle "do not discuss the council's activities as they affect Lilly."

As recently as March 10, 1999, Randall Tobias, the company's chairman emeritus, held a fund-raiser for Quayle. Family patriarch Eli Lilly II and a dozen or so executives have consistently and generously supported Quayle's campaigns over the years.

Gary Brinson, the president and managing partner of Brinson Partners, Inc., and the chairman and chief investment officer of UBS Brinson, manages the financial portfolios of corporations, public funds, endowments, foundations, central banks, and other investors. His firms are part of United Swiss Bank and are based in Chicago and New York City, with offices worldwide. He's a recognized expert in the field of investment management, and he's invested heavily in Quayle's 2000 campaign. He is Quayle's No. 4 career patron, having contributed at least $137,000, and all of it since 1997.

"My decision to give to Quayle really reflects his beliefs in managing down the size of the federal government, his emphasis on family values, and his experience," Brinson told the Center in July 1999. "It's a formidable challenge," he said of Quayle's quest for the nomination, but he added that he thought the former vice president might have a chance. "Dan's well-positioned if problems develop on the Bush side," he said. Nonetheless, Brinson acknowledged that the Bush juggernaut seemed unstoppable.

And, as things turned out for Quayle, it was.

DAN QUAYLE
Top Ten Career Patrons

Ranking	Company/Individual/Family Name	Total
1	Wilshire Financial Services Group, Inc., Portland, Oregon/Andrew and Tiffany Wiederhorn	$257,000
2	FirstPlus Financial Group, Inc., Dallas	$254,451
3	American Standard Companies, Inc., Piscataway, New Jersey/Emmanuel Kampouris	$139,000
4	Brinson Partners, Inc., Chicago/Gary and Suzann Brinson	$137,000
5	Archer Daniels Midland Corporation, Decatur, Illinois	$102,500
6	Crown Equipment Corporation, New Bremen, Ohio/Dicke family	$85,250
7	Hiler family and business interests, La Porte, Indiana	$72,550
8	Black Beauty Resources and affiliated companies, Evansville, Indiana	$71,500
9	Kelso & Company, New York	$55,000
10	Eli Lilly family and related interests, Indianapolis	$51,499

This list is based on individual contributions to Quayle's House campaign from 1977–1978; individual and PAC contributions to Quayle's Senate campaigns from 1979–1992; individual and PAC contributions to Quayle's vice presidential campaign from 1987–1990; all disclosed contributions to the Vice President's mansion fund from 1989–1990; individual and PAC contributions to Issues '94 and Issues '96; individual and PAC contributions to Campaign America from 1995–1998; all contributions to Campaign America's Virginia account from 1997–1998; and individual and PAC contributions to Quayle's presidential campaign through June 30, 1999.

Sources: Federal Election Commission; Center for Responsive Politics; Virginia State Board of Elections.

7. Includes contributions from Hiler family members; employees of Hiler Industries, Inc.; and employees of Accurate Castings, a Hiler Industries subsidiary.
8. Includes contributions from employees of Black Beauty Resources; Black Beauty Coal; and Ameriqual Foods, which was founded by Black Beauty Resources.
10. Includes contributions from Lilly family members; employees of Eli Lilly and Company; and employees of the Lilly Endowment.

OTHERS

Patrick Buchanan

||||||||||||

Patrick Buchanan moved into his first White House office three decades ago. The Vietnam war had cast a neat part through the men of his generation, with short-haired men falling to the right and long-haired men to the left. Pat was a short-hair. Writing in his frequent newspaper columns, the Nixon aide never missed a chance to open fire against draft-dodging liberals.

Angela Buchanan is ten years younger than her brother Pat. The women of her generation went to college and planned careers their mothers had never even dreamed of. Angela studied graduate-level mathematics at McGill University in Montreal. There she found herself surrounded by long-haired Americans, many of whom had come there because they preferred carrying books to rifles. Her big brother's tirades weren't helping her reputation, and she feared they would soon damage her grades. So she wrote him in response, "Could you calm down a little bit?"

Pat invited the sister he called "Bay" to work for Nixon's 1972 reelection campaign. She did. And though their disparate duties kept them apart—she was a campaign bookkeeper, he a White House speechwriter—they communicated frequently. Sprinkled through Pat's files are handwritten notes from his sister. "Here are the astounding figures," proclaims a page torn from a yellow legal pad. "See what can be done, if anything." Within these notes lay the seeds of a remarkable political partnership.

The Buchanans today operate a highly profitable political machine. Pat is the front man. Every four years he takes a break from his work as a television pundit to hit the campaign trail. He tosses out his trademark sharp-tongued barbs as quickly as he can think them up; his are often the best one-liners of the campaign. Bay is the back office. As compulsively organized as her brother is freewheeling, Bay keeps the campaign trains running on time with an attention to detail that aides describe as obsessive. Together, they have built a semipermanent political organization that both promotes conservative causes and earns millions of dollars for "Buchanan, Inc."

Pat and Bay Buchanan have accomplished nothing less than a complete overhaul of the rules by which the game of presidential politics is played. By embarrassing President Bush in 1992 and briefly sidelining Robert Dole in 1996, they prodded mainstream GOP leaders into queuing up behind a centrist like George W. Bush early in 1999. And by demonstrating the viability of an unabashedly right-wing candidate, the Buchanans encouraged rival Gary Bauer into the contest and pushed Malcolm "Steve" Forbes, Jr. further to the right.

In late 1999, however, the Buchanans abandoned their lifelong commitment to the GOP—"the party of Lincoln, Nixon, and Reagan," as Pat liked to call it—and moved to reincorporate Buchanan, Inc., in the Reform Party. Having raised less than $4 million—pocket change in the cash-flush GOP field—the Buchanans surely realized that their prospects for reaching the top of the Republican ticket were dim. In announcing his decision on October 25, Buchanan became the overnight front-runner in the contest for the third party's presidential nomination. "Today, candor compels us to admit that our vaunted two-party system is a snare and a delusion, a fraud upon the nation," he said. "Our two parties have become nothing but two wings of the same bird of prey."

Except for adding campaign finance reform to his political laundry list, Buchanan hasn't overhauled either his message or tactics in his switch to the Reform Party. He would restore America's "lost sovereignty" through a protectionist trade policy he has long called "economic nationalism." He would lift restrictions on gun ownership, call "a time-out on legal immigration," and ban all abortions.

The key to understanding what Buchanan will do as a card-carrying Reformer lies in the political events that shaped his worldview, the evolution of his sister's permanent campaign, and the way the campaign's direct-mail fund-raising tactics shape the message of Buchanan, Inc.

The Great Betrayal is the title Pat Buchanan chose for his 1998 book, which advocates his "economic nationalism." He could easily have chosen the same title to describe the dominant theme of his own life, which has been haunted by three powerful men—Joseph McCarthy, Richard Nixon, and Ronald Reagan, all of whom Buchanan believes were betrayed by a phantasmic liberal elite.

Senator Joseph McCarthy was a hero of Buchanan's boyhood. His father, William Buchanan, was a government accountant who steadfastly defended McCarthy's anti-Communist crusades. His mother, Catherine Buchanan, was a nurse and a teacher who raised seven boys and two girls in their home in northwest Washington, D.C. All nine Buchanan kids attended Catholic schools and the Shrine of the Most Blessed Sacrament.

Patrick Buchanan was a rowdy boy who inherited his father's belief that McCarthy, like Spanish dictator Francisco Franco before him, was felled by power-hungry leftists. He skipped military service to attend Georgetown University, from which he was suspended for punching a police officer who had stopped his car. He was ultimately readmitted, and graduated in 1961. After earning a master's degree in journalism at Columbia University, he took a job as a writer at the now-defunct *St. Louis Globe-Democrat*. There, he often editorialized against liberals and their causes, particularly the Reverend Martin Luther King, Jr., and the civil rights movement.

The youngest Buchanan brothers were still babblers when Angela was born. They were either unable to fully pronounce the word "baby," or were unable to finish a word with Pat and his father around, so they simply called her "Bay." The nickname stuck. She graduated from Rosemont College, a Catholic school near Philadelphia, before earning her master's at McGill.

In 1965, thanks to his newspaper job, Pat got a chance to interview another family idol: Richard Nixon. As soon as Buchanan learned that Nixon was planning a political comeback, he said, "Sir, I'd like to get aboard early." In 1966, Pat joined the Nixon team at a starting salary of $10,000 a year. Two years later the thirty-year-old Buchanan moved into an office next door to the White House.

The roots of Buchanan's present-day style of conservative populism were evident from his earliest days with Nixon. He coined the phrase "silent majority" and helped shape the strategy that drew millions of "hard-hat" Democrats to the GOP. "We should move to recapture the anti-Establishment tradition or theme in American politics," Buchanan wrote in a typical 1972 memorandum. "We need to shed the 'in bed with Big Business' image . . . we should seek out the opportunity to 'take on' some egregious, giant . . . corporation publicly—as Kennedy did with Big Steel in 1962."

And in a White House that became notorious for its dirty tricks, Buchanan quickly developed a reputation as the toughest trickster of all. He popularized the phrase "political hardball" and repeatedly showed his elder colleagues what it meant. He co-authored the 1972 "assault strategy" that promised "not only to defeat" Democratic nominee George McGovern, "but to have him indicted." He and assault strategy co-author Ken Khachigian are widely believed to have been the authors of phony pamphlets and forged letters that viciously attacked Edmund Muskie, one of which caused the Democratic frontrunner to break down in tears at a New Hampshire news conference and irreparably damage his own presidential prospects.

Buchanan's defense of Nixon grew even more pugilistic as the Watergate crisis began to unfold. In December 1972, after CBS News began reporting on the *Washington Post*'s allegations of a cover-up, he proposed drawing up the now-infamous "enemies list" of hostile reporters, and suggested "firing the first guy in the bureaucracy found talking to [then-CBS reporter] Daniel Schorr." When the White House tape recordings came to light the following summer, he advised Nixon to destroy the tapes. Nixon didn't. When special prosecutor Archibald Cox pressed the President to hand over the tapes, Buchanan told Nixon to fire Cox. Nixon did. The firing—which triggered what came to be called the "Saturday Night massacre"—turned leading Republicans against the White House. It was a critical miscalculation that made impeachment possible, and resignation inevitable.

At the height of the scandal, Buchanan received a call from his father. "Pat, why aren't you fighting?" his father asked. "That was the right question," Buchanan later wrote in his 1990 memoir *Right From the Beginning*. "Whether Nixon was wrong was not the relevant issue. Even if he had booted it, he had a right to be defended; and his friends had a duty to be there." Buchanan stood by Nixon until the bitter end.

Nixon's downfall was a blow to Buchanan. Though he emerged unscathed legally—back in July 1971, when his White House superiors asked Buchanan to investigate the President's enemies, he turned the job down and documented his decision in a memo—he was crushed emotionally. He'd been the first full-timer to join Nixon's comeback in 1966, and the last to leave in 1974. For those eight years, Buchanan's personal and professional lives revolved around Nixon's: He met Shelley Scarney at Nixon's New York City law office in 1967, courted her while she worked as a White House receptionist, and married her in 1971, with the President and his family in attendance. Nixon had become like a second father.

Bay was so disillusioned after Watergate that she quit both the United States and the Catholic church. After finishing her degree at McGill, she moved to Sydney, Australia, and found work as an accountant. There she dated a Mormon. The relationship didn't last, but her interest in the Church of Latter-Day Saints did. She converted shortly after her return to the states. Neither Pat nor her father attended her 1982 wedding to a Mormon lawyer.

After a failed bid to be named U.S. Ambassador to South Africa, Pat took up writing a syndicated newspaper column and wangled a seat on a Washington talk show called "The McLaughlin Group." He was angry at the liberal establishment he blamed for toppling both McCarthy and Nixon, and bitterness became the central theme of his commentary.

Bay returned from exile in 1976 to work on the long-shot presidential bid of a California governor. After he lost the GOP primary, Bay landed work as controller of "Citizens for the Republic," the organization that was created with money and mailing lists left over from Ronald Reagan's '76 campaign. Headed by Reagan confidant Lyn Nofziger, Citizens for the Republic used direct-mail solicitations to help finance (in ways later determined to be illegal) Reagan's political activities. Bay's hard work at Citizens for the Republic got her the job of treasurer of Reagan's 1980 campaign, which ultimately drew about half its receipts from direct-mail appeals to conservative voters.

President Reagan rewarded Bay by appointing her Treasurer of the United States. In that post she spearheaded a drive to sell more U.S. savings bonds, started making pennies out of cheap zinc (instead of copper) to save money, and lent her graceful signature to millions of greenbacks. At thirty-two, she was the youngest person ever to hold that post—though only the second thirty-something Buchanan to have an office next door to the White House.

Pat followed his younger sister into the Reagan Administration during its second term, serving as White House communications director from 1985 to 1987. Buchanan liked Reagan, and he accompanied the President on the historic Reykjavik summit and other high-profile trips. But he never became a part of Reagan's innermost circle, as he had been at the Nixon White House. By the time the Iran-contra arms-for-hostages scandal broke, though, those in Reagan's inner circle were working to keep the former actor away from the television cameras. They turned to Pat as stand-in.

Buchanan found himself in an eerily familiar place: defending a conservative President he loved against the liberal establishment that had betrayed him. He took Reagan's case to the public during halftime on ABC's "Monday Night Football," in a segment of an NBC News special, and in frequent bites on "CBS Evening News." The exposure raised his value as a pundit, and he cashed in after leaving Reagan's service. He rejoined "The McLaughlin Group" and soon became a highly paid regular on CNN's "Crossfire" and "Capital Gang."

It was Bay Buchanan who initiated her brother's transformation from TV pundit to what columnist Jack Anderson called "the Energizer bunny of the Republican presidential primary."

Pat Buchanan toyed with the idea of running in 1988, but he stayed out of the race in deference to Jack Kemp. He began attacking George Bush for "betraying Reagan's legacy" almost as soon as the election was over, and the accusations grew sharper as the year wore on. After reading a particularly critical column in December 1991, Bay rang up her older brother. "We don't have any time for any further discussions," she reportedly said. "If you're interested in running, give me a call."

He called. Bay urged him on and offered to manage the campaign. She was divorced, with three sons to support. Her career as a political consultant had stalled after managing a losing Senate campaign in 1986 and losing her own bid for California Secretary of State in 1990. Her primary source of income was a $58,500-a-year salary from the nearly moribund Citizens for the Republic, which was supporting itself by renting its contributor lists to marketers of everything from magazine subscriptions to cheese. Bay needed a new gig.

And so it was that, after decades of chasing each other around the pews of conservative politics, brother and sister Buchanan finally joined forces. In the years since, he has shaped himself into the candidate he spent years urging first Nixon and then Reagan to become. And she sits atop one of the most independent—and profitable—political machines in the country. "Bay Buchanan runs it like a general," Pat's wife, Shelley, told a reporter in 1996. "There wouldn't be a campaign if it weren't for Bay."

The Buchanans began their 1992 campaign by recruiting an exceptionally young but remarkably talented staff. Finance chairman L. Brent Bozell III, pollster Frank Luntz, political director Paul Erickson, and press secretary Greg Mueller were all still in their twenties when they started working for the Buchanans. Bozell, Luntz, and Mueller had cut their political teeth at the National Conservative Political Action Committee (NCPAC), renowned for hitting liberal incumbents with devastatingly dirty television ads. Also on board was Scott MacKenzie, a veteran of two Reagan campaigns who'd worked for Kemp in 1988.

Buchanan ran in thirty-three state primaries in 1992 and won 3 million votes. He humiliated President George Bush in working-class New Hampshire by winning 37 percent of the vote. The Buchanans carried their conservative crusade as far as the National Republican Convention in Houston, where Pat used a nationally televised speech to invite the faithful to join him in a "Culture War" against the liberal establishment.

As successful as Buchanan was at the polling halls, Buchanan, Inc., was even more so in the locked "caging rooms" where the envelopes containing contributions to the campaign were opened. Out on the campaign trail, Buchanan wrote and refined his own speeches, most of which urged supporters to join his "fight against" one liberal cause or another. Back at their headquarters in McLean, Virginia, a well-to-do suburb of the nation's capital, Bay Buchanan transformed her brother's various battle cries into tightly written fund-raising letters, which were mass-mailed to carefully selected target audiences. By the time the '92 campaign was over, Buchanan, Inc., had raised at least $7.2 million, most of it through direct-mail solicitations. It was a record-smashing haul. Not since Reagan had a candidate used direct mail so successfully.

Once the convention was over, Pat Buchanan rejoined the punditocracy. His quixotic campaign boosted his ratings—and his take-home pay. The year before the campaign he made $457,000. In 1994 he pulled down $608,579.

Bay Buchanan had no such career to which she could return. But there was enough money left over from the campaign to pay her a salary for two more years. She took home $112,538 from January 1993 through March 1995, and campaign treasurer Scott MacKenzie's consulting firm was paid $222,856 in the same period. She needed a way to keep the rest of her core team in place. And so, in February 1993, Bay changed the name of her defunct nonprofit organization to The American Cause, and moved it into the offices in McLean, Virginia, from which she'd run the campaign. The American Cause would allow Pat Buchanan to keep his name in front of conservative voters—and squeeze them for money at the same time. It raised $2,495,709 between the 1992 and 1996 elections, most of that from donors to the 1992 presidential campaign. An affiliated organization, the Coalition for the American Cause, collected millions more.

Through these noncampaign organizations the Buchanans were able to accept donations far larger than the $1,000-per-election maximum (for individuals) that's allowed under federal campaign-finance law. In 1994, for example, Roger Milliken, the owner of the nation's largest privately held textile company, gave $250,000 to The American Cause and another $1,902,000 to the Coalition for the American Cause. Milliken, whose businesses have been hurt by the flood of cheap textiles, received the Buchanans' help in lobbying Congress against adopting the General Agreement on Tariffs and Trade (GATT). The Buchanans received literally millions of dollars worth of television exposure. They bought ads on ABC, NBC, CBS, and CNN, which starred a very presidential-looking Pat Buchanan stating: "Bill Clinton is bringing back his rejected Congress to ram through his GATT trade treaty. That is a crime against democracy."

As a not-for-profit organization, The American Cause pays no taxes on its activities, but it has run afoul of the IRS for repeatedly failing to file its tax returns on time.

With an office and staff in place, the creation of a 1996 presidential campaign team was relatively simple. On the last Friday night in 1994, Bay locked up the generic glass-and-concrete offices of The American Cause. When she returned the following week, the offices once again were home to Buchanan for President. The name on the door had changed, but the faces inside all remained the same.

Buchanan did even better in 1996 than he had the first time around. He won high-profile early victories in Alaska, Louisiana, and all-important New Hampshire; and he almost won Iowa, in Bob Dole's backyard. Buchanan made the cover of *Time* magazine in February—and was briefly considered to be the Republican front-runner—until the GOP's moderate wing steamrolled him on Super Tuesday.

Once again, Buchanan's showing at the ballot box was exceeded only by Buchanan, Inc.'s take at the mailbox. It collected a total of more than $16.3 million, mostly through direct mail. In just the first three months of 1996, Buchanan had spent more than *four times* as much on direct mail as the campaigns of President Clinton and GOP front-runner Dole *combined*. And the Buchanans didn't stop there. Even after the nomination was hopelessly lost, Bay continued seeking funds. Around May 1—weeks after Bay had laid off half the campaign's hundred salaried workers—roughly 140,000 Buchanan supporters received a letter asking for money to continue Pat's fight for "the heart and soul of the Republican Party."

Buchanan, Inc., has proven itself astonishingly adept at collecting federal matching funds. In 1992, Buchanan got more than $5 million in federal matching funds; only Clinton and Bush qualified for more. And in 1996, Buchanan got nearly $11 million in federal matching funds. The Dole campaign—which stayed on the road more than twice as long as Buchanan—got only $13.5 million. Clinton got only $13.4 million. Altogether, Buchanan, Inc., has been the beneficiary of more than $16 million in federal funds.

Buchanan's success at the matching-fund game stems from how the money is raised. Only the first $250 from each donor qualifies for federal matching funds. As a result, candidates such as Clinton or Dole—each of whom received many contributions at the $1,000 limit—qualify for a lower percentage of matching funds than do candidates such as Buchanan, whose direct-mail solicitations produced greater numbers of smaller donations.

With so much money coming in through the front door, Bay Buchanan found a way to take some out through the back door. In addition to her $85,000-a-year salary as campaign chairman, she made an undisclosed sum from a media-buying company that she'd set up on the side. The company—named WTS, after her sons, William, Tommy, and Stuart—collected an eight percent commission on the roughly $4 million worth of broadcast advertising bought by the campaign, netting Bay some $320,000. WTS had no office—the checks were mailed to the home address of Carolyn Melby, Bay's friend and former campaign office manager—and no clients other than the Buchanan campaign. Shortly before the current campaign, Bay Buchanan changed the name of WTS to "Carmel Consultants"—as in *Carolyn Melby*. (Asked whether the firm would buy the Buchanan campaign's ads this time around, Bay Buchanan told the Center "I don't expect them to—they could put in a proposal.")

Shortly after the 1996 Republican National Convention in San Diego, Buchanan, Inc., metamorphosed back into not-for-profit mode. The American Cause was revived. The Coalition for the American Cause gamely sent out a fund-raising letter calling for abolition of the "rogue regime" at the IRS. And the red-hot Buchanan for President mailing lists sold for a quick $360,000.

Pat Buchanan's punditry—on and off the stump—has made him a wealthy man. He makes more than a million dollars a year, and is worth at least $4.4 million, according to financial disclosure documents filed in August 1999. Recent adjustments to his personal portfolio suggest that he's taken his own predictions of economic gloom-and-doom to heart: Since filing his 1996 disclosure statement, he has sold most of his foreign stocks and many of his shares of large U.S. companies—and moved the money into bonds and bank shares. He lives in a white-columned mansion in McLean, Virginia, directly across the street from CIA headquarters. Senator Edward Kennedy, General Colin Powell, and Sun Myung Moon (the Korean evangelist who founded the conservative *Washington Times*) live down the street.

At the beginning of 1999, when it was time to switch back to presidential-campaign mode, Buchanan, Inc., was ready. This year's campaign includes an 800 number where callers are asked for their name and address before the receptionist even takes the call, and a Web site where an e-mail-based "Buchanan Brigade" is slowly supplanting direct-mail as a fund-raising tool.

And where the other Republican primary campaigns offer yard signs that proclaim "Bush 2000" or "Dole 2000," this one's yard signs are ready-made to be reused. They read: "Buchanan for President."

Most big presidential campaigns are financed mostly with big contributions. Many of these are raised at huge $1,000-a-plate dinners, or are solicited by fat cats who deliver checks in "bundles" to their candidate of choice. To become one of Texas Governor

George Bush's "Pioneers," for example, a fund-raiser must bring in at least $100,000. As this book makes painfully clear, most such individuals are looking to buy something other than good government.

The Buchanan, Inc., donors are different. The average contribution is a mere $27, according to Bay Buchanan. Perhaps more important than the small size of the typical Buchanan donation is the intent behind it: Other than a small cadre of textile-industry executives who hoped to benefit from Buchanan's crusade against free trade, most of the donors to his 1996 campaign didn't expect anything in return.

Take Paul Zignego, for example, the owner of Zignego Ready Mix in Waukesha, Wisconsin. Zignego and members of his family were among the top donors to Buchanan's 1996 campaign. He told the Center for Public Integrity that he supported Buchanan's stand against abortion, as well as his advocacy of strict constitutional government.

Even more unusual is an elderly woman who lives just outside Houston. The woman, who asked that her name not be used, lives on Social Security and gave Buchanan, Inc., a series of small contributions totaling more than $7,000 in 1995 and 1996, though much of that money was eventually returned. She told the Center that she supported Buchanan because he is a "fine Christian man" who "knows the difference between right and wrong, and would never do anything wrong." Other than her desire to see the government returned to the way it was when she was young, she said, she expects nothing in return.

There is, however, a downside to the relentless grinding of the Buchanan money mill. To reap the harvest of disillusioned individuals such as Zignego and the woman in Texas, Buchanan, Inc., must sow discontent. Donors like these don't respond to junk mail that says "All is well." Rather, they whip out their checkbooks in response to crises, preferably ones that require immediate action in the form of a small contribution. Thus, to keep the money rolling in, Buchanan, Inc., must continually frame every complex and continuing issue in terms of a simple and urgent problem.

Which creates a simple and urgent problem for Buchanan. As soon as his rhetorical crises fade from the limelight, the ordinary

Americans who give money to his campaigns disappear. Of the four textile companies that gave heavily to Buchanan in 1996, only one gave early money to his 2000 campaign. (Several Milliken employees are supporting Bush this time around.) Zignego told the Center that he's sitting out the presidential race this time around; recognizing that he can't make a dent against the big-money interests behind Bush and Gore, he's backing conservative candidates for the U.S. House of Representatives instead. And the Texas retiree is making smaller contributions now.

The supporters who stand by Buchanan fight after fight tend to be from the fringes of American politics. Among them is Larry Pratt, the president of Gun Owners of America. Pratt, a co-chairman of Buchanan's 1996 campaign, was forced to step down after the Center for Public Integrity reported that he had attended rallies sponsored by white-supremacist groups and had also advocated the creation of "civilian militias." Also dropped from the 1996 campaign for similar reasons were William Carter of South Carolina and Susan Lamb of Florida, both of whom had ties to former Ku Klux Klan leader David Duke. (An investigation by *USA Today* found that the 1996 Buchanan campaign accepted nearly $12,000 from at least eighteen donors with ties to Duke.)

Likewise, Buchanan's rigid stand against abortion—he would outlaw it in all instances, including in cases of rape or incest—has attracted such fantatics as Michael Bray, who spent nearly four years in federal prison for his role in a series of abortion-clinic bombings. Michael Farris, another co-chairman of Buchanan's 1996 campaign, participated in events honoring Bray and Paul Hill, who was convicted of murdering a Pensacola, Florida, abortion doctor and his bodyguard.

Buchanan's top operatives are quick to point out that such extremists undoubtedly account for far less than one percent of their supporters and argue that they simply don't have the resources to screen every donor. (This point was proven for them by TV satirist Michael Moore, who mailed the '96 campaign $100 from "Abortionists for Buchanan." The check was promptly cashed.) But Pratt and Farris weren't mere donors; they were two of only four campaign co-chairs. Not coincidentally, both are also recognized experts in direct-mail fund-raisers.

Throughout the 1990s, Buchanan has become defined and re-defined by the many contradictions between his career as a Washington insider and the zealots his direct-mail-driven campaigns attract. He paints himself as an outsider running against Washington, yet he's lived inside the Capital Beltway for all but four of his sixty-one years. He appeals to evangelical Christians whose lives revolve around their families, though he himself is a devout Catholic who has never had children. And he speaks against immigration and affirmative action, while casting himself as the champion of America's working class, whose ranks in fact are being swelled by immigrants and racial minorities.

Such disenfranchised supporters pulled Buchanan slowly but steadily away from the Republican Party, and the party likewise moved away from Buchanan. Although he was a star of the GOP's 1992 convention, by the time of the 1996 convention Buchanan had become persona non grata—a rather remarkable turn of events for a man who served in both the Nixon and Reagan White Houses.

After the 1996 primaries, Buchanan openly floated the idea of bolting the GOP. And in the fall of 1999, he acted. "Both parties are addicted to soft money," he said. "Both write laws with lobbyists looking over their shoulders. Both embrace the unprincipled politics of triangulation. And neither fights today with conviction and courage to rescue God's country from the cultural and moral pit into which she has fallen."

Betraying the GOP undoubtedly was not easy for Buchanan, whose Republican roots ran deep and who valued loyalty over nearly everything else. This, after all, was the man who stood by Nixon, the man who defended Reagan, and a man who has defended a veritable parade of right-wing extremists associated with his campaign. And while the Reform Party welcomed his zeal for smaller government and his working-class message of "economic nationalism," the libertarian-leaning party—led by an ex-wrestler who once wore feather boas in the ring—merely tolerates his fierce stand against abortion rights.

But joining the Reform Party was a brilliant move for Buchanan, Inc. The party is sitting on $12.6 million in federal money that will flow to the nominee, and it gets another $2 million to spend on its August convention. An extended campaign will raise the public profiles of both Buchanans, bringing them even more lucrative media deals and speaking fees—whether or not Buchanan wins the party's nomination.

The reach of Buchanan, Inc., was dramatically illustrated in the wake of President Clinton's 1998 testimony before Kenneth Starr's grand jury. At one point, the Buchanans appeared on two TV networks at the same time, Pat on MSNBC and Bay on CNN. As they dug into Clinton, their hands struck the air in the exact same manner: pointing and poking in staccato spasms. And the theme they hammered away at was the same, too: America had once again been betrayed.

PATRICK BUCHANAN
Top Ten Career Patrons

Ranking	Company/Individual/Family Name	Total
1	Vopnford family, Blair, Nebraska	$19,000
2	Milliken & Company, Inc., Spartanburg, South Carolina/Milliken family***	$18,500
3	Duro Industries, Fall River, Massachusetts	$18,000
4	Zignego family, Waukesha, Wisconsin	$17,000
5	Hubner family, Goshen, New York	$12,350
6	National Right to Life PAC, Washington	$10,400
7	Buchanan family, Northern Virginia	$9,500
8	Knight family, Boston	$9,000
9	Leigh Fibers, Wellford, South Carolina	$8,000
10	Uihlein family, Northbrook, Illinois	$7,500

This list is based on individual and PAC contributions to Buchanan's 1992 and 1996 presidential campaigns; all contributions to Buchanan's federal PACs (America First PAC and PATPAC) from 1991–1998; and all individual and PAC contributions to the 2000 presidential campaign through June 30, 1999. Independent expenditures are also included, where appropriate.
Sources: Federal Election Commission; Center for Responsive Politics.

2. Includes contributions from employees of Milliken & Company. Also includes contributions from Milliken family members, some of whom live in New York City.

3. Includes contributions from the families of Edward Ricci, Robert F. Fischer, and Stanley B. Goldberg, who are all executives of Duro Industries. Many of the contributors live in Rhode Island.

6. This money consists entirely of independent expenditures for the 1996 presidential campaign.

7. Contributions are from Pat Buchanan, wife Shelley, since-deceased mother Catherine, sister Angela, brothers Thomas and Brian, and sister-in-law Phyllis Ann.

***NOTE: The Center for Public Integrity has learned that Roger Milliken donated $250,000 to Buchanan's not-for-profit organization, The American Cause, and another $1.9 million to an affiliated organization, the Coalition for the American Cause. Since complete donor lists for these groups are not available, these figures are not included in the above list.

Conclusion

The author of the Declaration of Independence, Thomas Jefferson, called it "an assembly of demi-gods." George Washington, James Madison, Alexander Hamilton, and, all told, fifty-five representatives from twelve states met in Philadelphia for a constitutional convention that lasted four long months. Ultimately, they produced a document, the basis for the world's longest-living democracy, that has endured for more than two centuries.

Benjamin Franklin, who at eighty-one was the elder statesman during that hot, historic summer of 1787, warned them, in words written down by James Madison: "There are two passions which have a powerful influence on the affairs of men. These are ambition and avarice; the love of power, and the love of money. Separately, each of these has great force in prompting men to action; but when united in view of the same object, they have in many minds the most violent effects. Place before the eyes of such men a post of honor, that shall be at the same time a place of profit, and they will move heaven and earth to obtain it."

Political and economic realities change, but ambition and avarice are as old as human history itself. Today, we face not a constitutional convention or the beginning of a new nation, but merely the start of a new millennium. The 2000 presidential election in the United States of America is a magnificent opportunity for our democracy to select its next leader, to ventilate the most salient issues of our time, to reflect back on the American Century, and to celebrate the most remarkable transfer of power in the world. It is a time to imagine what can be, what will be.

But amidst the grand reverie, let us not forget that this presidential election is also the Super Bowl of greed and opportunity, a two-year-long extravaganza that dramatizes the unattractive, everyday intersection of politics and commerce. There is simply no more obvious or compelling convergence of power and money in the world— for thousands of lobbyists and their clients; for the exploding campaign industry of pollsters, consultants, ad buyers, opposition researchers, and so on; for the thousands of television and radio stations saturated with political advertising; for the thousands of working journalists covering the spectacle. All of them—not to mention *we, the people*—are watching the candidates move heaven and earth to capture the most powerful public office on the planet.

Much of our writing has attempted to examine the "most violent effects" of the avarice and ambition in U.S. politics today. For the past four years, we have extensively investigated the 1996 presidential candidates, the U.S. Congress, the 2000 presidential candidates, and their collective patrons. Our research has been recorded in nearly 400,000 words in four "Congress and the People" studies and three books, *The Buying of the President, The Buying of the Congress,* and now, *The Buying of the President 2000.* Our goal is very simple: We believe that an informed citizenry is the best antidote to apathy, distrust, cynicism, and corruption, and we hope our investigative reports empower citizens to demand a higher level of accountability, from government, from elected officials, from vested interests. Our work—our reports, files, computer databases, investigative insight—is an increasingly valuable resource to journalists.

We understand that some of the information we impart is irritating and outrageous to some. And our unwillingness to exceed our self-prescribed function as an honest broker of information, our refusal to advocate solutions, can be frustrating, even to us. If we did make specific recommendations, then we would be criticized for being "biased" or "having an agenda." The true-to-life writing of

Upton Sinclair, the revelations of Ida Tarbell and Lincoln Steffens, the insight from public documents and statements gleaned by I. F. Stone were ultimately resonant not because of their personal opinions about recourse. The sheer power of the information is what was compelling and remains seared in our memory.

The fact is, this nonpartisan "watchdog" role of the Center for Public Integrity is difficult, constraining, and frequently unpopular. A sense of humor is essential. After reading *The Buying of the Congress,* Harlan Lewin, a political science professor, wrote in the *San Diego Union-Tribune* last year: "Reading Lewis's book alone is like drinking hot sauce out of a bottle without putting it on your food. All you can think of is the burn."

I would add the cold drink of citizen involvement in this democracy (not just voting, either), side dishes of serious information from all kinds of credible print and electronic sources, and for dessert? Try asking your local, state, or federal politicians— a.k.a. your employees—what favors they have given to their career patrons, and at what cost to the public at large. No one asks them such fair, reasonable questions. Try researching their positions, their backgrounds, their votes, their patrons, on the Internet or from other sources (our Web site links to both research and re- form-minded organizations that can assist you in this regard). You would do that when buying a car or a toaster, so why not when selecting a public servant who will make major decisions affecting your health, your safety, your pocketbook, your children's futures?

Lord Acton, the nineteenth-century English historian, once said, "Life is a matter of application." If you apply yourself to the public interest, the public's business, that is to say "politics," the result will be more satisfying and successful than if you sit back on your haunches and whine about "those bastards." Thousands of people don't deserve the disrespect they get, in state and federal government offices, processing your Social Security check or your tax return, defending your freedom or protecting basic human rights in the Armed Forces, protecting the environment, trying to achieve peace abroad—the list goes on. There are many fine offi- cials at the state and federal level who desperately need citizens to get more engaged, to increase the scrutiny of the public policy decision-making process.

But, beyond all this, what is our assessment of the current political landscape?

The American political process has become warped and distorted over time, so that we are left today with only a cosmetic democracy. The only people who can credibly seek the highest office in the land are millionaires or grip-and-grin Sammy Glicks willing to go out and solicit untold sums of cash. This money—which must be collected more than a year before the election—must then be used to purchase celebrity, also known as name recognition. Thus, celebrity status from other walks of life, such as sports, movies, or publishing, is not a prerequisite to success, but it certainly helps. Raising jaw-dropping amounts of political cash requires world-class schmoozing, day and night. It defies credulity that a human being can hobnob with the rich and powerful, on posh golf courses, at fancy resorts, in four-star hotels and restaurants, in their Learjets, and *not* be affected over time. You begin to dress like them, to talk like them, to invest (on a smaller scale, of course) with them, even to think like them. In short, you begin to forget whence you came. Maybe there is a reason Frank Capra never made a sequel to his wonderful 1939 classic film, *Mr. Smith Goes to Washington*—it becomes a Stephen King horror flick.

Meanwhile, because politicians must raise so much money from so many disparate interests, while also attempting to appeal to demographically, geographically, ideologically diverse voters, their *every* public utterance must be calibrated to please or at least not to offend. That is one of the reasons our politicians are so bland and innocuous. The best-financed campaigns are the ones with the most extensive polling and focus group research, enabling the politician to pander and to parse the perfect pablum.

Increasingly, the only way in which to reach the electorate is via "paid media," or television commercials. Why? Because local and national news organizations are providing less and less news coverage of political campaigns, on the presumption that the public is less interested. The Annenberg School of Communication at the University of Pennsylvania found that in the 1996 presidential election, broadcast campaign coverage, measured in words, was down 55 percent from 1992. Front-page campaign coverage in the *New York Times,* the *Washington Post* and the *Los Angeles Times* declined 45 percent. CBS News president Richard Salant was known for saying, "Our job is to give the people what they need to know, not what they want to see." There was a time when the national news media understood that they have a public responsibility to inform the nation, not pander to the lowest common denominator. Broadcasters recognized that a license to transmit also implied a public duty. For example, the Communications Act of 1934 and subsequent court decisions have affirmed that local broadcasters have an obligation to put on "programs of local interest and importance," not just to rebroadcast national programming. A 1998 study found that forty television and radio stations in five local markets broadcast "almost no programming that addresses local issues in the communities they serve," just one-third of one percent of all programming in a selected two-week period.

Regarding the money-politics equation, news organizations too often look at it the same exact way the candidates and donors do. Too often they see a candidate's contributions not as fingerprints of a politician-patron relationship that might have manifested itself in public policies, but as a litmus test of viability. "The ability to raise money is one measure of a candidate's political support and of the intensity of preferences," Thomas Mann of the Brookings Institution recently wrote, echoing the "conventional wisdom" inside the Beltway. "And contributing money to campaigns is one important channel for organized political action, an essential element of representative democracy."

But Mann's analysis grossly undervalues the power of money in the modern electoral process. Fact is, the candidates who best shake the money tree best shake coverage out of the news media. And like a cat chasing its tail, the more known or popular a candidate is, the easier it is to raise money, which draws news coverage about his or her fund-raising prowess and further helps to get the message out to voters, which in turn boosts the candidate's recognition, which helps with raising money, and so forth. For better or for worse, the year before the election that simple but exclusionary dynamic seemed to comprise the lion's share of U.S. political news coverage.

But the candidates, their handlers, and the news media are all part of an artificial exercise. It also substantially precludes candidates of perhaps terrific ideas but meager financial wherewithal—half a year to a year before any citizen can vote for or against them. These judgments make or break candidacies long before anyone can vote, limiting and basically preselecting our political choices. Substance about candidate positions is not exactly typical in this important, early phase, nor is sophisticated analysis of the origins and motives behind all of the cash. Certainly in the case of George W. Bush, it wasn't just the sheer amount of cash he amassed that drowned out his GOP competitors, or the stories about how much he raised, but the breathless reporting about his inevitability as President of the United States.

This has probably always been somewhat true about politics, but the emphasis on *money raised*—by the candidates, their patrons, and reporters—seems to be increasing, exacerbating the dynamic of superficiality.

Where does that leave the public? Disillusioned, feeling like the caboose in this so-called open election process. Not surprisingly and for other reasons as well, voter participation is at historic lows, and indeed, in 1996 only 24.1 percent of the American people actually voted to reelect President Clinton and Vice President Gore. Last year, pollsters Peter Hart and Robert Teeter did a national survey for the Council for Excellence in Government. Their report, *America Unplugged,* found that 60 percent of the American people feel disconnected from government. "This gulf between the citizens and their government," they wrote, "grows larger with each successive generation of Americans, a trend with ominous implications for the future." And while the amount of news coverage about public affairs is decreasing, the number of donors sponsoring our politicians remains tiny. As noted earlier, fewer than one percent of the American people write a check of $200 to any politician or political party, and only four percent give at all.

This is all a rather discouraging picture, admittedly. These days Abraham Lincoln's idealistic view of American democracy, as *government of the people, by the people, and for the people,* seems more than a little distant. Nonetheless, the fundamental, undeniable reality is that at some point the people will be heard.

I keep waiting for them to speak.

Acknowledgments

||||||||||||

"**I** am a firm believer in the people," Abraham Lincoln once said. "If given the truth, they can be depended upon to meet any national crisis. The great point is to bring them the real facts." These words convey the raison d'être for the Center for Public Integrity, which in slightly more than nine years has produced nearly forty investigative reports. The "real facts" we bring to the American people invariably relate to public service, public policy, and ethics-related issues. It is in that spirit that we have written *The Buying of the President 2000*.

That was certainly the context in January 1996, when we released the inaugural edition of *The Buying of the President*. Two years before that, it had occurred to us that we'd never scrutinized the electoral process itself. As author Kevin Phillips later wrote, "Washington is a giant influence-mongery, and the buying of the President is the hottest game in town." Who were the 1996 candidates, we wondered, and who were the real forces behind them? Weren't the American people entitled to know *before* the election? It amazed us that no one had ever investigated the backgrounds of the candidates for a book published before the presidential campaign.

And so, in late 1994, we embarked on our unprecedented

investigative project. For more than a year, six writers, sixteen researchers, and 103 student database researchers at two universities applied the Center's exhaustive, "no-stone-unturned" approach to this important subject. In January 1996, a month before the Iowa caucuses, we released *The Buying of the President,* the first systematic examination of the financial relationships and entanglements of America's major presidential candidates. We wrote: "The presidential campaign in the United States has become not so much a 'beauty contest' or 'horse race,' but instead a giant auction, in which multimillion-dollar interests compete to influence and gain access to the candidates who would be president . . . Before the first vote is cast in a presidential primary, a private referendum has already been conducted among the nation's financial elites as to which candidate shall earn his party's nomination."

Against this backdrop, *The Buying of the President 2000* was inevitable.

Roughly two dozen researchers, writers, and editors worked on the project this time around. The members of the "Investigative Team" are listed in the front of the book, and brief biographies of them are on the Center's Web site. I gratefully acknowledge the devoted efforts of each and every one of these wonderful, enormously talented individuals. Once again, I am humbled and thrilled most by the warm collegiality and willing submersion of ego for a greater good. In recent months, for example, we've seen the Center's new managing director, Peter Eisner, a former foreign correspondent, editor, author, and entrepreneur who happens to speak four languages, step up to the plate, cheerfully. We've watched a Pulitzer Prize-winning, thirty-year veteran journalist, Knut Royce, join our ranks and quietly sock a few home runs. And we've reveled at how effortlessly Bill Allison—our frighteningly bright chief of research, and project manager of the Center's next book—comes in from the bullpen in the late innings. Such self-effacing teamwork is hardly limited to these three. In general I benefited hugely from the best "bench" of research talent I have ever seen. Anya Richards tirelessly assembled much of my research for this book, and she kept in her sights all of those we sought—and actually managed—to interview, the former number being much larger than the latter. Nathaniel Heller, Marianne Holt, Melanie Strong, and Derrick Wetherell all played wherever and whenever they were needed. Simply stated, a work of this range and investigative breadth could not be remotely contemplated without extensive collaboration and patient perseverance of remarkable, dedicated professionals who also had more than a year to work their magic.

There are a few people who should be singled out for special thanks and mention. First and foremost, Bill Hogan, a nationally respected journalist and the Center's director of investigative projects, has now shepherded his fourth investigative, nonfiction book to print here in three years. On *The Buying of the President 2000,* Bill led weekly editorial meetings for eighteen months, edited all the copy, and, in his spare time, managed to break a perishable, important national story about Vice President Albert Gore, Jr.'s campaign chairman, Tony Coelho. For years here, he has been an inspiring blend of investigative instincts, insightful Washington knowledge, and good, old-fashioned, infectious exuberance.

No one worked harder or longer on this book than Russ Tisinger and Annys Shin, who were in the trenches for a year and a half. No one carried the full, overwhelming, editorial weight of *The Buying of the President 2000* more than they did. They were, and they remain—along with Monte Paulsen, a veteran journalist, and Shannon Feaster, a recent graduate of Columbia University's Graduate School of Journalism, who both came a year later—our in-house experts on the leading candidates. Their grace, good-natured perseverance, and generous spirit toward their colleagues were essential to this exhaustive project.

This book is dedicated to my teacher, mentor, and friend, James R. Soles, the distinguished professor of political science at the University of Delaware. I hope such an act is more of a blessing than a curse; please do not blame him for the specific content or any inadvertent errors contained herein. At the Center we have created the James R. Soles Fellowship—a guaranteed, one-year stipend with full medical benefits—awarded to the best political science graduate at Delaware. The first Soles Fellow has been Dan Steinberg, a truly exceptional young man who is so thoughtful and multitalented that we took the somewhat unusual step of putting him in charge of the Center's career patron analysis and compilation. Dan handled it with quiet dedication, good humor, and aplomb. He has set a dauntingly high standard, one that the second Soles Fellow, Nathaniel Heller, already shows signs of reaching.

In terms of our investigative methodology, we read dozens of books about campaign finance, the presidential election process, and the 1996 race and attendant scandals, as well as books by or about the candidates themselves. Using the electronic news libraries of Lexis-Nexis, we consulted tens of thousands of newspaper, magazine, wire-service, and newsletter stories, along with transcripts of television shows, congressional hearings, and the like. We frequently clicked on the pertinent Web sites of the candidates, the parties, and various political research organizations. We even queried the members of our new International Consortium of Investigative Journalists—more than seventy of the premier investigative reporters on the planet from some forty countries—for any relevant information or published stories about the U.S. presidential candidates abroad. (More relevant than ever before, in light of the money from abroad that poured into the U.S. political process in 1995 and 1996.)

Regarding primary sources, we analyzed tens of thousands of relevant Federal Election Commission records and state reports (Texas, for example) for campaign contributions going back, in some cases, more than twenty years. We examined thousands of pages of relevant congressional testimony and reports; federal financial disclosure and trip reports; federal and local court and real estate records; federal lobby registration records; filings at the Securities and Exchange Commission, company annual reports and incorporation records; and thousands of pages of public documents received from various Freedom of Information Act requests.

It was a difficult internal choice for us, but we decided to *not* use up valuable, finite "word count" space in these pages with complete, detailed footnotes. Therefore, and perhaps as a sign of these multimedia times we live in, the complete footnotes are available on the Center for Public Integrity's Web site, *www.publicintegrity.org.*

As with *The Buying of the President* (1996) and *The Buying of the Congress* (1998), we once again compiled the "Top 10 Career

Patrons" for each of the major presidential candidates, as well as a new feature, "Top 50 Party Patrons." For the candidate patron lists, these names came not only from FEC filings in Washington, but also from available records for state-level political committees and for not-for-profit organizations that are unequivocally functioning for or led by the candidate. Obviously the career patron calculation was different for novice candidates such as Elizabeth Dole and Gary Bauer. The former's career patron list necessarily is based only on her 1999 contributions; the latter's list includes only his 1999 campaign contributions and contributions to his PAC and its state account. We have more detailed profiles of the candidates' "Top 25 Career Patrons" on the Center's Web site. The party patrons were culled from soft-money donors to both major political parties from 1991 through June 1999.

Our "career patron" lists could not have been compiled, of course, without the basic campaign-finance data that federal candidates and committees must file by law with the Federal Election Commission. The public records staff at the FEC was unfailingly helpful to us throughout 1998 and 1999, and Bob Biersack was especially helpful in providing us with data not available on the agency's Web site (*www.fec.gov*).

The Center for Responsive Politics, under the fine direction of Larry Makinson, once again provided us with gracious access to its extraordinary computerized databases and its unique fingerprint coding of interest-group giving. Our daily work is now infinitely easier now because of the user-friendly, information-laden Web sites maintained by CRP (*www.opensecrets.org*) and Public Disclosure, Inc. (*www.tray.com/fecinfo/*), a research firm. Even with all of the straight numbers increasingly available, compiling a career-patron list entails remarkable patience and several subjective, difficult judgment calls. How, for example, do you identify and tabulate employed spouses? When you are compiling the largest donors over many years, as we have done, how do you describe and incorporate all of the changes that result from mergers and acquisitions? Once such tough decisions are made, another significant challenge then is how to maintain consistent, data-counting standards regarding all of the candidates, and how to ensure a certain discipline and uniformity.

Craig McDonald of Texans for Public Justice, professor Fran Hill of the University of Miami Law School, Ellen Miller of Public Campaign, Sheila Kaplan of *U.S. News & World Report,* veteran Washington lawyer and author Dan Guttman, Richard Miller, John Newman, and Rick Shenkman of TomPaine.com, among many others, provided valuable insights to us.

We conducted many hundreds of on-the-record and background interviews with campaign aides, federal and state government officials, lawyers, lobbyists, company and labor-union representatives, political scientists and public-interest activists around the nation, and campaign contributors—ordinary and extraordinary. For example, we interviewed Archibald Cox, the Watergate prosecutor who was fired by President Richard Nixon in the infamous "Saturday Night Massacre" of October 1973. We questioned the current chairmen of the Democratic and Republican parties, Roy Romer and Jim Nicholson, and the chairmen of the DNC and RNC during the controversial 1996 election, Donald Fowler and Haley Barbour. We talked to Pat Choate, the former vice-presidential candidate of the Reform Party, and Russell Verney, the party's former chairman. We also spoke with Stan Huckaby, a prominent campaign-finance accountant and consultant. The transcripts and audio of these and other interviews are also on the Center's Web site.

Regrettably, none of the presidential candidates would talk to us. We don't take this personally—indeed, to them the prospect of talking to us is probably as exciting a notion as root-canal surgery. For more than half a year we sent formal letters to the candidates requesting interviews, and we made literally scores of follow-up calls to every campaign organization.

Our research is almost entirely based on *public* records, *public* actions, and the expenditure of *public* money. Indeed, in a democracy, these would-be public servants and want-to-be residents of 1600 Pennsylvania Avenue each have a moral obligation to answer such inquiries. We therefore have put some of what we deem to be the most important "Unanswered Questions" for each of the candidates on the Center's Web site. Why? Because we have the quaint notion that the American people and working journalists might actually get an opportunity to ask the candidates serious questions. Even though personal contact with nondonor voters is decreasing each election, the candidates still occasionally must appear at public functions such as debates and town meetings where questions are put to them.

I want to thank our thoughtful, savvy attorney, Marc Miller, of McLeod, Watkinson & Miller, who has scrutinized every word coming out of the Center for almost a decade now. Kudos to our tenacious development director Barbara Schecter and development associate Megan Vaughan. We are very grateful to the Arca Foundation and Alida Messinger for specifically supporting this project. And our government accountability research at the national level generally (we also have investigations in the fifty states and internationally) is made possible by the terrific ($10,000 and above) support of the Carnegie Corporation of New York, the Everett Philanthropic Fund, the Hafif Family Foundation, the John D. and Catherine T. MacArthur Foundation, the New York Community Trust, the North Star Fund, the Park Foundation, the Pew Charitable Trusts, the Price Family Fund, the Scherman Foundation, the Florence and John Schumann Foundation, the Streisand Foundation, and the Town Creek Foundation. That is in addition, of course, to thousands of members nationwide who subscribe to our award-winning newsletter, *The Public i*. The Center does not accept advertising or contributions from corporations, labor unions, and governments. Major donors and the organization's IRS filings (Form 990s) for the past three years are listed on our Web site.

The most generous, steadfastly loyal patron of this organization has been the Schumann Foundation. I will always be deeply grateful to the members of the Schumann family, and certainly to Bill Moyers and John Moyers for their wonderful insights and steadfast support these past years.

The effects of the Internet and its technological and cultural reverberations on our daily lives seem to grow every hour. Thus, what we were able to offer you in terms of information in 1996 is almost primitive compared to today. The Center's Web site, *www.publicintegrity.org,* augments *The Buying of the President 2000*. There, directly or linked to other sites, you can find: full candidate profiles, including personal biographies; the most significant books and articles written by or about them; personal financial information about investments; speaking fees; all-expenses-paid trips; their adherence to U.S. campaign finance laws, according to the Federal Election Commission; their "Top 25 Career Patrons"; campaign contributions; major-donor profiles; candidate policy positions in their own words; their legislative voting records; and much, much more (undoubtedly including things we hadn't envisioned when the book went to press).

On a more personal note, as we celebrate the Center for Public Integrity's ten-year anniversary, I want to thank the magnificent members of the organization's Board of Directors, particularly Charles Piller, who was present at the creation of this excellent adventure. Charlie, co-founding board member Alex Benes, and I held the Center's first board meetings in places such as the outfield stands at Baltimore Orioles baseball games. The Center's board and outstanding Advisory Board members have been amazingly supportive of me and the difficult, not always popular work we do here.

Finally, I am surrounded, sustained, and steadfastly supported by four strong, independent, brilliant women. No one has put up with me more—and complained less—than they have, and I am truly blessed by their presence. I thank them here, in the order of their years of hardship in this regard: my mother, Dorothy Lewis; my sister, Mary Lewis; my daughter, Cassandra Lewis; and my wife, Pamela Gilbert.

And there is at least one thing about which we *all* completely agree. We all very much look forward to the day, hopefully in the near future, when the notion of a woman running for President of the United States—let alone getting elected or holding that office—is no longer "news."

Charles Lewis
September 1999
Washington, D.C.

Index

Index

About The Center for Public Integrity

||||||||||||

The Center for Public Integrity began operation in May 1990. It is a nonprofit, nonpartisan research organization founded so that important national issues can be investigated and analyzed without the normal time or space limitations. Described as a "watchdog in the corridors of power" by *National Journal,* the Center has investigated and disseminated a wide array of information in nearly forty published Center reports since its inception. More than 3,000 news media stories have referenced the Center's findings or perspectives about public service and ethics-related issues. The Center's books and studies are resources for journalists, academics, and the general public, with data bases, backup files of government documents, and other information available as well.

As with its previous books and reports, the views expressed herein do not necessarily reflect the views of individual members of The Center for Public Integrity's Board of Directors or Advisory Board.

To access the most recent findings of the Center, including additional or updated information about the presidential campaign not contained in this book, you can visit the Center's Web site at *www.publicintegrity.org,* or subscribe to *The Public i,* the Center's award-winning newsletter (*www.public-i.org*).

For more information, to buy books and other publications, or to become a member of the Center, contact the Center for Public Integrity:

The Center for Public Integrity
910 Seventeenth Street, N.W.
Seventh Floor
Washington, D.C. 20006

E-mail: *contact@publicintegrity.org*
Internet: *www.publicintegrity.org*
On-line newsletter: *www.public-i.org*
Telephone: (202) 466-1300
Facsimile: (202) 466-1101